Customer-focused Marketing

Customer-focused Marketing

Actions for delivering greater internal and external customer satisfaction

Ian Chaston

McGraw-Hill Book Company

London • New York • St Louis • San Francisco • Auckland
Bogotá • Caracas • Hamburg • Lisbon • Madrid • Mexico • Milan
Montreal • New Delhi • Panama • Paris • San Juan • São Paulo
Singapore • Sydney • Tokyo • Toronto

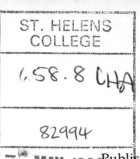
Published by
McGraw-Hill Book Company Europe
Shoppenhangers Road, Maidenhead, Berkshire, SL6 2QL, England
Telephone 0628 23432
Fax 0628 770224

British Library Cataloguing in Publication Data
Chaston, Ian
    Customer-focused Marketing. –
    (McGraw-Hill Marketing for Professionals
    Series)
    I. Title II. Series
    658.8

    ISBN 0-07-707698-2

Library of Congress Cataloging-in-Publication Data
Chaston, Ian
    Customer-focused marketing / Ian Chaston.
        p.   cm. – (Marketing for professionals series)
    Includes bibliographical references and index.
    ISBN 0–07–707698–2
    1. Marketing–Management. 2. Customer satisfaction. I. Title.
    II. Series: McGraw-Hill marketing for professionals.
    HF5415.13.C5117   1993
    658.8'12–dc20
    92-26506
    CIP

1234 CUP 9543

Typeset by Goodfellow & Egan Phototypesetting Ltd, Cambridge
and printed and bound at the University Press, Cambridge.

Contents

Preface

Over the last few years, discussions initiated by clients, participants on training programmes and students studying for postgraduate qualifications have increasingly focused on the issue of how to build successful organizations. The views expressed by each individual are influenced by their background, work experience and, in certain cases, which of the latest management theories is being popularized within their own organization. Frequently proposed solutions (to name just a few) concern one or more of such issues as organizational restructuring, changing company culture, performance appraisal, redefining job specifications, management training, improving interpersonal skills, Customer Care, Total Quality Management, JIT (Just in Time) and computer-based control systems (e.g. MRP2).

Like most of the human race, I was always hopeful that somebody somewhere would come up with the 'Holy Grail of Management' and with this purpose in mind avidly consumed each new best seller by experts such as Peter Drucker, Tom Peters, Rosabeth Moss Kanter and Michael Schonberger. Presenting the views of such writers to others frequently generated a positive response. But then as another management text entered the best-seller list or somebody produced evidence that the latest popular approach failed when applied to their organization, I embarked yet again on the search for the ultimate solution.

No doubt the reaction of some people to the above description of my activities is 'more fool you'. Nevertheless, it has taken me some years finally to come round to accepting that there is no universal formula for creating the successful organization. Instead I now believe that all one should hope for is to establish a philosophy of management which can be used as a unifying framework against which to implement actions most appropriate to specific organizational circumstances. I have settled on the concept that is increasingly being mentioned by various management theorists, namely that the common purpose of all organizations is to focus on meeting the needs of internal and external customers.

When I introduce this concept as a possible unifying philosophy to participants on management development programmes, a not uncommon reaction is to ask how this can be implemented in their organization where power is vested in senior managers who do not consider that greater customer focus is a high-priority issue. As demonstrated in recent research by the Chartered Institute of Marketing, my experience is not unusual. In fact, the Institute is sufficiently concerned about the attitudes of senior managers that it has now embarked on a national campaign to 'make marketing a Board-level agenda item' in UK organizations. Although external pressure from a professional body will have a positive influence, I feel an equally powerful mechanism is for marketers to utilize departmental level initiatives to demonstrate to senior management how the philosophy of greater customer focus can enhance organizational performance. Hence, over the last three years I have been involved in a fascinating period of reading, research, experimentation and reflection. The purpose of this book is to summarize my current perspectives on a range of techniques designed to enhance the level of customer focus within the marketing management process.

The text covers the issues of why customer focus has received insufficient attention in the recent past, establishing appropriate customer-oriented objectives, identifying alternative satisfaction opportunities in the marketplace, analysing internal capabilities and formulating feasible strategies. Coverage is then given to managing the processes of providing superior products and/or services and using the various aspects of the marketing mix such as price, promotion and distribution to achieve the goal of enhancing customer satisfaction. Subsequent chapters cover the specific organizational situations of service industries, the public sector and operating in overseas markets. The closing chapter then examines the challenge of how marketers can persuade senior management to accept that greater customer focus must be given a much higher priority on the corporate agenda if the organization is to be successful in improving long-term performance.

The text is primarily designed for practising managers seeking to understand the processes of building a more customer-focused marketing operation. The materials, however, are also suitable for use in company training schemes and on undergraduate or postgraduate management education programmes.

A frequently quoted phrase used by trainers introducing the concepts associated with Total Quality Management is, 'Quality management is not an achievable target, but more a journey upon which one embarks but cannot ever expect to arrive at a final destination'. I am now of the opinion that this truism is exactly the same for building customer-focused operations. Organizations can strive to be better, but cannot ever expect to achieve perfection.

As with all journeys, there are different routes and alternative ways of travelling. This text attempts to present one view of a unifying management philosophy. I hope the suggestions prove to be of benefit to the reader. Even more importantly, I would be grateful to hear from any managers who can add to my knowledge by describing new ways to improve the level of satisfaction delivered to the external and internal customers of their organization.

Ian Chaston

Dedication
For my constant source of support and entertainment –
Lyn, Miles and Annabel

1
Organizations – performance, problems and purpose

On the evening of 31 December 1899 a number of people gathered at Lands End in south-west England to light a bonfire in celebration of the arrival of the new century. As they watched the onset of night for the last time in the nineteenth century, it is doubtful whether anybody present would have predicted they would also soon be observing the sun finally setting on the world's most powerful economic force, the British Empire. Similarly, Americans who gathered on an evening in 1945 to celebrate the end of the war in the Pacific would never have accepted that within 30 years their country would be removed from its position as the world's richest nation by their now defeated enemy, the Japanese.

Changes in the economic fortunes of nations have been going on since the beginning of time. If one restricts this observation to the Western world since the birth of Christ, included in the list are countries such as Austria, France, Germany, Hungary, Italy, the Netherlands, Portugal, Spain and the UK. The only difference in this situation since the onset of the Industrial Revolution is the rapidity with which change occurs. Great Britain enjoyed almost 100 years as the leading creditor nation. America then assumed the role and held it for only 70 years until being overtaken by the Japanese in 1985. By the year 2010, the current holders of the title may face a strong challenge from either another Pacific Basin country or the post-1992, politically unified, European Community.

Factors influencing organizational success

Both the rise and fall of American multinational companies are events that have acted as catalysts for an information explosion of articles, books, videos and television programmes on building successful organizations. The subject has attracted the interest not only of management theorists in business schools around the world, but also of experts from disciplines ranging in diversity from anthropology through to zoology.

During the period 1950–70 many of the theories about organizations were biased towards technical issues such as strategic management, the design of structures with optimum spans of control, standard cost manufacturing control systems, management accounting, centralized budgetary control and computerized information systems. Many of these concepts grew out of lessons learned by American companies such as the Ford Motor Company or the GE Corporation, which enjoyed the huge profit growth that accompanied exploitation of the economies of scale associated with the creation of mass production and manufacturing systems.

Even before the Second World War, research such as the experiment of changing work conditions at the Hawthorne plant in Illinois had raised question marks about assuming employees were merely an extension of the other equipment used to sustain productivity. It was not until the early 1960s, however, that organizations began to accept the importance of managing both the human and technical aspects of the work environment. This acceptance resulted in a rapid expansion of management theory in the areas of interpersonal skills, participative versus autocratic management, the nature of the management role, performance appraisal, effective leadership and the performance of individuals as members of a team.

Over the last ten years the declining fortunes of both American and European companies has led to recognition of the social costs of industrial reorganization. Researchers have begun to report on individuals who selected a career path and loyally committed themselves to an organization, only to be confronted with the disappearance of their job in the latest round of cut-backs and/or restructurings. When such people began to search for new employment, they faced the personal trauma of discovering that their skills, expertise and age were not compatible with the job specifications described in recruitment advertising.

The 'quick fix'

Not surprisingly, the extremely competitive business environment now confronting organizations throughout the developed world and the reduced job security at all levels of management have provided a growing market for experts offering 'quick-fix' solutions for both organizations and individual managers. The reality, of course, is that any adviser with integrity who is asked to supply an elixir to guarantee future success is forced to point out that organizations are complex structures and their external environment composed of numerous interactive variables. Consequently a 'quick fix' may make things seem better in the short run but it is very likely that, unless other more fundamental changes are implemented, the long-term prognosis is that the troubled organization will eventually develop a terminal illness and die.

More realistic advice must be that, in order to ensure an organization attains and sustains a winning level of performance, managers must:

1 Comprehend basic general concepts about the role and purpose of organizations.

2 Fully understand the key variables both within and outside the organization which are likely to influence future purpose.

3 Recognize the need to create management systems which provide information on the relationship between performance goals and changes in influencing variables.

4 Appreciate the importance of assigning responsibility to individuals capable of (a) defining an appropriate response plan and (b) acting as facilitators to ensure plans are implemented across all relevant areas of the organization.

A model of organizational purpose

The basic role of an organization (Figure 1.1) is to acquire inputs which undergo transformation to produce output that is utilized by others external to the organization. Some of the inputs are the ingredients which are combined to create the output (e.g. the chemicals used to manufacture detergents). Other inputs (e.g. plant, direct labour and money) are consumed by the organization but do not usually become physical ingredients of output. The usual way of measuring process flows associated with both input acquisition/ transformation and output disposition is to apply some form of monetary value.

A fundamental purpose of all organizations is to ensure that the value of outputs exceeds the combined value (or 'costs') of inputs and the transformation process. In commercial organizations this

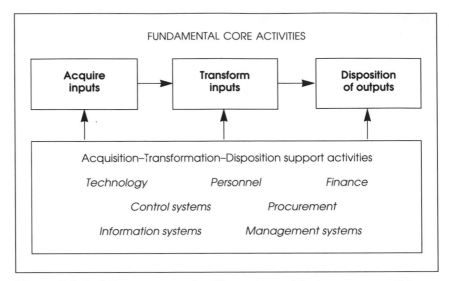

Figure 1.1 Activity components of the value-added processes within an organization

difference in value is the profit generated by the business. For public sector organizations, one frequently finds that monetary exchange for output is made available to the nation on the basis of a subsidized or zero price (e.g. socialized medical schemes in many European countries). In reality, the customer usually makes an indirect revenue contribution by paying taxes, although the level of consumption by individuals is rarely directly proportional to their personal contribution to the taxing body.

No matter whether an organization is in the private or public sector, if it continues to have costs greater than the value of the output (accepting that value may be measured in non-financial terms, e.g. parents' satisfaction that their children are being educated to a level which enhances employment prospects), eventually the organization will either cease to exist or be usurped in the market by a more effective alternative supplier.

In most situations there is a time lag between input acquisition/transformation and the receipt of value from the exchange of output (e.g. the lawyer who incurs expenses discharging his responsibilities for handling the sale of a property but does not receive a fee until the contract is exchanged with the purchaser). Hence the organization is forced to borrow money, and in many cases this is from an external source. Such sources expect reward for the risk of lending and are either paid interest or, if an equity stake is purchased, receive payment through dividends and/or an increase in the market value of their shares. As lenders can choose where to place their money, commercial organizations have to do more than ensure that output value is greater than costs; another goal is to fulfil the lender's desire to obtain a reasonable return on monies invested. Under these circumstances, if an organization's performance is poorer than that of the competition, the lenders may consider withdrawing their support and thereby accelerate the process of organizational demise.

In the public sector, the lender is usually a government body and they will also be unwilling to support an organization if they decide that another group is more able to fulfil the specified responsibilities. Government lenders are not usually concerned about the return on their investment. Performance requirements are more typically based upon some form of output requirement such as lowest possible cost, value for money or quality (e.g. a government may employ a civilian contractor to provide repair services for military aircraft as this is seen as giving 'greater value for money' than funds being provided for the country's air force to undertake the work).

Process functions

The core activities associated with generating output values in excess of costs are the technical functions of procuring inputs, transforming these into a product or service and negotiating purchases by customers. As these functions become more complex, it is usual to divide the technical role responsibilities into specialist sub-tasks such as procurement, manufacturing (or service provision) and marketing.

Given the vital importance of ensuring achievement of output values in excess of cost, another key function within the organization is the recording and measuring of value flows. This has led to the creation of the disciplines of accountancy and financial management. Managers of these functions are also responsible for ensuring that the financial status of the organization allows additional borrowing at times when the organization's internal resources are insufficient to underwrite value-generation activities.

With the exception of the one-person business (and possibly the futuristic situation of a company managed by robots), organizations contain people who require guidance on how to do their job. Furthermore, because humankind is not renowned as a species in which individuals are totally self-responsible, organizations need to monitor the performance of employees and, where appropriate, implement actions to enhance performance (e.g. an organization may improve the communication skills of its computer programmer staff so that other people can understand what they are talking about). It is this process of providing guidance, monitoring performance and implementing actions to improve employee performance that forms the basis of the third function within the organization: namely, people management. Unlike the technical or financial functions, which are often assigned as specialist roles, however, people management is a skill required of all employees.

The impact of process failures

Research by Argenti in the US and Slatter in the UK has identified a number of factors as the cause of decline in commercial organizations. Their studies confirmed that the following problems are found to occur with depressing regularity.

A fall in market demand

A decline in total generic demand is likely to place pressure on all organizations which are dependent on revenue from the market sector in question. If the product type is rendered obsolete (e.g. the replacement of the slide rule by electronic calculators), then the decline will be irreversible. In some situations, however, the decline is of a temporary nature reflecting the business cycle of boom and bust that is a characteristic of 'free-market' economic systems. There is some variation in the degree to which different industries are affected by economic cycles. Capital goods manufacturers (e.g. companies making heavy turbines for power stations) face extreme fluctuations in revenue. Others (e.g. the food and tobacco sectors) are much less influenced by changes in prevailing economic conditions. Whether a company survives a cyclical downturn usually depends on its financial status. A firm with a strong balance sheet is usually able to weather the storm. In contrast, a company facing cash flow problems and/or achieving an inadequate profit performance is less likely to live through a recession.

Another possible cause of demand decline is where there is a change in market behaviour to which the company is unable to respond. For example, the advent of desk top computers in the late seventies caused many organizations to favour providing managers with their own PCs and to restrict further expansion or updating of their mainframe computer. Demand for computers in business remained strong, but for those companies with limited capability in the personal computer market (e.g. the UK company ICL during the early eighties) sales suffered because they could not fulfil the change in equipment needs in the marketplace.

Shift in market demand is often caused by the actions of a competitor who has moved more rapidly to exploit an alternative technology or new product pathway for fulfilling customer need (e.g. Apple Computer's introduction of the personal computer versus mainframe producers such as IBM or Hewlett-Packard). However, even where market demand remains unchanged, a company may face a decline in sales because competitors are perceived as offering a better proposition (e.g. the successful entry of Chilean apple producers into the European market over the last decade). In the past, competitors tended to use aggressive pricing to create an initial beachhead in a new market. This was frequently the pattern of entry into the American and Western European markets by new Pacific Basin producers in the seventies and early eighties which led to accusations against the exporter nation of 'dumping'.

More recently it would appear that organizations are beginning to recognize that aggressive pricing can trigger off a 'price war' and/or the erection of tariff barriers. Hence it is now more probable that a competitor entering a new market will tend to exploit the proposition of greater product performance for the same price in preference to deep price cuts to stimulate product switching among customers.

Cost problems in the transformation process

An organization which incurs substantially higher costs in transforming inputs into outputs will be at a disadvantage if competitors are using a more efficient transformation process. In a world where socio-cultural differences are shrinking by the minute, the small, single-market company often faces a relative production cost disadvantage versus large multinationals. This is because the latter operate vast processing facilities and can enjoy the benefits offered by economies of scale.

Absolute cost disadvantages between organizations can be independent of size due to such factors as plant location (e.g. a plant in a developing country may enjoy the benefits of access to a low-cost source of labour and not be required to invest in expensive pollution control equipment), variations in public sector support (e.g. government grants for new equipment for plants located in economically depressed regions of a country) and access to raw materials (e.g. Japanese versus American steel plants – the latter are self-sufficient in ore and fuel whereas the Japanese have to import all such materials).

The other possible source of an absolute transformation cost disadvantage is that caused by poor management who have permitted the organization to acquire expensive habits such as over-manning, union-inspired demarcation rules reducing workforce flexibility, inadequate stock control relative to demand, excess production capacity and bureaucratic administrative processes involving a large number of clerical and supervisory staff. This problem seems to be very characteristic of large, complex organizations that have evolved multi-layered hierarchical structures and numerous satellite operations. Under these circumstances, any scale advantages which may have accrued from being big are then dissipated through the operating inefficiencies which have developed within the organization. In the UK it is this effect that has been the cause of concern about public sector organizations such as the National Health Service and British Telecom. The solution in the first case has been an attempt to make the organization more responsive to market forces and cost control management by redefining long-term strategies, restructuring the organization and appointing 'commercially oriented' managers. The British Telecom situation was resolved by privatizing the organization.

Inadequate financial information

Given the critical requirement of ensuring that output values exceed costs and that the organization has sufficient cash to fund the operation on an ongoing basis, there is a vital need to provide accurate and timely financial information to the management team. Lack of adequate financial controls, such as a failure to prepare cash flow forecasts and compare projections with budget, can result in a funding crisis. Furthermore if the accounting system is poorly designed it will not provide data in a form that can be used by management to analyse performance and implement remedial action where appropriate, to avoid costs continuing to increase and/or revenues to fall.

Inappropriate funding decisions

Given that most organizations need to borrow from external sources to support periods when internal financial resources are inadequate, then performance of the organization may be damaged if an inappropriate funding decision is made. For example, the organization may take on a high debt burden on the assumption that continued profit growth will cover the interest charges. In the mid-1980s, many property development companies in America and the UK borrowed heavily from the banks to cover expenditure on the construction (sometimes speculative) of office blocks. When the economy downturned at the end of the decade, demand for office space declined, leaving these companies unable to generate revenue sufficient even to cover interest charges. This has pushed many of these companies into a severely weakened financial position and, in the case of some, into receivership.

Another form of inappropriate funding decision is to borrow short-term money from the banks to support long-term projects. This is a common error in the SME (small and medium size enterprises) sector. In the mid-eighties, for example, UK firms in this sector relied heavily on bank overdrafts as a source of funds because the low interest rates which then prevailed meant this was the 'cheapest' way of borrowing. As interest charges rose at the end of the decade, many companies in this sector realized with hindsight that it would have been more prudent to have borrowed using fixed-term loans and/or raised equity capital.

Failed investments

Where a significant proportion of available resources is directed into a new endeavour which then fails, the organization is usually placed in a weakened position from which recovery may prove difficult. The two common forms of this type of error are (a) big projects that encounter unforeseen problems and (b) acquisitions that do not generate an adequate return on the purchaser's investment. An example of the big-project scenario is the Channel Tunnel linking Britain and France, which has faced actual construction costs significantly greater than those forecast by the participating companies at the start of the project. The subsequent need to raise additional capital has proved difficult. Furthermore, in the face of such a cost over-run, there must now be concern over whether the eventual revenue from tunnel traffic will be capable of generating an adequate return on whatever the final investment figure turns out to be. (And this was before the announcement of a Japanese invention of 'submarine trains' which run along tracks laid on the sea-bed, thereby possibly vitiating the need for tunnels under the ocean.)

Growth by acquisition has become an increasingly popular strategic tool for both large and medium firms in the last thirty years. Unfortunately, every now and again, the hopes of the purchaser are not borne out by subsequent events. An example of this scenario is Midland Bank, which decided to acquire Crocker Bank in California as an entry mechanism into the American market. The acquisition did not provide the rewards expected and the outcome was Midland being forced to rethink their entire strategy for the US market.

Management capability

The blame for most of the problems described above must be laid at the door of the management, for it is they who lacked the skills to make correct decisions. It would not be fair in most situations, however, to condemn all the managers in the organization. In some cases, for example, the errors are made by a chief executive whose highly autocratic style means that objections expressed by the Board or other senior managers go unheeded. Another possible problem may be that an effective, innovative senior management team is frustrated by middle management who do not like the idea of changing their ways. Their subsequent lack of response, intentional or unintentional, sabotages implementation of any new strategic or organizational initiatives.

In complete contrast to the above scenario is the organization growing at a rapid rate where there are insufficient numbers of middle and lower level managers to provide effective supervision of the corporate expansion. This is not an uncommon problem in the SME sector where market success has been so rapid that the owners have just not had time to implement the organizational developments necessary to underpin servicing of a, now, much larger customer base.

Finally, another common problem in both Europe and North America is the fact that managers are not incompetent but have simply not been trained in the interpersonal skills required to supervise, motivate and lead subordinates effectively. In the past, great emphasis has been given to ensuring that individuals in organizations have the knowledge to fulfil the technical aspects of their job role. This is evidenced by the massive expansion since the Second World War of the number of people entering higher education and the increasing number of years people spend in obtaining formal qualifications. The result, however, is reflected by organizational situations such as projects that fail because engineers in the team do not cooperate with each other, qualified accountants who are unable to communicate with clerical staff, data-processing manuals which nobody other than the computer manager can understand, and technicians who are frustrated by the lack of guidance provided by the doctor who is responsible for the analytical laboratory in a hospital.

Organizations have been forced by such events to become much more aware of the need to ensure that individuals who are assigned the responsibility of managing others are equipped with the necessary interpersonal skills to undertake this aspect of their job role effectively. Hence organizations are moving to install appraisal systems and, where necessary, provide appropriate training. These efforts are complemented by many professional associations (engineers, doctors, lawyers, accountants, etc.) and educationalists who now recognize the importance of placing equal priority on technical and managerial capabilities in the skills development process. Hence both educational and continuing professional development programmes are being revised to reflect greater emphasis on the acquisition of transferable interpersonal skills such as effective communication, leadership, assertiveness and time management.

Single-factor solutions

Given the multitude of factors that can affect organizational performance, it is not surprising to find that success depends on the capability of managers to handle a large number of influencing variables simultaneously.

Most people, however, would seem to prefer to hear that, for any problem, there exists somewhere a simple solution, despite being confronted with overwhelming evidence that the problems they are seeking to resolve are extremely complex. This desire for simple solutions is possibly the reason why some organizations embark on performance-enhancement projects which focus on resolving only one aspect of the organization's activities. The prevailing popularity of single-factor solutions seems to rise and fall like the tide. In the days of scientific management when mass production was seen as the only pathway to success, time and motion studies leading to incentive schemes were all the rage. This approach appears to have then fallen into disuse (although interestingly enough in recent years I have been contacted by various firms asking whether the Business School could mount time and motion courses for their younger production managers). Currently, concepts such as Total Quality Management (TQM), Customer Care, MRP computer systems, time management and the building of flatter, more 'organic' organizations, all have some disciples who preach that theirs is the only true path to organizational immortality.

As with all religions, there are elements of truth within these concepts which are appropriate to meeting the needs of their congregation.

My view, however, is that blind acceptance of any prescribed rules of behaviour involving acceptance of an 'only-way' solution to resolve all performance problems can cause a degree of myopia which may ultimately lead the believers down a road that ends at a cliff. Unfortunately, it does seem that some managers actually share the attributes of the lemming, and this may explain why organizations fall over cliffs as a result of their blind obedience to the latest appealing magic formula being preached by a popular management guru.

Managing organizational performance

Although one cannot specify one single solution which can be applied to enhance performance, it is worth examining the following analysis of how one might avoid the types of problems that cause companies to fail:

- **Total market demand decline** The scale of impact of demand downturns could be reduced if managers assessed market trends more carefully and avoided basing decisions solely on perpetual growth once performance decline indicators began to appear in the marketplace.

- **New product competition** Damage to sales from this source may be avoided if the company has an effective programme for monitoring customer needs and creating products which outperform any other products in the market.

- **Threats from new technology** In a similar way to avoiding competitive threats from new products, the monitoring of advances of relevant technologies, linked to an R & D capability that focuses on fulfilling carefully researched customer needs, will permit the company to avoid being rendered obsolete by competititon.

- **Cost problems** These will not develop into an unmanageable situation if departments such as manufacturing strive to respond to customer needs by optimizing internal productivity.

- **Inadequate financial information** This is a situation which can be avoided if the accounting staff are aware of, and respond to, the needs of other departments for timely and meaningful data.

- **Poor funding decisions** These will cease to be a risk if the external source of finance acts with integrity and regards client needs as more important than the objective of lending money. Greater emphasis on client satisfaction and integrity could also contribute towards avoiding weak investment propositions or acquisitions which offer minimal opportunity for significant growth.

- **Management skills deficiencies** These will disappear if all managers regard subordinates as internal customers, are aware through the medium of an effective appraisal system of their development needs, and then act to ensure that appropriate training is made available.

The common theme associated with the various possible responses described above is the idea that, if one is prepared to focus on customer needs both inside and outside the organization and uses this knowledge to provide the best possible product or service, most organizational problems would never occur in the first place. Or in other words, it is suggested that if a 'customer satisfaction' philosophy is adopted to handle all aspects of the management process then organizations would be able to avoid situations which could adversely impact future performance.

Adopting a customer-focused approach

Given the intuitively appealing concept of basing all managerial response on the philosophy of responding effectively to employee needs within the organization and to customers external to the organization, it is surprising that many executives are more than a little sceptical about the benefits of adopting a customer-focused orientation. The reason for this situation is that very frequently the concept has been proposed by the marketing department. Unfortunately, advice from this source may be rejected because senior management's prior experience of marketing personnel has often caused them to feel that such individuals:

- are selfish to the point of always placing personal goals before the needs of either colleagues or the employer;

- when criticized for inadequate analysis of information prior to reaching a decision will defend their actions on the grounds that marketing is based on 'creativity', not reasoned thought;

- when working with other departments often appear conceited, deaf to alternative suggestions, inexperienced, uninformed and inflexible;

- rarely seem to learn from their mistakes.

Ultimately neither people nor organizations are likely to accept the benefits of applying a customer-focused approach to any aspects of the management process until they have ceased to hold such a negative opinion of marketers. The purpose of the balance of this text, therefore, is to examine how the marketing group can manage various aspects of the customer satisfaction process more effectively. Once the improved performance of marketers persuades other people of the appealing nature of the philosophy, it is hoped that it will be adopted across operational activities within all departments, leading ultimately to the creation of a much larger number of excellent organizations.

2
Prior to marketing planning – fix the culture

Given the heavy emphasis on the rising economic fortunes of Pacific Basin countries in the writings of many of today's management theorists, it is perhaps understandable that people tend to forget just how successful American industry has been during the twentieth century. Both at home and at work, we are surrounded by products either developed or commercialized by US companies. Domestic examples include the refrigerator, colour television, the washing machine, instant coffee and frozen food. Photocopiers, wide-body aircraft, and mainframe or desktop computers running various software systems including spreadsheets and word-processing packages are just a small sample of industrial sector examples. Further proof of American success is the fact that many US companies have become household names in virtually every country around the world (e.g. Du Pont, Ford, General Motors, IBM, McDonalds and Pepsi Cola). These organizations could rightfully expect to be allocated space in any international hall of fame for businesses that are, or have been, outstandingly successful in identifying and satisfying customer need. Thus it does seem important to explain why, over the last 10 to 20 years, so many US corporations have yielded their market leadership to competitors from overseas.

The decline of the American Dream

In the twenties and thirties, Hollywood first presented to the world the 'John Wayne' image of men who walked tall, believed in God, country and apple pie, and overcame all odds in their fight to defeat the 'guys in the black hats'. Fiction turned to fact when the US applied its industrial might to winning the Second World War. As reward for this achievement, American corporations were able to move into and dominate world markets until that fateful day in the early 1970s when the Arab nations invoked their ownership rights by creating OPEC and took control of world oil supplies. Economic growth came to a shuddering halt and it is unlikely that planet Earth will ever again see the high levels of economic growth that were enjoyed by Western nations during the period 1946–72.

Unfortunately, the response of America to the oil crisis was not to accept that economic conditions had changed. Instead the investment community demanded that US corporations should continue to sustain their financial performance. As in all situations, if you are willing to pay enough, you will always find somebody to do whatever is asked of them. Hence, to keep Wall Street happy, some managers were willing to promise growth even when economic conditions would make this an extremely unlikely proposition. Their solution was frighteningly simple – if sales are not increasing, then reduce expenditure, lay off employees, freeze fixed asset renewal programmes and halt all new product activity unless such investment can reduce manufacturing costs. As US management techniques had provided the basis of Western nation economic revival after the war, this new style of management was also happily adopted by many leading companies in Europe. Such short-term expediencies were able to sustain profitability for the balance of the decade. To be successful, however, managers were not permitted to question the fact that this new orientation placed financial performance on a pedestal, well above such concepts as planning for the long term, the importance of placing the customer first or offering job security to the workforce. Customers became a poor second, well behind profits in the list of corporate priorities. In addition employees came to be seen merely as another asset, to be discarded or left untrained because investment in their welfare was just as damaging to ROI as the purchase of new plant and equipment. To remain successful, senior managers had to learn to be both insular and selfish. If you expressed any doubts about what the new management creed would do over the long term to either customer or employee loyalty, then you would be unlikely to keep your job.

In contrast, over this same period, the Japanese were investing heavily in moving their industrial base into sectors of industry such as electronics which were less affected by the impact of rising oil prices. Furthermore Japanese corporations were persuaded by their government to place emphasis on retaining the loyalties of their workforce by accompanying the shift in strategic direction with major investment in retraining schemes to minimize the level of unemployment during the period of industrial change.

CASE STUDY   Meltdown at Classic Ices Ltd

The disguised case of Classic Ices illustrates many of the key features of the management philosophy which evolved in Western nation economies in the period subsequent to the OPEC oil crisis. Founded by Joseph Clean in the mid-fifties, Classic Ices was initially a regional company supplying up-market ice creams to restaurants and specialized delicatessens. The company's core competence was responding to catering sector requests for new and different formulations to meet specific menu needs. Customer loyalty was further strengthened by the company's extremely flexible attitude to producing small quantities of unusual flavours and the high service levels achieved by the company's direct delivery, van sales operation. Geographic expansion was accompanied by the opening of satellite manufacturing operations around the country in order to sustain the 48-hour order placement/delivery cycle which customers considered extremely important.

By the early eighties, Classic Ices was a national operation with annual sales of £10 million, net profit before tax of £800 000 (i.e. 8 per cent sales) and a combined net current and fixed asset balance of £5.6 million. Borrowing to fund growth had come through the medium of issuing shares on the Unlisted Securities Market (USM) and this eventually opened the door to acquisition by a large multinational organization. Mr Clean was elevated to chairman and day-to-day operations were handed over to Graham Lick, previously marketing director in another of the new parent company's subsidiaries. Lick's assigned objective was to grow the company, especially in terms of absolute profits and ROI. He identified an increasing interest in Classic Ices products among the larger supermarket chains and immediately obtained contracts to supply own-label ice-cream to this sector. Sales demand was strong and this placed pressure on the company's abilities to continue to fulfil, concurrently, the needs of established customers for small-quantity, high-variety orders. Having reviewed the implications of incompatibility of order patterns between the catering sector and large retail customers, Lick initiated a programme of replacing part of the van sales operation by redirecting product distribution through wholesalers. When this provided only a partial solution, Lick closed most of the satellite processing plants and consolidated manufacturing onto two sites where new automated machinery was installed to increase productivity. Sales rose by 50 per cent to £15 million. Growth in profits was even more dramatic, reaching £2 million (13.3 per cent of sales) within three years, accompanied by an ROI improvement to 30.8 per cent. At this point, in recognition of his achievements, Lick was transferred to the managing directorship of another company within the group and his place was taken by Allen Green, promoted from marketing director.

As chairman, Mr Clean had expressed severe concerns about the new strategy, pointing out that it was destroying the customer base upon which the business had originally been built. Furthermore he felt that, as the company became increasingly reliant upon own-label business, national supermarket chain customers would be in a stronger and stronger position to dictate future prices. His views were ignored by the parent company and eventually he cashed in his stock options and left to start a new business producing sorbets and frozen yoghurts.

Within three years of his departure, his predictions about the vulnerability of Classic Ices proved to be all too accurate. Over this period sales fell by 20 per cent as established catering sector customers, frustrated by declining service levels, went elsewhere for product and large national frozen ice-cream manufacturers began to offer the supermarkets Classic Ices-type own-label formulations at much lower prices. To protect sales volume, Classic was forced to lower prices, eroding profits down to 10.0 per cent of sales and reducing ROI to 21.8 per cent. The situation was aptly summed up in an unusually honest report by the parent company's corporate planning department, who concluded that Classic's fundamental problem lay in the fact that 'it had been moved from an industry leader in meeting customer needs to being just another ice-cream producer in a remarkably short space of time'.

The financial community joins the party

By the end of the 1970s, US and European companies had exhausted the ephemeral profit growth offered by the rape of balance sheets. Their only real achievement was to have created a generation of managers who were very adept at surviving by being selfish. Growth was still a requirement of the shareholders but, if one cannot manipulate balance sheets from within, the only solution left is to create a financial services community willing to support concepts such as junk bonds, management buy-outs and insider trading to sustain the illusion that the Western world was still enjoying economic good health. By the mid-1980s, both Hollywood and American industry had discarded the John Wayne example and replaced him with a more 'macho' cult hero. Hollywood's version of the new role model was Sylvester Stallone. On Wall Street and in the City of London it became the young financial whiz-kid (or 'yuppie'), living in the make-believe world of success where their ability to 'screw the competition at all costs' permitted them to surround themselves with such evidence of wealth as an expensive German car, a car phone, a fax and (by being mortgaged to the hilt) a luxury apartment in the best part of town. It could not go on for ever, of course, and when the bubble burst in the late 1980s many of these success stories found that their personal empires were built on sand. Even more regretfully, however, they left behind them major banks, saving institutions and even large insurance companies in a severely weakened position. The full impact of this inheritance will probably not be totally understood until well into the 1990s. On the basis of such examples as the sorry state of the American Saving and Loans industry and the weakened balance sheets of certain UK banks, it does not seem unreasonable, however, to suggest that the games of the late 1980s may have damaged some financial sector organizations to the point that they will never be the same again.

The well managed company

By the beginning of the eighties, a few people had begun to sense that something was wrong and this led to a sales boom for books about companies that still remained successful. Sparked by people such as Tom Peters and Rosabeth Moss Kanter, the reader seeking a new Holy Grail was introduced to companies such as Nordstrom and Milliken. The former is a speciality retailer who in less than twenty years grew to be one of America's most successful department stores. Their secret is apparently based on a concept which is as old as the hills: namely 'the customer is always right'. To deliver this proposition the company has focused heavily on creating an internal philosophy of placing the customer first and then delegating to all employees sufficient authority to permit them to deliver an outstanding level of customer service. Stories such as sales people knowing your name after one visit to the store, gift-wrapping on the spot and keeping the store open late for a single customer have all contributed to Nordstrom becoming the retailer that management gurus believe should be emulated by the rest of retail industry.

The Milliken story is perhaps of even greater interest because the company has remained successful as a US manufacturer in an industry which entered maturity late in the nineteenth century, namely textiles. The secret, similar to Nordstrom's, lies in putting the customer, not short-term profitability, first. One of the key ingredients in their formula to retain leadership in the face of intense overseas competition is their Customer Action Team concept. This involves the formation of multi-disciplinary project teams who work in partnership with customers to seek new market opportunities which can be exploited through creative ways of further improving an outstanding record for Total Quality Management and Just in Time (JIT) manufacturing systems.

These examples of effective management are now so rare because, in most organizations, values such as putting the customer first have been replaced by short-term thinking associated with sustaining immediate profitability in the hope that tomorrow will probably be somebody else's problem. Even more regrettable is that these latter philosophies have now been adopted by politicians seeking to resolve public sector problems in education and health care under the banner of responsiveness to 'market forces'. Unfortunately, when one hires managers from the private sector who are deemed successful for their abilities as 'hard-headed', short-term results-oriented individuals and places them alongside civil servants promoted for their skills in ensuring that nothing changes (except possibly a steady increase in the number of employees needed to run the administrative systems), a possible outcome is not that customer service levels will decline but that the needs of customers will cease to have any relevance at all in any evaluation of organizational performance.

Is the effort really worth it?

For the marketer proposing a fundamental shift towards a position where the organization is more customer-oriented, the near-term outlook is that programme implementation will probably increase total expenditure, lower internal morale and generate critical comments from the financial community. Furthermore, if, after major efforts have been expended, the creation of a more customer-focused organization is not achieved, then the organization will probably be sufficiently weakened to be vulnerable to a hostile take-over bid. In view of this situation, it does not seem unreasonable for the reader to question what evidence exists to justify risking the whole organization in redirecting the marketing effort towards delivery of superior customer value.

Robert Buzzell and Bradley Gale's extensive studies of the vast amount of data on the performance of companies and industries, accumulated as part of the long-running PIMS project, possibly provide the most convincing answer. Their conclusions are that companies which deliver the highest possible level of customer satisfaction are able to enjoy the benefits of:

● Greater customer loyalty resulting in higher repeat purchase rates which lowers marketing costs by reducing the number of customers lost to competition.

● Reduced vulnerability in price wars because customers are less likely to be attracted by lower prices being offered by competition.

● An ability to command a price higher than the prevailing average price in their respective industrial sectors.

- Greater success in continuing to expand the total customer base and a high probability that most new business comes via word-of-mouth referrals, thereby reducing the need for heavy promotional spending.

- The combined effect of higher margins from premium prices and lower marketing costs permitting a greater proportion of resources being available for reinvestment into new products capable of further widening the superiority gap over competition in the future.

For those companies that are able to take a long-term perspective (i.e. they are not on the edge of bankruptcy or managed by individuals interested only in balance sheet manipulations to create the appearance of adequate financial performance), the conclusions based on the PIMS data must be that, in today's increasingly competitive world, seeking to deliver superior customer satisfaction appears to be the most viable operating strategy for any organization.

The concept of appropriate culture

The behaviour of an organization is guided and influenced by the values and attitudes of the employees. If marketing managers have been selected and promoted because of their ability to think short-term, and loyally never question objectives such as profit maximization at all costs, then do not expect to find an organization that will behave like a Nordstrom or a Milliken.

In modern management parlance, the term 'organizational behaviour' is now usually replaced by the phrase 'organizational culture' as the shorthand to describe the values and attitudes exhibited by the employees. Culture is reflected in the commitment of employees to a common purpose and determines the skills or competences required of the entire workforce to fulfil their respective job roles effectively. As illustrated in Figure 2.1, establishing an appropriate culture must be the first step to be considered in the strategic processes associated with the creation of an organization that seeks to focus more on meeting the needs of customers.

Management by example

It is very probable that in most organizations the prevailing culture is that which reflects the beliefs and values of senior management.

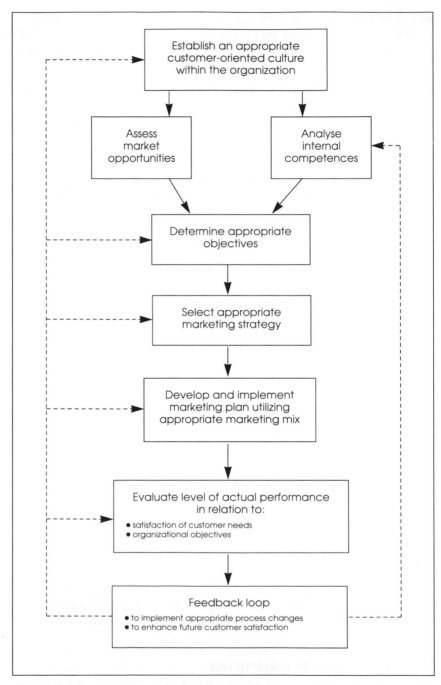

Figure 2.1 The process steps to effective implementation of enhanced customer satisfaction

Hence it is understandable that the reader who is employed in an organization where customer satisfaction is no longer a primary concern may feel that culture can only be changed following an attitude shift at the top. Undoubtedly one of the fastest ways of implementing change is to replace the senior management, but in many situations this is an impractical solution. An alternative suggestion is to establish the marketing operation as an intra-departmental example of a customer-oriented culture. Over time, this will hopefully be seen as more productive than an orientation of short-term profitability and will serve as an example to be adopted gradually elsewhere within the organization.

It is proposed that what is needed is a marketing department which judges the worth of all activities both inside and outside the organization on the basis of values which may seem somewhat old-fashioned: those of honesty, integrity and trust. Initially, one must expect that both customers and other employees will observe this change in behaviour with more than a little scepticism because it will probably be incompatible with their previous experience of how marketers normally behave. Over time, however, inter-departmental mutual trust will emerge and gradually the new culture will begin to be seen as a genuine attempt by marketing to improve organizational performance.

Once this has occurred, the marketer will begin to reap the rewards of enhanced external customer loyalty. Inside the organization, a growing sense of mutual cooperation will greatly assist achievement of the important goal of delivering a level of customer satisfaction well above that offered by competitors. At this point, assuming the revised culture can be sustained, the long-term future of the organization will be secured.

Installing the new culture

Managing the marketing process involves the coordination of product (or service) and information flows between the market and relevant departments within the organization. The start point in creating a new culture is to undertake a survey of current attitudes and perception of (a) staff relationships within the marketing department, (b) what other departments feel about the marketing department and (c) how the customers and market intermediaries view the company's products and services relative to competition. The actual issues raised will vary by organization, but some key areas that should probably be investigated are illustrated in Table 2.1.

Table 2.1 Areas of analysis to be considered in a culture survey

A Survey of intra-departmental staff perceptions of senior management within the marketing operation

Question: When working with senior managers do you find them:

Rating scale	Always	Most of the time	Sometimes	Rarely	Never
Knowledgeable					
Responsive					
Informative					
Helpful					
Innovative					
Cooperative					
Supportive					
Decisive					
Sympathetic					
Competent					
Committed					
Willing to delegate					
Trusting					

B Survey of senior marketing managers' perceptions of staff within their department

Question: When working with staff do you find them:

Questioning
Creative
Self-disciplined
Confident
Motivated
Committed

C Survey of other departments' perceptions of the marketing operation

Question: When working with the marketing group do you find them:

Knowledgeable
Informative
Cooperative
Sympathetic to your problems
Pro-active
Self-critical
Competent

D Survey of customer and intermediary perceptions of the organization

Question: In your dealings with Organization X, do you find:

Products are the best available
Products offer value for money
Products are continually being improved
An immediate response to your questions
Effort made to solve any problems
Staff give honest answers
Staff care about customers
Prompt response to after-purchase service requests

In a customer-oriented company one would expect to find that virtually every factor achieves an 'Always' rating. For the majority of organizations, however, it is likely that intra-departmental, inter-departmental and customer perceptions will reveal many factors classified within the range 'Sometimes' to 'Never'. Thus significant culture change will have to be achieved if the marketing department is to move towards becoming an excellent operation. The process should begin by improving the intra-departmental skills and competences with the aim of creating a participative, team-based marketing group that puts the long-term needs of others before any personal objectives. This will not happen overnight and may require the use of external management development advisers to assist in the planning and implementation of a programme to change work practices at all levels within the marketing team.

Once the culture change operation is well under way within the marketing group, attention can then be turned towards improving relationships with other departments and the market. The former can best be handled by meeting with representatives from other departments to discuss what behaviour traits of the marketers are the basis for their poor image with others inside the organization. Once these have been identified, action can be taken to build a more positive working relationship with other departments. In most cases, however, the new intra-departmental culture being established within the marketing operation will, in itself, begin to create a more cooperative and constructive attitude towards managing interactions with staff from elsewhere in the organization.

Building a new relationship with external customers will require an improved customer interface through the creation of a Customer Care programme. This programme will have the effect of raising customer expectations. Hence it is imperative that concurrently the longer-term marketing strategies are revised to ensure products and services are (a) genuinely designed to fulfil the needs of customers and (b) superior to anything offered by competition either now or in the future.

Patience and minimal promotion

The human animal is a creature of habit and does not respond positively to changes in its environment. Hence the marketer must accept that it will be a long time before a radical shift in culture is totally accepted by either employees or the market. Under these circumstances, an important managerial skill required of the marketer is that of patience. Furthermore, having determined what actions are necessary to implement the culture change, subordinates in the marketing group must also be cautioned about expecting to see any immediate benefits from the adoption of a more caring attitude when working with customers within and outside the organization.

Most management consultants assisting clients to adopt a more customer-focused attitude place great emphasis on the benefits of publicizing the scheme, especially where there is evidence of success. There is, however, a significant risk in this approach because it may raise expectations among internal or external customers of improvement which may not be deliverable given current product quality, resources or staff competences. In the UK, for example, many government employees have recently been sent on customer care training schemes to be taught how to be more pleasant during contacts with the general public. Subsequent research has shown, however, that when the public servant is pleasant but then goes on to explain that, as before, they cannot help (e.g. a hospital administrator informing a patient that it is necessary to cancel an operation because of budget restrictions), this has an even more negative impact than if they had acted in the blunt, unfriendly way characteristic of their behaviour before participating in the customer care training.

People are usually more convinced about any issue when they have acquired their knowledge through personal experience rather than by being informed through promotional campaigns mounted by a supplier. Until the 1970s, the Japanese had a reputation for supplying inferior quality copies of Western company products. They recognized that to succeed in markets such as America they would have to produce higher-quality, more innovative products. Having embarked on major R & D projects to achieve these objectives, they did not then usually spend huge sums on promotional campaigns to tell Western nation customers about the superiority of their products. Instead they tended to let customers find out for themselves. The advantages of this low-key approach are that customers who learn from personal experience about improvements in products and/or services will (a) become extremely loyal and (b) actively communicate their positive experience to others. Furthermore, because there has been no large-scale promotional campaign to raise expectations, if something goes wrong during initial implementation the customer is much less likely to notice that problems are being encountered. This will provide the organization with sufficient breathing space to determine an appropriate solution.

Hence, the recommendation to the marketer undertaking a change programme to revise aspects of organizational culture is initially to handle communication of these activities in a very low-key way. Let positive experience and word-of-mouth comments provide the primary vehicles through which the workforce and the market learn about your more positive attitudes towards customer service. It is accepted that this advice is probably in conflict with the more conventional wisdom of 'if you have it, then flaunt it'. Undoubtedly there are some short-term image gains to be obtained by featuring excellence in your promotional campaign. If, however, something then goes wrong or has to be changed, the reaction from customers can be extremely adverse. Take for example, the exploitation by many major airlines of their company-wide customer care reorientation schemes in the late 1980s through advertising campaigns to promote themselves as caring companies. This view was accepted by the general public and it was on the claim of superior service that these airlines were judged by their passengers. Then at the beginning of the nineties, the general slump in airline travel apparently necessitated a cut-back in service on some flights, such as not offering free nuts or cocktail stirrers with drinks. My observation, based on the comments of businessmen who use these airlines, was that they interpreted this very minor change in service as an early indication that the companies were slipping back into their bad old ways. This adverse reaction may not have been so prevalent among their customers had the airlines not so overtly featured claims of improvement in service levels in their promotional campaigns.

3

Identifying opportunities in the marketplace

As countries in the Western world began to enjoy major growth in per capita income during the fifties, companies that adopted the marketing-oriented philosophy of first determining the nature of customer need and then, satisfying this with appropriate products, outperformed firms that still used the more traditional approach of creating a product and then seeking out potential customers. Lessons learned during this era by companies such as Unilever, Procter & Gamble, General Foods and Nestlé have provided the foundations upon which many of the current theories of marketing management have been built. These organizations were the creators of what today are frequently referred to as the 'blue chip f.m.c.g.s', that is, those companies that dominate the fast-moving consumer goods sector of the economy.

Growing by spending

The 'blue chips' directed their efforts towards selecting large, non-durable consumer goods markets where there were huge revenue opportunities available from developing a product which had the potential to achieve market leadership. In many of these markets (e.g. coffee, soap, beer) there is no real tangible difference in the physical performance characteristics of the various products on offer. Hence leadership is usually achieved through reliance on heavy promotional spending to create perceived differences based on the creation of some form of unique product image.

Marketers who observe the power of promotional spending to improve market share in consumer goods markets frequently ignore the fact that most brand leaders originally achieved their dominant position by being first to enter the market with a different and/or superior product proposition (e.g. brands such as Persil detergent in

the UK or Ivory Soap in America). Therefore, when faced with the
objective of stimulating sales growth, the marketer will ignore the
importance of product performance and instead immediately initiate
an increase in promotional spending to steal a few share points from
the competition. This type of behaviour is possibly the reason why
the trade press is continually packed with articles describing the next
spending battle about to erupt between giants such as Pepsi versus
Coca Cola, McDonalds versus Burger King or Ford versus General
Motors.

Growth through exploiting new opportunities

Some years ago, management theorists recognized that there were
analogies to be drawn between the theories of military warfare and
the management practices of large corporations. Reading a press
release on the latest plan of a corporate giant to gain a few share
points from the competition by starting yet another promotional
spending war, one is reminded of the First World War generals who
placed their faith in frontal assaults to achieve a minor gain in
territory, but at the cost of millions of lives.

It seems a pity that marketers do not bother to read a few books on
military strategy. For in doing so they would learn that most strategic
reversals inflicted on the enemy have been caused by the
introduction of a new warfare concept (e.g. the submarine, the
aeroplane, the aircraft carrier, the tank, the guided missile and the
atomic bomb). This might then make them reflect on the fact that,
over the last thirty years, very few permanent business victories have
been achieved merely by outspending the competition. More
typically, similar to a military situation, winning has usually been
achieved through the introduction of a superior technical solution
which renders the competitors' products obsolete (e.g. Boeing
Corporation's launch of their 747 Jumbo Jet) or by a move to occupy
an area of market territory which has been overlooked by myopic,
and frequently much larger, competitors (e.g. the success of
Volkswagen in America at the point when US car manufacturers
were only interested in selling large cars).

Another fascinating aspect of military history is the recurrent theme
of an individual challenging the majority view and eventually
proving the superiority of their solution (e.g. Billie Mitchell's fight
with US Navy admirals to vindicate his belief in the ability of aircraft
to sink battleships). Analogous situations can be found in the world
of business. For in cases where a large company has been beaten, the

victor is often a new entrant who has been willing to challenge the conventional wisdom of the existing companies, which believe they are in an impregnable market position (e.g. Swiss companies that lost their hold on the world watch market to newcomers such as Seiko and Casio, who were prepared to exploit the advantages of incorporating microchip technology into their products).

In view of this situation, it should be concluded that the decision of many marketers to focus virtually all efforts on supporting increased expenditure to steal a few share points from a competitor is rarely a wise decision. Obviously, an organization should normally allocate sufficient resources to protect the existing customer base. The main focus of marketing effort, however, should be directed towards analysing market trends and identifying indicators of impending change, with the objective of seeking ways to exploit newly emerging opportunities in order to satisfy customer needs more effectively ahead of competition.

One possible approach for identifying future opportunity is to examine the market system of which the organization is a part and to isolate indicators of change by carefully analysing the key factors of influence. The basic core constituents of most systems comprise four elements: suppliers, producers of end products or services,

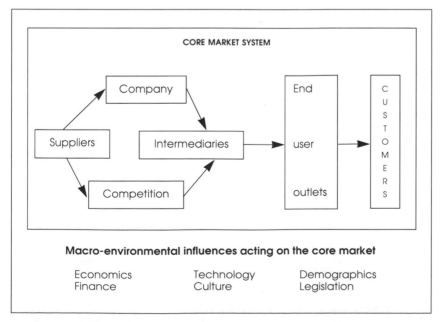

Figure 3.1 A generalized market system model

intermediaries and end users (Figure 3.1). Fundamental influencers of core system performance are macro-environmental variables such as economic conditions, the composition of customer profiles, socio-political values and technology. All these have the potential to affect customer buyer behaviour directly or indirectly.

The influence of economic conditions

In examining the potential impact of economic conditions on buyer behaviour one has to distinguish between cyclical and long-term permanent change. Management of cyclical situations depends on the organization achieving a balance between market conditions and the capacity to respond to variation in demand. There is usually a time lag between deciding to increase or decrease capacity and then implementing appropriate actions. Hence, as illustrated in Figure 3.2, it is probably wise (a) to expand capacity in anticipation of an increase in market demand and (b) to be willing to forgo some sales at the peak of the growth cycle in order to avoid being left with expensive, underutilized capacity when the market finally downturns.

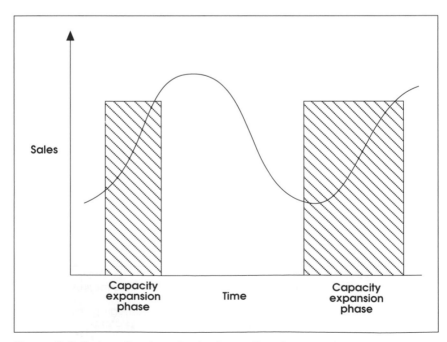

Figure 3.2 Generalized cyclical sales pattern in response to changing economic conditions

Suggesting this approach is easy. Nevertheless it must be recognized that, in practice, it takes a very brave marketing team to suggest terminating investment during the euphoric period when markets are growing or, alternatively, suggesting that funds be directed towards new product development involving a complete re-tooling of the manufacturing operation in the middle of a recession. The construction industry, for example, in both the UK and America, has recently learnt the expensive lessons of having misread sales trends in the late eighties and being left with excess, over-valued assets at the time the market suddenly plunged into recession.

In addition to managing capacity, the marketer must also recognize that the nature of product demand will vary across the economic cycle. When there is an upswing, customers not only spend more but they also tend to demand greater variety. Hence, during this phase of the economic cycle, the marketer must ensure that the organization offers an appropriately broad range of products. In contrast, during a downturn customers typically become more conservative. They may opt for a low-cost, 'no frills' offering or, alternatively, reduce frequency of purchase but seek higher quality to ensure product durability is maximized. Whichever is the case, the company must ensure either that their product position is recession-proof (which is often the case for the leading brands) or, alternatively, that the product range can rapidly be revised to suit prevailing economic conditions (e.g. the move by many supermarket chains in the late 1980s to expand their range of own-label products and give in-store prominence to national brands willing to offer increased sales promotion activity such as price pack or coupons).

In the search for the most appropriate way of satisfying changing customer needs, there are possibly very significant implications in the observations of researchers such as Professor Hirsch who have demonstrated that, as nations acquire wealth, their populations begin to exhibit the characteristic of seeking a greater diversity of choice when selecting goods or services. At this point, organizations which focus on the provision of a single uniform product on the assumption that price is still the dominant influence in the purchase decision may find their market position weakened by competitors who are prepared to respond to an increased desire for diversity of choice. An early demonstration of this phenomenon was provided in the thirties by the Ford Motor Company which, having created the mass-production technologies that made automobiles affordable for the average consumer, continued to place strategic emphasis on seeking new ways of remaining price competitive. Their philosophy was encapsulated in the now infamous offer of 'any colour as long as it is black'. General Motors, realizing that the American public had begun to exhibit a desire for a much greater degree of choice, responded by offering a broader portfolio of product options and toppled Ford from their dominant position in the market.

Over the last two decades, the concept of satisfying the needs of a newly emerging subset of specialist demand has become known as 'market niching'. It has proved extremely popular for smaller companies that wish to attack a more dominant competitor but without becoming involved in a costly and drawn-out frontal assault on the latter's well entrenched market position. Examples of the strategy are provided by Cray Computers' success against the large mainframe computer manufacturers with their 'supercomputer' and, in the UK, Mercury Communications' successful challenge to British Telecom by concentrating on the provision of telecommunications services to large companies.

The market niching approach has also proved effective for companies that have sought to establish a beachhead in new overseas markets. Once an initial victory has been accomplished in one market segment, the company may then further exploit the reputation created by their first success and launch a broader portfolio of products. Examples of this strategy are provided by companies such as Sony in consumer electronic goods and Canon in photocopiers, and more recently by the entry of certain American banks into the European financial services market.

Customer profile composition

The profile of customers in any market will have significant influence on overall demand. In consumer goods markets, for example, the age composition of a population will have a dramatic positive or negative impact on product demand. The sales revenue of a manufacturer of children's shoes is directly influenced by the size of the population, per capita disposable income and the prevailing birth rate. If a large proportion of newly married couples decide they cannot afford to start a family, or it becomes fashionable to have only one child, the birth rate will fall and subsequently so will the demand for children's shoes. This change in the age compositon of the market will also affect intermediaries who specialize in the children's market (e.g. retailers of baby clothes) and companies that provide industrial goods and services to this sector (e.g. an engineering company which designs and installs food-processing lines for canned baby foods). The ripple effect will also spread into the public sector because the declining birth rate may lead to a fall in the demand for the provision of educational services.

As the wealth of a nation increases, this is typically accompanied by a declining birth rate and an increase in average life expectancy. Hence population demographics is an important factor in creating new opportunities for virtually any organization, no matter whether it is in the public or private sector. Take for example the provision of medical services. Public sector providers have to direct more resources to the provision of caring for the aged. Drug companies need to concentrate R & D towards better treatments for conditions such as heart failure and renal disorders. Insurance and pension firms have to create policies which can fund the provision of services for people who can be expected to live for many years after retiring from full-time employment.

Customer profiles in industrial markets may also undergo change if once-dominant members within a sector are replaced by new and more successful organizations. For example, a company specializing in the manufacture of plate steel for the shipping industry in the period immediately after the Second World War would probably have key customers among shipyards located in America and Western Europe. The ship construction industries in these countries have long since been overtaken by Pacific Basin producers such as Japan and, subsequently, Korea. Unless the company had identified this trend and moved to develop a base of sales in the Far East or, alternatively, diversified into another sector such as the supply of plate steel to the off-shore oil exploration industry, then by now these radical changes in customer profiles would probably have had a terminal effect on the organization.

It should also be recognized that changes in customer profiles are sometimes caused by the new entrant launching a superior product or service which utilizes different manufacturing technologies. This in turn will require revised specifications for the components they purchase from their suppliers. An example of this situation is provided by the European Airbus Consortium who sought to improve the performance of their new generation of aircraft through the introduction of 'fly by wire' technology. Some companies which had traditionally supplied components for hydraulic control systems suddenly found that this new specification was completely outside their field of experience. As a result, they lost sales to competitors who had already acquired expertise in the field of electronic avionic systems through their previous involvement in defence industry contracts.

Socio-political values

The behaviour of individuals is greatly influenced by the prevailing attitudes and values of the society of which they are a part. Furthermore, in a democracy, the manifesto of the ruling party has to reflect the prevailing views of the population if they wish to remain in power for any significant period of time. Hence all organizations need to monitor carefully the market environment to detect newly emerging changes in social values, because these can represent new opportunities or, if ignored, may have disastrous consequences for future performance.

In the early eighties a small minority of people began to be concerned about the impact of the human race on the environment. At first most organizations considered this to be a fringe movement that would have no real influence on their business, so no real attempts were made to avoid being accused of causing damage to planet Earth. By misreading the situation, companies such as McDonalds were suddenly confronted in America by a massive threat to their sales because outlets were picketed by large numbers of people accusing the chain of using environmentally unfriendly packaging and being a contributor to the destruction of South American rainforests.

Although the usual inclination of organizations is to see value shifts as a threat, in reality one can expect any change in buying behaviour to provide new opportunities for the perceptive organization prepared to act ahead of the competition. For example, during the 1980s two companies in the UK, Ark and Ecover, launched environmentally friendly washing powders. Their success has subsequently influenced the larger companies (e.g. Procter & Gamble's Fairy washing powder brand) to reformulate their products to provide the basis for counter-claiming that their products now use fewer chemicals and less packaging and contain no phosphates.

A shift in the cultural values within a society is usually very gradual, which means that forecasting the speed with which new attitudes will affect buying behaviour is quite difficult. This is rarely the case when governments take action to respond to the prevailing mood of a nation, because they can introduce legislation to invoke more rapid change. Recent political scenarios – the growth of fundamentalist religious sects in the Middle East and the impact of perestroika in the Warsaw Pact countries – provide two very contrasting examples of how politics can affect demand. In the case of the Middle East, religious fervour has dramatically curtailed sales of Western-type consumer goods for the foreseeable future, whereas in the Eastern bloc the move to replace communism with a free market economy represents a major new source of revenue for Western nation producers.

Technology

Whether in the home or at work, we are all surrounded by machines, products and processes which represent examples of how technology can radically alter our whole way of life. The challenge facing the marketer is to comprehend which scientific or technical advances offer the greatest potential to enhance the organization's ability to satisfy customer needs in the future.

The magnitude of opportunity offered by new technology will to a certain degree be influenced by whether the technology is evolutionary or revolutionary. The latter event is much rarer, but when it occurs the impact is likely to cause severe alteration in the competitive position of companies within the industrial sector that is affected. One example is the impact on the aviation industry of the discovery of jet propulsion. Although pioneered by Germany and Britain, the technology was more effectively exploited by the Americans and permitted them to move to a dominant position in both the civilian and military aircraft markets.

Evolutionary change typically involves effort being focused on further improvement in an established process. Consequently it is easier for existing companies within an industrial sector to monitor progress and react by ensuring any advances are incorporated into current operations. Even in this situation, however, there are numerous examples of leading companies who were aware of a technical advance but underestimated potential opportunity and handed market leadership to competitors. This scenario is illustrated by the electronics industry where the leaders in vacuum tube technology underestimated the potential of the transistor, the transistor companies paid insufficient attention to LSI semiconductors and they, in turn, were not the major exploiters of VLSI technology.

In view of the major opportunity for growth offered by technological change, the marketer must continually monitor the scientific environment to obtain adequate warning of a revolutionary technology. Marketers working alongside technical staff within the organization can then jointly assess the potential that new technologies offer for entering new markets, expanding product portfolios and/or creating obsolescence within the existing product line. An example of this situation is the development of the plain paper copier by Xerox Corporation in the sixties. This technology

offered not just a superior product alternative in the stencils/
duplicator market but also opened up completely new markets by
radically altering, on a global scale, many aspects of the entire
process of reproducing printed information.

In the case of evolutionary change in established (or 'base')
technology, the impact of changing technology is likely to be less
dramatic. Again, however, the marketer needs to work with technical
staff in determining whether technological advances might create
new opportunities (e.g. the Winchester disk drive which radically
altered the computing power of desktop computers relative to
mainframe and minicomputers) or support a more competitive
market position (e.g. the mini-mill technology which permitted small
regional steel companies to compete more effectively against the big
mills, whose large integrated steel plant previously allowed them to
enjoy very large economies of scale within their operations).

Opportunities within the core system

Although change in macro-environmental variables offers numerous
ways to satisfy customer needs more effectively, the marketer must
also be alert for similar opportunities made possible by changes
within the core system. Many of the features in the latest computers,
for example, have only become feasible because suppliers in the
electronics industry have repeatedly found ways of miniaturizing
and enhancing the processing power of the microchip.
Organizations can also benefit from advances made by suppliers of
the equipment used in value added processes within the
organization (e.g. the impact of robotics on enhancing product
quality in the automobile industry).

Intermediaries can also be major sources of ideas which can be
exploited by producer companies. In part this comes from the fact
that the intermediary often has more contact with the end user and
can more rapidly identify newly emerging needs. For example, as the
computer industry has grown, many manufacturers have turned to
distributors to manage the customer in place of the more traditional
approach of using a direct sales force. The larger distributors are now
a very important source of information on customer needs and often
provide suggestions to the manufacturer on opportunities for new
machine configurations and software systems.

Ultimately, of course, the destiny of producer, supplier and
intermediary are all bound together by the common objective of
seeking ways to satisfy customer needs. In the past the more usual

practice of companies was to keep suppliers and intermediaries at 'arm's length' on the grounds that this enhanced the organization's ability to control these external forces. The more forward-thinking companies have realized that all parties in the core system have a common goal. Hence they now see that there are major advantages to working together in the continued improvement of existing goods or services and in the development of new product concepts.

As well as monitoring the changing needs of the final customer, the marketer must also work on creating more effective working relationships with external organizations and to use this medium of information interchange as an important element in the process of continually seeking new ways of further building customer satisfaction. In the car industry, for example, forging closer and closer partnership with component suppliers is now widely accepted as a vital ingredient for any manufacturer attempting to produce vehicles that will outperform the competition. Linking with other members of the core system may even in some cases mean entering into collaborative relationships with companies that in theory are potential competitors (e.g. the recently announced product development alliance between Apple and IBM). This is now quite accepted in those sectors of industry where the complexity of technology makes it virtually impossible for companies other than a dominant world market leader to manage successfully the development of new, superior products. In both the US and Europe, companies in sectors such as computing and telecommunications are now forming consortia and/or joint ventures to manage the creation of the next generation of new products.

Marketing by listening and learning

If one visited most marketing departments and enquired about their search for new opportunities, they would proudly point to numerous market research reports and describe lengthy sessions held regularly with their advertising agency in the search for new ways of outmarketing the competition. All this is well intentioned. But regretfully it runs the risk of being incestuous because, even with the best will in the world, the most likely outcome of such activities is that the marketing department and/or their external advisers will be biased towards their own views on how the customer should be treated.

There is a growing awareness of the need to involve others from within and outside the organization in the search for new opportunities. A move that is enjoying widespread popularity in many companies at the moment is to install a company-wide 'suggestion scheme'. The justification for this activity – frequently mentioned in popular management writings – is the fact that Japanese companies can expect to receive up to 50 000 suggestions per year. It must be recognized, however, that this level of achievement is only likely after one has established a deep commitment by all employees to contributing towards enhancing organizational performance. If a Western company puts up suggestion boxes without having previously created an internal culture centred around strong employee loyalty, they should not be surprised to find that the commonest items deposited in the boxes will be cigarette stubs and chewing gum wrappers.

The initial objective for the marketer seeking to widen internal participation in the opportunity search process must be the more humble goal of getting others interested in the activity. How this might be done will vary by organization but, whichever methods are adopted, the message to communicate is that the marketing group recognizes it does not hold the monopoly on new ideas. They need to broadcast their desire for help from others and establish an 'open-door' policy to anybody interested in helping to find even more effective ways of satisfying customer needs. Concurrently, of course, the marketer must create an image of complete integrity. This will dispel the fear that, if someone from another department has a good idea, they will have recognition of their achievement stolen by the marketing department.

The following is just a sample of some of the approaches I have observed in working with various organizations on consultancy and/or management development projects:

• Installing a machine to brew endless supplies of fresh coffee, buying fresh pastries every day and broadcasting that the marketing group is always happy to entertain visitors at the beginning of each day.

• Asking other departments to deliver seminars or attend regular meetings with the marketing department to focus on aspects of their work and on current concerns about the working relationship with company marketers, and to examine forecasts of change in their areas of functional expertise which might affect products and/or customer service.

• Sponsoring seminars for or by industry suppliers to review trends and changes at their level in the market system which might offer new opportunities to improve the organization's products and services.

- Organizing seminars with intermediaries with objectives similar to those of the in-company and supplier meetings.

- Holding open days when suppliers, intermediaries and/or end-user customers are invited to wander round the organization meeting with employees and discussing common problems or opportunities.

- Producing a marketing department newsletter for the entire organization (or taking regular space in the organization newsletter if one exists) communicating information on issues such as future plans, recent examples of customer complaints and new initiatives to enhance customer service. The editor should actively promote feedback from other departments which can provide the basis for future articles to stimulate further debate across the entire organization.

The common focus of the above examples is that they provide evidence of the most important skill required of the marketer, the ability to listen. This must be accompanied by an active willingness to learn. In part, the learning process will come via the knowledge gained from hearing the views of others. The learning process must be taken further, however, to ensure the marketer is exposed to the widest possible range of new concepts which will contribute to stimulating the search for new opportunities. Hence it is recommended that marketing departments actively promote this learning process by actions such as persuading staff to read articles and books on a wide range of subjects, attend trade seminars, commit to attending courses at educational institutions and travel extensively both at home and abroad.

The move to a listening and learning marketing department will not happen overnight. It will demand dedication and effort to establish successfully this type of marketing culture. The final rewards, however, are immense because ultimately it will result in an entire organization where employees, working in close collaboration with external sources such as suppliers and intermediaries, are directing their efforts towards the common objective of identifying new opportunities for the further satisfaction of the customer.

4

'But can we deliver what the market wants?'

Although the orientation of desiring to satisfy customer need is fundamental to success, there is little point in pursuing such a strategy if the organization lacks the internal capabilities to meet the market's product and/or service needs. Hence the marketer seeking ways to outperform competition should not just study external opportunities. Concurrently an in-depth understanding will have to be acquired about all internal operations which have any influence on customer perceptions of how well the organization's output fulfils market demand. In today's competitive world, there is no future in just finding markets in which to operate. The successful organization must also have an internal capability to win the race to satisfy customer requirements ahead of competition.

A very popular tool for studying organizational potential is a technique known as SWOT analysis, where the acronym stands for Strengths, Weaknesses, Opportunities and Threats. The first two variables cover internal operations and the accepted logic is to focus on exploiting those organizational characteristics that are seen as strengths. Although there is some merit in this philosophy, in most markets the intensity of competition is such that, if a weakness is identified, significant attention must be given to ensuring that this variable does not place the organization in a vulnerable position.

EXAMPLE In 1991, the food and drinks giant, Allied-Lyons, received its auditors' report quantifying a loss of £147 million stemming from mistakes made by its international currency dealing centre. The company has an outstanding track record as a producer and marketer of branded products. Unfortunately the finance director, Cliff Hatch, appears to have made an error in assuming the currency dealers he hired were as good as they thought they were in trading currency options. From the report prepared by the auditors. KPMG Peat Marwick, it appears the currency centre was dealing in options to a much greater extent than was needed to support the company's mainstream activities. In early March 1991, due in part to the influence of the Gulf War on the value of the dollar, the company incurred huge losses from currency trading. Long-term success in the food and drinks sector demands an ability to sustain massive promotional budgets while concurrently investing heavily in entering new markets and launching new, improved products. Although Allied-Lyons still retains all its marketing and manufacturing expertise, it does not seem unreasonable to suggest that the trading losses will significantly weaken its ability to fund mainstream operations in the near term. If the Board does not find a way of overcoming this weakness, then for the foreseeable future the company will probably be very vulnerable to attacks by other multinational food and drinks operations. Thus it would probably be most unwise of its marketing staff to ignore consideration of this corporate reduction in financial circumstances when preparing plans for the balance of this decade.

Dissecting the product

One starting point for the marketer engaged in examining organizational competences is to focus on the department whose primary function is production of output. In a tangible goods company, this will normally be the manufacturing group operating production lines and factories. In contrast, a service company production centre will often be composed of numerous employees based on office environments (e.g. a company offering insurance cover for private cars where staff are engaged in the information transmission and storage processes associated with providing clients with policies for their vehicles and handling any subsequent claims).

Theodore Levitt has suggested that one needs to consider the product as composed of two elements: the 'core product' which represents the standard benefit sought by the customer, and the 'augmented product' which comprises the additional attributes that surround the basic offering. In the airline industry, for example, the core product is the seat on a flight. Augmentation is provided by factors such as the reservation system, passenger-handling facilities at the terminal and in-flight services. The augmented product is often the key element in delivering a product different to that of competition (e.g. American Airlines who reached market leadership in the 1980s through service efficiency based on their internally developed computerized passenger-handling system). If, however, the basic product is flawed, then this has to be rectified before any attempt can be made to exploit opportunities that may be offered through product augmentation. This point was sadly demonstrated by the UK car industry in the last decade. In this industry there was little point worrying about improving their dealer-network or incorporating advanced technology into their post-purchase service and parts operations as a mechanism for product augmentation until they had overcome the basic problem that mechanically their cars were seen as inferior to overseas competitors such as the Japanese.

Manufacturing competences

Required manufacturing competences for core and augmented products will vary dramatically between industrial sectors. Factors which influence this variation include product and manufacturing technology, stability of market demand and intensity of competition. In examining internal capability, the marketer will need, therefore, (a) to understand how such variables influence internal competences to fulfil the product performance expectations of the customer and (b) to judge whether potential exists to meet these demands both now and in the future.

In a capital goods sector such as heavy engineering, product technology is often complex (e.g. aero-engines), specifications are continually changing to reflect incorporation of new scientific advances, products are frequently 'one offs' to meet a unique customer specification and the time period from order placement to delivery is very long. Yet financial success often hinges on an ability to meet an exact delivery date many months after work on the contract was first initiated. Under these circumstances, the marketer's evaluation of manufacturing competences will include the ability to carry out successfully complicated R & D tasks, accurately specify delivered prices early into the contract (even when the real costs of the product technology are not yet fully understood) and manage large multi-disciplinary project teams engaged in the manufacture and assembly of highly complex products under very tight time schedules.

The manufacturing competences in a sector engaged in producing high-volume, standardized products at competitive prices, although just as demanding, will be very different from those of the capital goods situation. A company making plastic pipes, for example, would have to be very competent in the area of plant capacity planning and utilization. This is because their customers (e.g. house builders) seek a standard product at the lowest possible price. This requirement can only be achieved if the manufacturer runs a more productive plastic extrusion line than the competition and is thus able to meet market pressures over price while still returning an adequate profit to the stakeholders. In such a high-volume production environment, the company will also need to be competent in such areas as feed stocks procurement and Just in Time processing philosophies in order to minimize working capital being tied up in raw materials, work in progress and finished goods.

Augmentation competences

The ability of an organization to offer an augmented product may lie within the core production group (e.g. a lawn-mower company which is able to offer a number of product models ranging from the simple feature of an electric start option through to complex concepts such as cutting heads which automatically adjust to variation in lawn surface and a computer-based engine fault diagnosis system). It is equally possible, however, that augmentation will be delivered by departments involved in processes outside mainstream manufacturing operations. In consumer goods markets, for example, supermarkets face the difficult problem of creating store and shelf layouts which maximize profitability per square metre while concurrently ensuring appropriate products are made available to the general public. One way of managing this problem is to develop a computer model which examines market trends and then develops an optimal shelf layout planogram which relates facings to brand performance. Already market leader, the UK company Mars Petfoods has over recent years augmented their product range by developing a computerized store management decision model for the canned petfood sector. Data collected by field sales staff are used to develop shelf layout recommendations which are made available to the major supermarket chains. Although undoubtedly Mars recovers the cost of the system from improved in-store movement for its product range, the even greater benefit is that the analysis service augments the core product, thereby further differentiating the company from other manufacturers in a highly competitive market sector.

Customer service interface competences

The customer may come in contact with a number of different departments of the organization during the various phases of selecting a product, making the purchase, taking delivery and then using the item. Take for example the very simple process of going out to eat at a restaurant. The customer may telephone to reserve a table and also enquire about certain aspects of the menu. The quality of telephone response of the switchboard operator and the head waiter will cause opinions to be formed. Upon arrival the service of the doorman, the barman, the coat-check person, the head waiter, the wine waiter and the table waiter will probably have more influence on customer attitudes than the kitchen's ability to prepare and serve the meal in a timely and enjoyable form. At the time of departure, the skills of the person at the till in efficiently processing the credit card will have an impact. Other aspects of the event such as cleanliness of the table linen and towels in the rest-room, which are hired from an industrial services group, can also have a negative or positive effect depending on the restaurant's skills in selecting competent suppliers. Finally, it is not until the next day that the customer realizes he has left his favourite umbrella behind. The perception of the previous evening can now be enhanced or reduced, depending on how the cleaner who answers the telephone responds to the early morning enquiry about locating the item of lost property.

Simultaneously managing all the interfaces in the restaurant example is not easy. Imagine how rapidly the complexity of the task is magnified within a much larger organization such as the Ford Motor Company or ICI. Yet if an adequate assessment is to be made of all aspects of the internal capability of an organization to satisfy market need, then it is necessary for the marketer to evaluate fully the impact of every interface with which customers come in contact during all the phases associated with reaching and implementing their purchase decision.

Financial competences

If managers are to be effective then it is imperative that they are held both accountable and responsible for their actions. A major aspect of the management role is to ensure that all departments are fulfilling their obligations to contribute to the processes associated with adding value to organizational outputs. Although specification of policies by which value addition activities are measured is usually the preserve of the accountant and/or external auditors, it is the individuals undertaking line management activities who have the responsibility for balancing expenditures against revenue in order to optimize profit performance. Hence key areas that must be assessed by the marketer are (a) the internal capabilities of all departments and their staff to be financially competent and (b) the accounting team's ability to create information systems that permit everybody to understand actual versus budgeted performance.

It is imperative, however, that both revenue and cost management activities are driven by the primary goal of satisfying customers, not achievement of some arbitrary profit figure which is seen as appealing to external stakeholders and thereby avoids a short-term decline in the value of company shares. In May 1991, for example, the giant of customer-oriented UK retailing, Marks & Spencer, announced a freeze on graduate recruitment and redundancies at Head Office. If these actions are not merely designed to sustain the 1991 share price, but instead are an integral part of a carefully planned strategy to permit the company to offer an even better level of customer service in the nineties, then such actions are to be applauded. At this juncture, however, it does not seem unreasonable to ask the questions of (a) how much accumulated service experience will be lost in the departure of several hundred corporate staff and (b) will a graduate entry recruitment freeze now create a store-level management resource problem in a few years' time? Only time will tell which is the correct interpretation of current events.

Financial performance is not just measured by profit on sales. The organization is entrusted with the guardianship of assets and is obligated to achieve a return on investment (or return on capital employed – ROCE) sufficient to satisfy the perceived risks of the stakeholders who have loaned money or purchased shares. The balance sheet as the financial statement of assets and liabilities is often seen as the preserve of the finance director and/or board of directors. Unfortunately, it is all too easy to manipulate balance sheets over the short term to enhance ROCE and thereby endear oneself to the financial community. If the organizational priority is to meet the demands of such people to the detriment of customer satisfaction, then ultimately the company will pay the price in terms of undermining its long-term market position.

CASE STUDY   Arlington versus Bernwick Engineering

To demonstrate this effect one can compare the disguised case of two UK engineering companies both operating as subcontractors supplying components for defence industry Original Equipment Manufacturers (OEMs). In the late eighties, the 'peace dividend' offered by perestroika had serious implications for small UK engineering companies, because suddenly they could no longer be certain of a steady flow of orders from their customers who supplied military hardware to NATO forces in Europe. The response by the Board of Arlington Engineering Ltd was reflected in a press statement in which they talked about 'tough times ahead, the need for belt tightening to build a slimmer, fitter organization with the capability to sustain the level of financial performance expected by our shareholders'. This latter group was no doubt pleased over the next three years to see a growth in sales, profits and ROCE (Table 4.1). It was achieved by cutting all but the most necessary

Table 4.1   Comparative financial results for two UK engineering companies

	£'millions		
	Year 1	Year 3	Year 5
Arlington Engineering Ltd			
Sales	5.0	5.3	5.0
Total operating expenses	4.5	4.6	4.5
Net profit (before tax)	0.5	0.7	0.5
Profit as % of sales	10.0%	13.2%	10.0%
Net current assets	1.25	1.5	1.3
Net fixed assets	2.0	2.0	1.5
Total net assets	3.25	3.5	2.8
Capital employed	3.25	3.5	2.8
ROCE	15.4%	20.0%	17.9%
Bernwick Engineering Ltd			
Sales	5.0	5.5	7.0
Total operating expenses	4.5	4.9	6.1
Net profit (before tax)	0.5	0.6	0.9
Profit as % of sales	10.0%	10.9%	12.8%
Net current assets	1.25	1.4	1.8
Net fixed assets	2.0	3.0	3.2
Total net assets	3.25	4.4	5.0
Capital employed	3.35	4.4	5.0
ROCE	15.4%	13.6%	18.0%

expense, halting R & D, laying off shop-floor production staff and permitting capital expenditure only on the most urgent renewal of obsolete plant and equipment. The increase in net current assets (i.e. current assets less current liabilities) reflected negotiations with certain customers who were willing to place orders if Arlington were prepared to carry larger than usual finished goods inventories and not press for prompt payment. The increase in debtor balances was partially compensated for by a significant lengthening of the period that Arlington suppliers were made to wait before they were paid. This improvement in financial performance proved to be ephemeral; within two years sales had declined and, to fill their order book, Arlington were forced to accept some contracts at prices at or below breakeven.

In contrast the strategy adopted by Bernwick Engineering Ltd was somewhat different. The marketing director recommended that it would be necessary to find mechanisms to retain defence industry customers by investment in new technologies that permitted the company to offer upgraded specification components. He also believed that in order to avoid redundancies it would be necessary to diversify into new markets. The Board accepted this philosophy and approved a decision to embark on a medium-term product/plant modernization scheme that required a significant injection of new capital over a five-year period. In announcing their plans to the business press, the company explained that 'we have a responsibility to secure the future of our workforce, investors and suppliers in what will be difficult times. Cut-backs will hurt everybody and most importantly undermine the foundations upon which this company is built: namely, our reputation for outstanding engineering quality and customer service'. No doubt there were some nervous people both inside and outside the company because, although new markets were found and defence industry orders did not fall too dramatically, the heavy expenditure on new technologies and market diversification resulted in ROCE declining from 15.4 per cent to 13.6 per cent over the next three years. Two years later the ROCE performance of Arlington and Bernwick were very similar. The trends, however, were very different with the latter heading on upwards and the former having nowhere to go except down.

It is hoped that marketers assessing asset management competences within their own organization will find the philosophy is similar to Bernwick, where the balance sheet reflects a dedication to serving markets and stakeholders appreciate the importance of creating strategies designed to secure the company's future. Unfortunately, based on events over recent years in many Western economies, one is forced to accept that all too frequently organizational cultures are clearly biased towards placing the financial community before the customer. Over the longer term, this philosophy will be to the detriment of everybody – customer, employees and ultimately entire nations.

Organizational structure competence

Human beings are independent-minded animals and, as the number of employees rises, so do the problems associated with organizing them into an effective and coordinated workforce. Business school libraries are crammed full of books offering theories on the perfect organizational structure. Possibly the only unifying factor which the reader is likely to find in such texts is that the authors rarely agree with each other. There are concepts about how many people should be under the control of one individual (often known as 'managerial span of control'), about layered versus non-layered (or 'flat') organizational hierarchies, and about centralized versus decentralized managerial control styles. Possibly the best way of handling this huge variance of expert opinion is to accept that different structures suit different situations and to adopt some form

of unifying parameter of measurement that can be used to evaluate
actual practice.

CASE STUDY   Car parts for DIY enthusiasts

One parameter which does not seem too fanciful is to suggest that
organizational structures might be assessed against the simple measure of
the competence of the structure to optimize customer satisfaction. How the
organizational structure can sometimes fail against this criterion is
demonstrated by the disguised case of Roger Parr Ltd. This company
supplies car parts to DIY enthusiasts through a chain of 25 retail outlets. Trade
customers can also obtain parts at these locations or have them brought to
their garages by the Parr van delivery fleet. The company's success is
founded on the philosophy of having a well trained sales staff, a helpful
attitude over resolving customers' car maintenance or repair problems and
a willingness to let managers have complete discretion to stock whatever
items seem popular with customers in their locality. Three years ago, the
company encountered a cash crisis and was acquired by a national
company in the parts supply business. Their analysis of their new subsidiary
revealed excess stocks, poor inventory control, insufficient attention to price
in negotiations with suppliers and a very liberal policy towards slow-paying
trade customers. The solution was to install a computerized stock control
system with terminals in outlets linked to a mainframe at Head Office, a
complete ban on any purchasing except by the newly created central
buying office, determination of a common store layout policy for all outlets,
Head Office shipping replacement stocks based upon a computerized
national stocking level decision model and a very hard-nosed attitude over
trade accounts, with court action frequently being invoked to speed up
debtor payments.

Initially these policies had a beneficial impact on overall financial
performance because profits and ROI both increased. Within 18 months,
however, the year-on-year sales growth which was the accepted 'norm' in
the past came to a grinding halt. Furthermore, even though the total UK
market for car spares continued to increase, this cessation of sales growth
indicated that Parr was beginning to lose market share. A market survey
revealed a significant decrease in customer loyalty and analysis of the
research data revealed that customers saw Parr as a 'distinctly less friendly
firm' with employees increasingly exhibiting an attitude of 'if we haven't got it,
then you will probably be better off trying somewhere else'.

Discussions with outlet managers revealed that the computer system was
seen as a distinct improvement over the way stocks and ordering processes
had been managed in the past. These managers also felt, however, that the
Head Office centralization of virtually all decisions (a) ignored regional
variation for many parts, (b) created an impression among customers that
Parr was not interested in selling anything other than standard car parts and
(c) indicated a complete lack of trust in employees among senior
management at Head Office.

After careful consideration of these findings, the marketing director realized that, in responding to a clear Board directive to improve financial performance, he had overlooked the need to sustain concurrently the reputation for customer service upon which Parr Ltd was originally founded. He raised his concerns with the finance director and together they examined ways to improve customer service. Eventually they decided that, although procurement and distribution of high-turnover items would remain under Head Office control, each manager should be granted authority to source and stock up to 25 per cent of outlet inventory to meet local needs without involving Head Office. In addition, management of trade customer accounts receivables balances would be handed back to the outlets. Over this issue, however, Head Office did reserve the right to intervene where the average age of debtors dramatically exceeded the corporate average or if their analysis revealed a growing debtor problem with the same trade customer across a number of outlets.

In addition to the issue of whether authority is retained by senior management or transferred to managers operating nearer to the market interface, another aspect of organizational competence is the interpersonal skills within each department. Empowered employees are of little use if they are ineffective in key areas such as communication, delegation, problem solving, decision making, time management or motivating others. Hence it is also necessary for the marketer in any review of customer service processes to determine if this is impaired because of deficiencies in the selection, training and development of staff. For example, there is little point in implementing the new delegated authority processes at Roger Parr Ltd only to find that a personality clash between the warehouse manager and the fork-lift truck drivers means that urgently requested items have been omitted from shipments to outlets.

Assessing perception of competence

When determining the relationship between customer satisfaction and relevant internal competences, it is necessary first for the marketer to establish which factors form the basis of how the performance of the organization is perceived in the marketplace. Once this is known, research will be needed to evaluate current performance for each of the dimensions which have an important influence on customer attitudes. Those areas seen to be inadequate should be targeted for improvement if the organization is to achieve the objective of eventually having the competences necessary to outperform competition. Examples of issues which it may be beneficial for the marketer to evaluate are described in Table 4.2.

Table 4.2 Assessment of some internal competences which may influence customer perceptions of organizational performance

Possible scale for assessment of competence	Very adequate	Adequate	Just acceptable	Inadequate	Very inadequate
Output production					
Product design					
Product performance					
Product value					
Availability					
Product range					
Repair service					
Technology					
Capacity					
Distribution					
Procurement					
Marketing					
Market knowledge					
Promotions					
Sales force					
Customer service					
Order entry					
Finance					
Information					
Enquiries					
Credit control					
Asset management					

Organization
Delegated authority
Structure
Cooperation
Staff skills
Communication
Motivation
Flexibility
Training

5

Optimizing satisfaction – balancing opportunity and competence

An important contribution to management theory was the recognition that organizations are more likely to succeed if they carefully determine their current situation relative to market conditions and internal capabilities. This knowledge can then be used to develop a specification of future direction that will permit achievement of desired performance objectives. This aspect of the management task is encapsulated in the concept which has become known as strategic planning.

The concept of strategy

Popularized by management writers in the 1960s, strategic planning has subsequently been criticized because of a tendency by some organizations to undertake the process mechanically without giving sufficient thought to linking strategy to overall corporate purpose. To overcome this problem, it is now in vogue to precede planning of the strategy by the formulation of a mission statement for the organization. The advantage of this technique is that it provides a qualitative statement of philosophy against which the viability of the strategy can be assessed. Like all new ideas, however, it presents management with a dilemma: should the mission statement be sufficiently broad to permit maximum freedom of purpose – but then how does one ensure that excessive breadth does not create the situation of misinterpretation or misunderstanding? My experience based on observation of various clients has left me uncertain about what is best. Very generalized statements about 'seeking to contribute to society through serving our customers' seem to be understood, and hence effectively exploited, by employees of companies with their roots in the Pacific Basin. Yet within Western companies this type of statement appears at best to confuse employees and, at worst, to create further cynicism about what are the real motives behind senior management's new-found faith in the importance of having a mission. Hence, although I believe there are real benefits from using the concept of mission to define a generalized statement of organizational purpose, the Western mind does seem more comfortable with a certain degree of specificity (e.g. a European computer manufacturer's mission of 'harnessing science to benefit the information processing requirements of our customers' is probably more likely to help managers responsible for strategy formulation than the alternative of 'seeking to help our customers decide').

The Harvard professor, Michael Porter, has made a number of important contributions to our understanding of how organizations can misuse or misapply the principles of strategic planning. His research has revealed that all too often companies successfully determine strategy by relating opportunity to capability, but then fail to include in the planning process any evaluation of how future performance might be influenced by the behaviour of existing or new sources of competition. This seems especially prevalent among:

● companies that for many years have faced little opposition (e.g. the Xerox company's domination of the world photocopier market which caused them to underestimate the potential threat posed by the Japanese companies who decided to enter the office equipment sector);

● recently established companies that fail to appreciate that once they begin to take a significant number of customers away from larger corporations they will no longer be ignored (e.g. Laker Airlines in the UK who pioneered cut-price Atlantic airfares. As the size of the Laker operation moved from small to significant it became a major threat to the large carriers such as British Airways and eventually the company was driven out of business by the magnitude of the response of the larger airlines).

In contributing towards the formulation of an appropriate organizational strategy, the marketer should incorporate consideration of competitive threats while undertaking the processes described in Figure 5.1, designed to give sequential answers to the questions of:

● Where are we now?
● Where are we going?

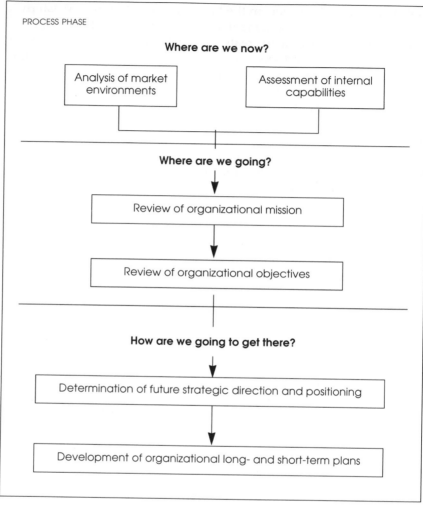

Figure 5.1 The strategic planning process

● How are we going to get there?

The outcome of these activities is that the marketer will have determined how best to (a) balance market opportunity against internal capability and (b) position the organization in a way most likely to nullify the impact of competition.

Variability of market opportunity

Not all markets are created equal, some markets offer much greater opportunity than others. Factors which can influence market attractiveness include absolute demand, growth rate, variation in the nature of demand and, as mentioned earlier, the level of existing or potential competition. By examining each of these in detail, it is possible to develop a specification of market sectors where there are the greatest opportunities for totally satisfying customer needs now and/or in the future.

Absolute demand is a direct function of both the total size of the buying population and the per capita expenditure of the customers. The US remains the world's largest consumer goods market because the population is large and per capita wealth extremely high. Hence most companies are more likely to include North America in their list of priority markets than, for example, Russia which has a large, but extremely improverished, population. Limited market size is often the stimulus that forces companies to enter world markets. An example is the Volvo car and truck group that originally established its reputation for quality and durability in their home market of Sweden. Given this country's small population, however, to sustain sales growth Volvo was forced, as are many other Swedish engineering companies, into marketing its product overseas. A similar situation is found in the Swiss banking industry which many years ago became extremely active in attracting new clients from elsewhere in the world because their own population could hardly be expected to provide enough business to sustain more than a very small number of banks in the country.

The profitability of sales generated by attracting new users to a market or increasing purchase frequency among existing customers is much higher than from sales generated by persuading people to switch from buying a competitor's products. Furthermore, in those markets where the only source of incremental business is stealing customers from other organizations, profitability will be further reduced by the expenditure needed to defend the company against retaliatory attacks by the competitors. A very recent graphic example of this situation occurred in the UK consumer banking market in the late eighties. Although total annual promotional spending rose from less than £10 million to over £100 million, the proportion of the population opening checking accounts remained virtually unchanged. When linked with the rise in the level of bad debt following a period of somewhat liberal lending policies, this behaviour resulted in a massive decline in the profitability of the High Street banks by the end of the decade. Hence, newly emerging market sectors are usually a much more attractive proposition than ones which have reached saturation. Two markets currently exhibiting exciting growth prospects are the information technology (IT) and telecommunications industries.

An exception to the rule of assuming static markets are always unattractive occurs where the dominant companies have become lazy and are no longer delivering the level of customer satisfaction upon which their leadership position was originally based. In these circumstances a more market-aware, innovative competitor will find that huge profits can be generated by attracting disgruntled customers away from their traditional sources of supply. The Pacific Basin countries have specialized in this approach when expanding into global markets by successfully taking business from the leading incumbent brands (e.g. from the Germans in the camera industry and the Americans in the television manufacturing industry).

This loss of leadership in mature markets is usually due to companies becoming complacent, thereby permitting competitors to catch up and then overtake the previously dominant brand in the key area of product performance (e.g. the Japanese destruction of the UK motorcycle industry). In some cases, however, a new opportunity will arise because, although overall market size may remain static, customer needs have changed. If smaller companies recognize this trend and react more rapidly than their larger and often more slow-moving competitors, then this can also result in the latter group being toppled from their leadership position. The American car industry in the seventies, for example, ignored their customers' desire for smaller, more energy-efficient vehicles and thereby opened the door to competitors from both Japan and Europe.

Possibly the most worrying type of competition is that created where there is excess supply, competitors are unwilling to reduce capacity and/or leave the market, and to sustain plant throughput a massive price war breaks out. At this juncture, efforts to defend a market position based on superior product performance or quality of service may become impossible because customers cannot ignore the financial benefits of accepting the bargains on offer. In Europe, for example ECC (English China Clay) has established a leadership position through emphasis on product quality, technological support and customization of their clays to suit specific customer needs. The downturn in demand for clay in America, linked to the lower production costs of open-cast clay pits in that country, has recently caused some US producers to enter the European market offering highly attractive prices. Under these circumstances, ECC is facing a certain degree of difficulty in sustaining customer loyalty based on a positioning strategy of premium price/premium quality.

Most price wars that are caused by an imbalance in supply and demand eventually come to an end as companies leave the market and/or gradually reduce their production capacity. Unfortunately, by the time market equilibrium returns, customers may have become so price-sensitive that it is virtually impossible to build a successful business on any basis other than being the lowest cost producer. Rarely will any company in this situation be able to make more than a minimal profit over the long term. Hence the wisest advice is to avoid opportunities which lead the organization into operating in markets where, either now or in the foreseeable future, the key determinant in the purchase decision is lowest possible price.

A classic example of this type of market is the bottom end of the mass car market where the customer is seeking a basic low-cost vehicle. Most developing countries early in their industrialization phase will be attracted by the idea of establishing car-assembly plants. As exporting of cars will generate hard currency, the governments will provide investment support and this, when linked to low labour costs, will permit the country to be extremely price-competitive. Profitability will initially be high, but as rising living standards force up labour costs and governments find difficulty in sustaining ongoing financial support, the country's car industry will find it can no longer compete on the platform of offering the lowest possible price. The Japanese car producers, for example, have moved out of this sector in the face of growing competition from the Koreans. Within Europe, the Spanish are placing pressure on other producers at the bottom end of the market. No doubt, however, within a few years the Koreans will need to reconsider their marketing strategy as the Chinese move into the industry and, similarly, the Spanish will face a growing threat from Eastern European producers.

Determining an appropriate strategic direction

To select the most appropriate strategic direction for an organization, the marketer will need to balance opportunity against internal capability. A simple but effective tool for this activity is the directional policy matrix (DPM). This technique was pioneered by GE Corporation in the US who, working with the management consulting firm McKinsey, were seeking a decision model that could be applied to identifying appropriate strategies across their very diversified range of manufacturing operations.

The process first requires the development of a framework for assessing different opportunities. One approach is to classify markets in relation to the degree of opportunity to deliver customer satisfaction. A list of common factors will need to be established

against which each market opportunity can be evaluated. No doubt
there will be different viewpoints about which factors should be
used, depending on which industry or public sector is being
examined. In some cases, added weight may be given to certain
factors because they are felt to have more influence on market
behaviour than others.

Possible factors that are often considered in the analysis are:

- market size

- growth rate

- stability of demand

- the relative importance customers attach to price in reaching a
  purchase decision

- customer emphasis on quality

- level of customer pre- and post-purchase service demands

- breadth of requirement for performance specification alternatives

- customer desire for product innovation

- intensity of existing and/or potential competition

- the primary focus that forms the basis for competitive activity (i.e.
  based on price or product performance).

Each market sector is rated by factor using a scoring system where
the maximum rating is 10. The summated factor scores are divided
by the number of factors to calculate an overall average score. By
assigning a range (e.g. 0–3 for low, greater than 3 up to 7 for average,
and greater than 7 for high), each market sector can be classified in
terms of the level of opportunity for delivering customer satisfaction.

Analysis of internal capabilities will be based upon a review of those
internal competences described in Chapter 4, which it is felt will
have a significant influence over the organization's capability to
satisfy customer needs. Factors which might be considered could be

- manufacturing (or service process) capacity

- ability to incorporate and exploit technology

- product or service quality

- ability to customize product

- financial resources to invest in product development

- the capability of the R & D group to develop new products

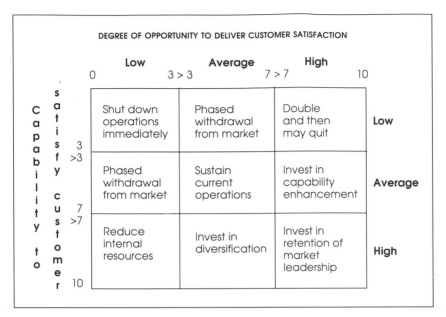

DEGREE OF OPPORTUNITY TO DELIVER CUSTOMER SATISFACTION

	Low	Average	High	
	0	3 > 3	7 > 7	10
3 >3	Shut down operations immediately	Phased withdrawal from market	Double and then may quit	Low
	Phased withdrawal from market	Sustain current operations	Invest in capability enhancement	Average
7 >7	Reduce internal resources	Invest in diversification	Invest in retention of market leadership	High

Capability to satisfy customer

Figure 5.2 The directional policy matrix

- marketing group understanding of market needs
- effectiveness of promotions to communicate with customers
- ability of the sales force to manage the client relationship
- integration of the customer order/production scheduling/raw material procurement cycle

Similar to the market assessment, each internal factor is rated out of 10, and an average calculated to express the degree to which the organization has the capability to satisfy customer need in a specific market sector.

The scores for market and capability then permit each opportunity to be placed into a sector within the DPM. As illustrated in Figure 5.2, this permits determination of the most appropriate strategic direction at (a) the macro level of the overall organization or (b) the micro level of an individual item within the product portfolio.

CASE STUDY   Strategic direction for ABC Systems Ltd

Application of the DPM technique can be illustrated by examining the disguised case of the computer distributor operation, ABC Systems Ltd. Founded some 10 years ago, the company specializes in the SME service sector supplying computer hardware, software packages, system design

Table 5.1   Market sector scores

Sector	Market	Capability	Comments
Open access training	2.8	5.4	Local colleges deliver at much lower prices
Standard software	2.6	8.2	Customers don't need level of expertise offered by ABC
Standard hardware boxes	6.2	1.8	Cannot match lowball prices of 'no frills' competition
Specified office systems	6.0	6.4	Uses ABC expertise in areas of specification and operations
Company specific training	5.8	6.2	Compatible with knowledge gained from installation
Integrated SME systems	6.6	8.8	Expertise could be utilised in other markets/ systems
Networked AIMIS[1]	9.4	2.8	Rapidly growing sector but complex technologies
Networked MIS[2]	8.6	6.0	Operating at boundary of ABC staff expertise

Additional information
[1] Artificial Intelligence Management Information Systems are organization-wide decision support systems (DSS) which not only permit managers to examine 'what if' scenarios, but also the systems 'learn' as they accumulate data on outcomes and events.
[2] Basic Management Information Systems which integrate databases from across the organization and allow management to examine (a) the interdepartmental impact of alternative decisions scenarios and (b) the future performance implications of variance in current performance trends against plan.

services (including the development of customer-specific systems packages), open access and company-specific computer training programmes for operatives and a computer system maintenance service. The company uses a broad mix of promotional tools including mail shots, a direct sales force, telemarketing, exhibitions and trade advertising. There are sales showrooms in major cities where clients can inspect a broad range of PC-based systems. These showrooms have training suites, office space for sales and administrative staff, plus a warehouse/local distribution/ system repairs service area. The overall company operation is directed from a head office/central warehouse complex based on a science park in south-west England.

The factors selected for assessing relative attractiveness of market sectors and capability to deliver customer satisfaction are as follows:

Market factors

- Total market demand
- Market growth rate
- Rate of technology change
- Intensity of competition
- Customer price orientation
- Service response time
- Quality of advisory services
- Provision of training

Internal capability factors

- Understanding of technology
- Financial resources
- Hardware/software procurement
- System design capability
- Sales force skills
- Service capability
- Installation/training capability
- Administration/distribution

Results of the factor analysis are shown in Table 5.1. Insertion of these results into a DPM model (see Figure 5.3) provides the marketing department with a clear specification of the degree of matching between company capability and the attractiveness of the opportunities to satisfy customers' needs.

On the basis of this analysis the marketing director's recommendations on future strategic direction are as follows:

- *Open access training*   Given there is no way to compete with the local colleges on price, ABC will gradually withdraw from this market.

- *Standard software*   De-emphasis of this product line by the existing sales force will make more time available to call on clients likely to purchase complex systems. To sustain customer service levels on standard software (because some of these will upgrade to more sophisticated systems over time), the telesales operation would be expanded and an on-screen telemarketing system introduced to provide a more focused approach for responding to this type of customer.

- *Standard 'boxes'*   The market has become extremely price-competitive due to the activities of manufacturers seeking to sustain output from their factories and increasingly aggressive national firms who operate 'no frills' mail order operations. Profit margins for ABC are very thin for this type of product because the company does not have a sufficiently large sales volume to be able to negotiate large discounts from the manufacturers. Hence the company will gradually phase out their involvement in this sector and refer enquiries to other suppliers.

- *Standard specified systems*   This sector is a major source of income but, given a gradual slowing in total market growth rate and probable intensification of competitive activity, resources will be added only when necessary to sustain current market position.

- *Company-specific training*   The same philosophy will apply as to standard specified systems.

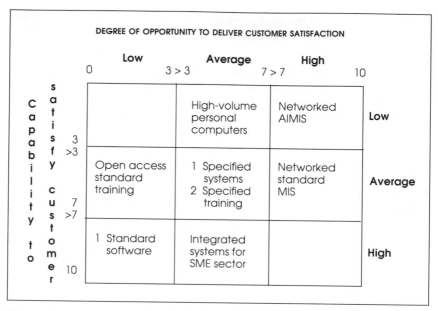

Figure 5.3 Directional policy matrix for ABC Systems Ltd

● *Integrated SME systems*   The company has developed a strong reputation among SME service sector organizations. This capability can be used as the foundation upon which to seek more clients in larger companies and to diversify into SME manufacturing environments.

● *AIMIS*   This sector is expected to grow very rapidly over the next ten years but ABC has very few staff with the systems design expertise necessary to succeed in this market. To develop these skills in-house will be virtually impossible, so the company will make one last effort by seeking to acquire an existing UK specialist software company or entering into a joint venture with an American supplier.

● *Networked MIS*   This is also a rapidly growing market, but ABC has only limited capability to develop the software needed for effective integration of data systems within client companies. The strategy will be to invest in upgrading of internal capability through in-house staff development and also the recruitment of programmers experienced in this area of systems creation.

At the moment, ABC Systems Ltd has no product which provides them with a market leadership position in a highly attractive sector. It is necessary that this be achieved and the two most likely prospects are the AIMIS and standard MIS sectors. By analysing the existing product portfolio the company can now see that certain sectors should receive more attention while others should be de-emphasized over time. This clearer perspective will probably result in a focusing of resources to the point where achieving a market leadership in either AIMIS or specified MIS sector is now a feasible proposition.

Selecting a suitable market position

Having determined the strategic direction for an organization, the next step is to decide market positioning in relation to the dimensions of (a) what proportion of the market to serve and (b) the basis on which to compete against others. Michael Porter's very useful decision model (Figure 5.4) suggests that organizations can opt for supplying the majority of customers or focus on a specific market sector. The organization also has the choice of competing on the basis of offering the lowest possible cost (i.e. price competition) or by being differentiated (i.e. perceived as offering a proposition uniquely superior to competition).

Differentiation can be based on some form of tangible evidence (e.g. a pharmaceutical company which holds the patent on a superior drug treatment). For a product category where there is minimal technical difference in the performance of products available, however, differentiation may be achieved through the use of a promotional campaign to establish a perceived difference (e.g. Castlemaine's television advertisements which exploit the strong appeal to the 18–25-year age group of the Australian lifestyle in the UK lager market).

		COMPETITIVE STANCE	
		Cost leadership	**Differentiation**
M a r k e t **c o v e r a g e**	**M a s s**	Cost-based market domination (usually lowest price)	Performance-based or perceived differentiation domination
	f o c u s e d	Focused cost leadership	Specialist position differentiation

Figure 5.4 Alternative strategic positioning matrix

Porter has suggested that cost leadership is a 'low level' advantage because the advantage lasts only for a short time (e.g. over recent years Spain has exploited low land and labour costs to become the lowest cost supplier of horticultural products in the EC. Operating costs are now beginning to rise. Within the foreseeable future, the Spanish will be threatened by Eastern bloc countries which are now beginning to direct into the West European food market output which they previously sold to the Russians). Hence Porter proposes that differentiation is a safer competitive stance than cost leadership to ensure survival of an organization over the longer term.

In recent years, American mass market corporations have been increasingly threatened by attacks from Pacific Basin producers, whereas US companies which focused on servicing an up-market, specialist niche have been less vulnerable to competition from overseas. This has caused the management expert, Tom Peters, to suggest that the best strategy for most Western nation companies is to avoid mass markets and occupy specialist niches. As has recently and very eloquently been pointed out by the managing director of the Swiss Swatch Watch Corporation, however, this suggestion is not always valid; in the end the Pacific Basin competitors may eventually come looking for you in the specialist niche (e.g. the entry of Mazda, Toyota and Honda into the luxury car market which is putting a significant dent in the sales of Mercedes and BMW). Hence the marketer may wish to question the strategy of 'always specialize' and, instead, consider dominating as much of the market as possible. If a company has limited internal capabilities, however, then it may be eminently sensible to be a 'nicher'. This decision is not suggested merely because of evidence that it has proved beneficial to US corporations, but because this type of company probably lacks the resources sufficient to permit it to succeed against larger competitors that are more adequately equipped to service the needs of a mass market.

CASE STUDY   Positioning response – Baldwin Chemicals Ltd

Baldwin Chemicals Ltd, a disguised case example, manufactures a broad range of industrial cleansing agents which are sold direct to large customers and through regional distributors to users of smaller quantities of their product range. The company is a market leader, positioned on a premium price/ premium quality platform. This platform is sustained by (a) a reputation by their large R & D facility for creative practical solutions to unusual cleansing problems and (b) a sales force able to undertake situation surveys to advise clients on how best to meet the rapidly changing UK legislation on industrial safety and effluent discharge from factories. Over the last three years, the leadership position has been increasingly threatened by national and smaller regional companies importing lower standard cleansing chemicals in bulk from overseas, repackaging and selling on the basis of significantly lower prices.

In response to this situation, Baldwin sought advice from a management consulting firm who recommended that the company should respond to this new trend in competition by (a) supplying a lower grade of agents under a second label and (b) marketing this new range through a telesales operation. The Porter market positioning model can be used (Figure 5.5) to examine the implications of these proposals. It can be seen that Baldwin offers a differentiated range of products across the entire market. The emerging threat is from competitors who are operating a cost leadership positioning on both a total market and geographically focused market basis. The risk of adopting the consultants' recommendation is that the new product range marketed on a price platform could endanger Baldwin's existing and, until now, very successful differentiated positioning. Furthermore, as there is nothing to be gained from becoming a Tom Peters' style 'nicher', the preferred solution for the company is to ignore the advice of the consultants. Instead the marketing department should seek mechanisms to protect themselves from price competition by strengthening their total market product performance reputation.

The R & D group, working in partnership with some major customers, undertook a number of comparative studies on the magnitude of absolute cost savings, using the imported chemicals versus Baldwin products in relation to cleansing power, effluent chemistry and operative safety. The results revealed that, because Baldwin products were more effective cleansing agents, there was actually little difference in the total costs at Baldwin and competitor products to achieve a specified cleansing

COMPETITIVE STANCE

Market coverage	Cost leadership	Differentiation
Mass	Other recently established national firms	Baldwin Chemicals Ltd
focused	Newly established regional firms	

Figure 5.5 Analysis of the industrial cleansing chemicals market

standard. More importantly, the cheaper chemicals sometimes created their own effluent problems and in certain cases were in breach of industrial safety guidelines.

The short-term tactical response of Baldwin Chemicals marketing department was to mount an educational/promotional campaign to advise the market of the possible fallacy of assuming low-price products could reduce cleansing costs. The marketing director recognized, however, that over the longer term strengthened forms of differentiation were needed to protect the company adequately from the increasing threat of lower-cost products manufactured elsewhere in the world. A number of alternative projects have now been implemented. These include examination of 'greener approaches' in the formulation of cleansing products and the initiation of a joint venture with a machine tool company to develop automated cleansing equipment which would lower costs by reducing the labour content of cleansing tasks. The company is also aware of the unique cleansing problems facing the IT industry. Consequently, a collaborative relationship has been established with a university to research new product opportunities that may exist within IT industry manufacturing environments.

6

Innovate or vegetate

CASE STUDY   Dorset Foods Ltd

Dorset Foods is a disguised case which provides an interesting example of how the product line in many companies can change over the years. The organization was originally founded to process and market whole, cooked crabs. Over time, demand for cooked crabs has gradually declined and the company's main revenue now comes from being one of the largest processors of fresh and frozen crab meat in the UK. Output is sold direct to large supermarket chains and to wholesalers who service smaller retail shops and outlets in the catering industry such as public houses, restaurants and hotels. The company has become involved in various other products either because they were offered the raw material by contacts in the fishing industry or because customers enquired about sources of supply. These other items include scallop meat, cooked shrimp (peeled and shell-on) and crab pâté. Total UK sales volume for both crab and scallop meat has remained flat for some time and Dorset is an extremely minor player in the scallop meat market. Seafood pâté and cooked shrimp are both markets exhibiting healthy growth, but again Dorset is not seen as a major supplier in either sector.

The product life cycle concept

An extremely useful conceptual tool in analysing product performance over time is the product life cycle (or PLC). As illustrated in Figure 6.1 it is suggested that products go through four phases: introduction (where customers are trying the product for the first time), growth (additional customer trial and existing customers beginning to repeat purchase on a regular basis), maturity (the phase of maximum sales) and decline.

Of even greater interest than the sales curve over time is the profit trend during each of the four phases. Throughout most of the introduction period, profit is negative because expenditure on market introduction is greater than revenue from sales. Profit increases in the growth phase and peaks out as the market enters maturity. In the maturity phase there is no opportunity for further sales growth because no new customers will enter the market. The

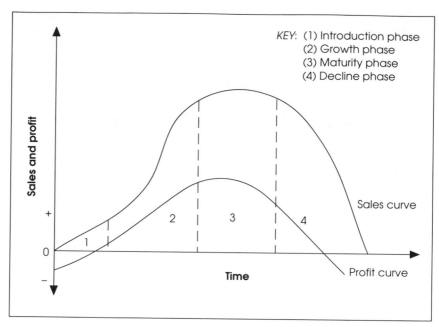

Figure 6.1 The product life cycle curve (PLC)

only way to sustain growth is to rely heavily on promotional spending to steal sales from competition while concurrently defending against other companies seeking to persuade your customers to switch to them. The longer a market remains in maturity, the greater will be the scale of promotional battles and as total marketing expenditure increases, profits will shrink. As sales revenue begins to slip with the onset of the decline phase, profits will fall even faster and eventually the product will be selling at a loss.

There has long been a debate whether the PLC exists in the real world or is merely a figment of academic imagination. Much of this argument has centred around the shape of the curve. Certainly, various authors have justified their opinion that the PLC is a fallacious idea by producing examples of some very strange-looking sales curves which have no resemblance to that shown in Figure 6.1. My position in this debate is that undoubtedly there are huge variations in the shape of the PLC curve. What is of importance to the practising manager, however, is that all products are born, grow up and then eventually die. This means that the organization which ignores long-term sales trends may find its products are obsolete and, with no new products in its portfolio, total revenue will begin to fall as existing products move into the decline phase.

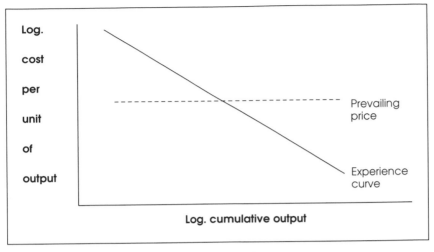

Figure 6.2 The experience curve concept

The Boston Consulting Group product matrix concept

Examination of Dorset Foods in the context of the PLC concept would reveal that total sales have remained virtually unchanged for some years despite the prolonged decline in sales of cooked, whole crab. The reason for this situation is that the falling sales for whole crabs have been compensated by increasing sales of pâté and cooked shrimp as products that are still in the growth phase.

Merely to be concerned about performance in the context of balancing sales of products at various stages in their respective life cycle is not sufficient. Product profitability also needs to be included in the equation. A well accepted technique for analysing product portfolio profitability is that pioneered by the Boston Consultancy Group. This firm had been studying a phenomenon that the knowledge an organization acquires over time will cause unit costs to fall as output increases. Known as the experience curve, its beneficial effects are illustrated in Figure 6.2 where, at the prevailing market price, the lower costs enjoyed by the larger company will usually permit the organization to be more profitable than a smaller competitor. The Boston Consulting Group combined the two concepts of the PLC and the experience curve to create what is now known as the BCG matrix.

As illustrated in Figure 6.3, it is suggested that there are four product types. A high market share product in the mature phase of the life cycle will generate extremely large profits because the product occupies a position well down the experience curve. This product is termed a Cash Cow and a good example of such an animal is Kelloggs

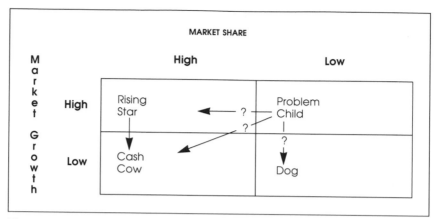

Figure 6.3 Boston Consulting Group (BCG) market product matrix

MARKET SHARE		
	High	**Low**
High	Rising Star	Problem Child crab pâté cooked shrimp
Low	Cash Cow crab meat	Dog scallop meat

(Market Growth on vertical axis)

Figure 6.4 The Boston Consulting Group matrix applied to Dorset Foods Ltd

Cornflakes. Once a market enters maturity, it is virtually impossible to topple a major brand from its leadership position. Products with a small share in a mature market will be positioned further up the industry's experience curve. As such products cannot be expected to expand sales volume by stealing significant share from larger companies, they will provide only a minimal level of profit. Such products are called Dogs and, instead of keeping them alive in the hope that just one more attempt will improve market position, it would be kinder if they were put to sleep.

Even Cash Cows' sales will eventually move into decline and need to be replaced with a new product. The earlier in the PLC a new product achieves a high market share, the greater is the probability that it will remain in a dominant position as the market moves into maturity.

Hence the high-share product in the introduction/growth market phase is known as a Rising Star. In contrast, new products which perform poorly and achieve only a small share are likely to grow up to be the next generation of Dogs. Thus this type of product is termed a Problem Child.

The BCG matrix suggests that an optimal portfolio is one which contains only Rising Stars and Cash Cows. The matrix is useful in assessing the current state of a company's product portfolio and thereby indicating possible areas for a revision in marketing activity. To demonstrate this effect we can construct a matrix for Dorset Foods (see Figure 6.4). It is apparent that although crab meat provides the company with a Cash Cow, scallops are a Dog and need to be assessed as candidates for discontinuation. Even more critical is the fact that both pâté and cooked shrimp are Problem Children. This indicates that the company's new product activity has been somewhat unsuccessful over recent years. Unless immediate action is taken to establish a Rising Star, then the future prospects for Dorset Foods could become quite bleak.

Managing the new product process

Given the importance of new products in guaranteeing the existence of an organization over the long term, it is not surprising that since the 1950s there have been significant research efforts to determine the most appropriate ways to manage this aspect of the marketing task. Writers are in general agreement that two key factors are (a) the level of commitment to the importance of new products within the organization and (b) the existence of some form of structured process to ensure that only successful concepts are progressed through to market launch.

Employees read situations; they realize it is politically expedient to place priority on those issues which are seen as important to senior management. One way to read the political climate is to observe the organizational structure which has been created to manage a specified task. In the area of new product management, two approaches – the new product committee and allocating new products as a secondary task among managers primarily responsible for existing products – are both seen by employees as evidence that this is not priority activity. The committee is usually made up of senior managers from across the organization who meet on an *ad hoc* basis. No single individual is seen as being accountable or responsible and, not surprisingly, the group rarely achieves any positive outcomes. In the case of allocating the task to managers responsible for existing products, managerial competence is mainly assessed on the basis of maximizing total sales. Under these circumstances new products will usually be relegated to being something that receives attention on Friday afternoons if there are no outstanding problems on existing products which the marketing department must resolve before the weekend.

A common solution to register the importance that should be placed on new products is to make this task the primary responsibility of one or more individuals within the organization. Many companies locate these managers within the marketing department working alongside individuals responsible for established products. If new products are seen as a junior assignment and seniority is vested with individuals responsible for high sales volume mature products, however, this approach may be ineffective. This situation occurs because continuity in the project management process is impaired as individuals actively seek to get themselves promoted out of new products and into the team responsible for managing established products. To overcome this problem, some companies create a separate department solely responsible for marketing new products. Furthermore, in order to register the priority given to the activity, it is not unusual to find that the department head may report directly to the chief executive instead of the more traditional approach of being supervised by the marketing director.

Structuring the development process

The objectives in new product development are maximizing the number of ideas generated and minimizing the number of ideas that are progressed only to fail in the marketplace. In many organizations these concurrent objectives are managed through the creation of a control process of the type illustrated in Figure 6.5.

At the idea generation stage, the net is spread as widely as possible by drawing on sources which may include customers, intermediaries, competition, sales force, employees from other departments, suppliers and external experts. Screening is undertaken by assessing each idea against specified parameters such as sales volume, profits, ROI, uniqueness, potential for future market or product diversification, and compatibility with internal organizational resources. Ideas which survive the screening stage are then developed into concepts that most effectively describe the benefit proposition to potential customers. Reactions to the product concept are evaluated through market research which also provides

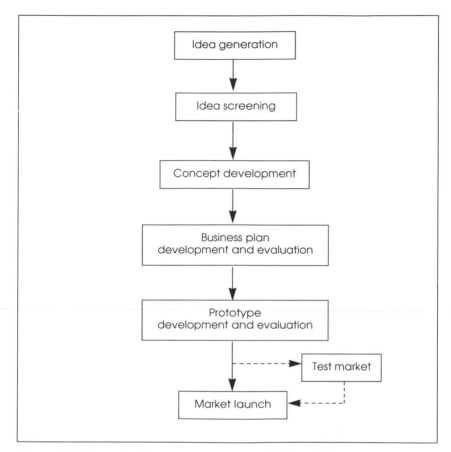

Figure 6.5 Phases in the new product development process

the information used to validate the sales forecast upon which the business plan is then based.

Especially for products involving complex production technologies, prototype development can be extremely expensive and hence this phase is postponed for as long as possible. Once prototypes have been constructed, the reaction of potential customers will be assessed through placement studies where people are asked to use the product and comment upon actual versus desired performance. In industrial markets, these tests are often undertaken by the company's largest customers who frequently suggest significant modifications likely to enhance further the performance capabilities of the new product. This close level of involvement in the prototype evaluation phase (often known as ß -testing) in industrial markets has the added benefit of greatly increasing the probability that these customers will place orders immediately the new product becomes available. In consumer goods markets, the launch will often require massive expenditure on promotional support to generate a high level of customer awareness and hence rapid product trial. Given the financial risk that the promotional campaign may be unsuccessful, many companies precede the launch with a test market. The test is a 'mini-version' of the intended launch and is implemented by placing the product in a restricted area of the country (e.g. a small number of cities or a single television transmission area). Product performance in the test area is monitored until trial and repeat rates can be assessed in relation to those forecast in the business plan. Assuming the test is successful, the product is then launched for real.

The decline of the innovator

In view of the widespread understanding of the existence of the PLC, the importance of new products and methods whereby their development can be managed, it must be of major concern to Western nations to find that in market sectors such as consumer electrical goods, cars, office equipment and machine tools virtually all of the most successful new ideas are spawned by Pacific Basin firms.

A key reason that many Western nation organizations have done so badly in the new product race over the last two decades is that this area of the marketing process can be both risky and expensive. Hence, by the end of the seventies, when marketing managers were being selected on the basis of their ability to control expenses and manipulate assets to deliver non-sustainably high ROIs, it was not surprising that new product programmes were already being de-emphasized or directed towards projects designed to extend the life of existing products. Evidence of this trend was starkly demonstrated in research undertaken by the consulting firm Booz Allen Hamilton, which found that the majority of new product effort in US corporations was directed to improving profitability of existing products (Table 6.1).

At the beginning of the eighties, this research and the growing success of the Japanese in using new products as an important mechanism in their fight to increase their share of world markets should have set off warning bells in Western organizations. But it seems that nobody was prepared to listen. Even by the end of the decade, research comparing the internal cultures of British, US and Japanese companies in the UK demonstrated that there still remained huge differences between Western and oriental management philosophies. This is especially evident in the vital area of the

Table 6.1 US companies' allocation of resources by area of new product activity

Proportion of corporate effort %	Nature of project activity
11	Cost reduction – existing products
7	Repositioning – existing products
26	Improved performance – existing products
26	Line extensions – existing products
70	Total of resources allocated to existing products
20	Products new to the company
10	Products new to the world
100	Total of all activities

(*Source:* New products for the 1980s. Booz Allen Hamilton, 1982)

emphasis placed on growth through innovation. The findings of this study (see Table 6.2) show that British firms continue to emphasize short-term profits, concentrate efforts on cost reduction, operate more in the lower end of the market and have a management philosophy which is centred around rigid hierarchical structures. In contrast, Japanese firms have a much longer-term outlook, seek to build share through product performance, operate in the middle to upper end of the market and use much looser, flexible management structures.

Reawakening the innovative spirit

New product management in Western organizations over the last twenty years has gradually evolved into a process of risk minimization and, by sustaining the existence of products for the longest possible time, profit maximization. One justification for this philosophy is that, by offering the same product over many years, prices will be kept at a reasonable level because the company can spread recovery of the original R & D investment over the life cycle of the product. In reality this rationalization is in direct conflict with the concept of customer satisfaction, because optimizing purchase value is more likely to occur through emphasis on development of new products which offer even greater benefits at the same price. The obsolete item can either be withdrawn from the market or offered at a much reduced price. The validity of this latter scenario has repeatedly been proven in recent years by the IT industry with such products as televisions, computers, photocopiers and facsimile machines.

Table 6.2   A comparison of attitudes in different firms operating in the UK market

	Proportion of firms responding to an issue (%)		
	UK	American	Japanese
Issue 1: Primary objective is 'good, short-term profits'			
	87	80	27
Issue 2: Primary focus of market share strategy			
a. Prevent decline	27	7	3
b. Defend	17	3	0
c. Maintain	23	17	0
d. Steady growth	13	23	17
e. Aggressive growth	13	33	57
f. Dominate market	7	17	23
Issue 3: Descriptions of strategic focus			
a. Enter new sectors	40	50	77
b. Beat competition	53	73	83
c. Stimulate demand	40	83	67
d. Cost reduction	83	70	43
Issue 4: Technological capabilities			
a. Advanced R&D	33	63	68
b. Process R&D	30	60	77
Issue 5: Attitudes to product superiority over competition			
a. Quality superiority	47	77	93
b. Breadth of range	43	63	60
c. Product performance	54	61	69
Issue 6: Product positioning			
a. Down-market	20	3	0
b. Middle market	43	27	43
c. Up-market	37	70	57
Issue 7: Management style			
a. Non-hierarchical	17	43	65
b. Informal communication	40	47	69
c. *Ad hoc* jobs	33	30	73
d. Team orientation	50	63	73

Table 6.2   continued

| | Proportion of firms responding to an issue (%) | | |
	UK	American	Japanese
Issue 8: Budget criteria most scrutinized by senior management			
a. Profitability	60	87	7
b. Cash flow	40	33	7
c. Sales	47	33	53
d. Market share	27	67	67

(*Source:* adapted from V. Wong, J. Saunders and P. Doyle, 'The quality of British marketing', *Marketing Management,* Vol. 4, 1988)

Once the marketer accepts that it is customers, not accountants, who should drive the new product development process then there are several different pathways by which to enhance the level of innovation within the organization. One approach is to replace the attitude of extending the PLC with one of seeking to speed up the rate at which existing products are rendered obsolete. Conventional wisdom, for example, suggests launching a single product and delaying product line expansion until the onset of market maturity. An alternative proposed by the American professors, Wheelwright and Swanson, is the concept of 'product mapping'. Essentially their approach is that, at the development stage, marketers should not consider just a core product idea but extend their thinking to include enhanced performance and 'no frills' models, all of which are launched simultaneously. Market response to this broad product range will rapidly stimulate demand for customized products. These in turn, when combined with other items in the range, will spawn development of hybrids and, possibly in a very short time, a completely new generation of core ideas.

In Japan, the pressure on organizations to beat the competitor to market has led to a move away from the traditional linear new product management model of the type described in Figure 6.5 to systems where there is significant overlap in the various phases of the development process. For example, the company will move into concept development and evaluation even while an idea is still undergoing screening. Construction of early prototypes may be progressed even before a detailed business plan has been completed. Although reduction of 'time to market' has been the primary motivation for adoption of this new approach, further stimulus has been provided by the advent of computer technology. The designer can now use computer aided design (CAD) systems to simulate product performance for alternative propositions, determine manufacturing viability using software to assess the practicality of a specification and then rapidly move into the production phase using integrated computer aided design/compuer aided manufacturing (CAD/CAM) software.

Another important contribution to enhancing the level of innovation is for the marketing department to be prepared to relinquish their control of the new product development process to multi-disciplinary teams drawn from across the entire organization. Leadership can be from any source and may be varied depending on which point has been reached in the development process (e.g. business planning might be led by finance and then, on the move to prototype development, they abdicate their role to manufacturing). The important impact of this approach is that new product ownership is now not seen to be aligned with any single department, but vested with all the employees in the organization. This will increase the breadth of sources from which ideas are drawn and also avoid delays, because all departments wish to show themselves in the best possible light. It will often have the added advantage that product performance will be enhanced because, by everyone talking to each other, they will avoid decisions being made which may cause problems at a later date (e.g. designers will design to simplify the tasks of colleagues in manufacturing; manufacturing will be aware of plans by marketing to broaden the product range soon after launch and specify flexible production systems which can be rapidly modified to handle product diversification).

Marketers who have accepted the benefits of the multi-disciplinary approach will often realize that an even higher level of innovation can be achieved by also involving people from outside the company. By discussing new products at the idea stage with customers, intermediaries and suppliers they are able to draw upon incremental skills and knowledge sources which may further improve product performance and/or reduce production costs. Suppliers, for example, may be able to suggest a more durable raw material or an alternative machine tool which can increase output. An intermediary may propose a packaging specification that will reduce storage and handling costs. Customers may identify a potential problem with the first design or suggest an additional feature which can greatly expand the applications to which the new product might be put.

Initially a move to much greater involvement of outsiders in the new product development process will raise concerns about industrial espionage and information being leaked to competitors. This risk, however, is greatly outweighed by the advantages of launching a new product which offers a better performance specification and, even more importantly, exactly meets the ideal needs of the customers because they have been involved in the development project from the outset.

Once the organization has accepted that customer satisfaction is the primary goal of new product development programmes, it will rapidly abandon the classic 'not invented here' syndrome and widen the search outside the company for additional sources of ideas. Mergers and acquisitions have traditionally been the preserve of managing directors and senior finance staff. This leads to the myopic attitude that the main benefit of the activity is to enhance share values by the manipulation of balance sheets. At the extreme, this philosophy leads the organization down the very dangerous path of growth through acquisitions which offer the opportunity for asset stripping and/or issuance of junk bonds. Under these circumstances, the organization will soon lose sight of the fact that the fundamental purpose of management is to find new ways to achieve an even greater level of customer satisfaction. This risk can be avoided, however, by persuading the Board to involve the marketing group in the search process and by realigning the objectives of acquisitions and mergers to one of seeking potential purchases or alliances that will enhance the organization's capabilities to develop even better products in the future. In high-technology industries, even the largest companies are now accepting that they may lack all the skills needed to create their next generation of products. There is now a growing tendency to consummate friendly take-overs of smaller specialist companies and to form joint ventures or R & D consortia with others traditionally considered their competitors (e.g. the Rover Group's joint venture with Honda in the car industry; GEC and Siemens in electrical engineering; the European Airbus consortium which has brought together the main players in the European aerospace industry to make an effective challenge to Boeing Corporation's dominant position in the world passenger jet market).

Creating innovative cultures

Companies, like products, exhibit a life cycle. When first founded they are small (or 'embryonic'), then success stimulates the onset of sales growth and eventually, as sales begin to plateau, the company enters the maturity phase. If the core business is poorly managed, then gradually sales will decline and eventually the company may disappear from the market.

During the embryonic and growth phases, the company is often managed by the founder. The culture is one of opportunistic unpredictable activity, with individuals granted a high degree of autonomy, permitted to operate without the creation of clearly defined layers of authority or specified boundaries of functional responsibility. Resources are made available without detailed discussion, people are allowed to take risks and to challenge the conventional wisdom of senior staff. Eventually the company may become very large and concern begins to develop that the business is running out of control. If financial performance has become very volatile, this view is reinforced by external financial stakeholders becoming worried about the security of their investment.

It is at this stage that conventional wisdom suggests the company should be 'professionally managed'. The individuals assigned the task of managing this type of change will tend to favour a more focused, cohesive approach to planning, demand central control of information, instigate creation of tightly specified job roles and delineate departmental areas of authority. Resources will be allocated on the basis of corporate policy, risk taking will be frowned upon, major decisions will be taken only by senior managers and more junior staff discouraged from questioning the views of their superiors within the organization.

As management theorists began to study innovation management in recent years, they soon discovered that the move towards becoming a professionally managed organization is typically accompanied by a stifling of any attempts by employees to take an entrepreneurial attitude towards new product development. Over time, new or improved products will cease to have the capability of keeping the company ahead of the competition. This very frightening conclusion is now causing many large corporations to consider how to revise their culture, organizational structures and systems to motivate their employees in a desperate bid to recreate the innovative internal climate which contributed to the major successes enjoyed in the period just after the company was founded.

Different organizations have found alternative ways of creating a more innovative internal environment. Some are promoting the concept of intrapreneuring, in which employees with a new idea are granted permission to create new 'mini-businesses' inside the organization. Others promote the concept of 'skunk works' in which employees covertly redirect resources to support personal projects which they run alongside their approved job role. One of the most famous examples of this approach is at Boeing Corporation where it is claimed that many new concepts that have kept this company ahead of competition in creating new aircraft often started out as unauthorized research programmes. Having proved their worth, they are then legitimized and incorporated into the formal R & D programme of the organization.

CASE STUDY   Making innovation happen at 3M Corporation

Minnesota Mining and Manufacturing, now more commonly known as 3M Corporation, has an impressive record for developing more new products and launching them more quickly than possibly any other Western nation company. One of their most widely known innovations is the 'Post-It' note, those little pieces of paper with the sticky edge which are so heavily used to pass on informal written communications both at work and at home. The 3M product portfolio is now amazingly diverse, ranging across antistatic videotape, translucent dental braces, synthetic ligaments for damaged knees, reflective coatings for warning signs, industrial abrasives and heart–lung machines, to name just a few. In 1988, 32 per cent of 3M's $10.6 billion annual turnover came from products which it had introduced within the past five years.

The cornerstone of their success is continually to strive to retain an entrepreneurial culture directed towards new ways of delivering customer satisfaction. Rules are kept to a minimum, salaries are tied to the success of new products and people are encouraged to be inventive. The 25 per cent rule requires that a quarter of a division's sales came from products introduced within the last five years. Meeting the 25 per cent rule is a crucial yardstick at bonus time, so managers are forced to take it seriously. Any barriers or turf fights are kept to a minimum and the 'not invented here' syndrome is actively discouraged. Divisions are kept small, on average about $200 million in sales, and there are now more than 40 divisions within the corporation.

Staying close to the customer is an ingrained cultural trait. Researchers, marketers and manufacturing personnel all regularly spend time in the field and customers are routinely invited to join regular brainstorming sessions at 3M. Once a 3Mer comes up with an idea he or she is encouraged to form an multi-disciplinary action team to progress the concept through to market launch. The success of the product is accompanied by promotion for the originator. At the $5 million sales level, the individual becomes a project manager, at $20–30 million a department manager, and a division manager as sales approach $75 million. To give people space to think, there is the 15 per cent rule, which allows virtually anyone to spend up to 15 per cent of the working week doing whatever they want as long as it is product-related. Nevertheless, in 1983, some employees complained that, despite this rule, worthwhile projects were going unnoticed because guaranteed free time did not also mean there would be money made available to fund the development of a prototype. 3M therefore created the Genesis grant which gives inventors up to $50 000 to progress their projects past the idea stage. A panel of experts reviews the grant applications and, on average, approximately 90 new projects are funded every year. In total, 3M investment in R & D has regularly exceeded 6 per cent of total sales, which is twice the level of spending among the top 50 industrial corporations in the US.

Despite 3M's preference for divisional autonomy, the company encourages interchange of technology and expertise. Experts on abrasives, for example, cooperated with the technologists from the non-woven fibres group to create the extremely successful Scot-Brite scrubbing sponge. This type of interaction, when linked with all the other elements associated with creating an entrepreneurial culture, is the reason why 3M has created an entity which continues to succeed in delivering customer satisfaction by 'out-innovating' the competition on a global scale.

7

Planning promotions to benefit the customer

For most organizations the largest single component of marketing expenditure is promotion. In the 'blue chip' f.m.c.g. companies, the promotional budget may even exceed the total annual corporate expenditure on fixed assets. The magnitude of spending will be influenced by variables such as market structure, product type, product positioning and status of the product on the PLC. In most industrial markets, characterized by a small number of customers each representing a significant proportion of total company sales, promotional spending is mainly directed towards funding a large sales force. This is contrasted by branded, non-durable consumer goods markets where promotional support will be heavily skewed towards advertising.

Products in the growth phase of the PLC with a performance superiority marketed under the manufacturer's name will be allocated a large promotional budget, whereas an item in the decline phase of the PLC offering only parity performance, supplied as an own-label good to supermarket chains, will probably receive virtually no promotional support at all.

The '3Ms' of promotion

Given the important influence of promotional spending on total organizational costs, one would expect marketers to be highly skilled in the effective management of this aspect of the marketing process. Unfortunately, numerous studies have repeatedly revealed evidence of the '3Ms' of promotion: Misuse, Mismanagement and Misconception.

Misuse of promotions

Misuse is most clearly demonstrated in the case of sales (or below line) promotions which, through mechanisms such as coupons, price

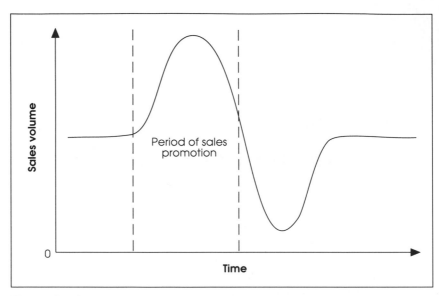

Figure 7.1 Sales volume over time to illustrate short-term impact of a sales promotion

pack, and trade allowances, offer the customer a temporary price reduction. As illustrated in Figure 7.1, these promotions have only a short-term positive impact on sales and once the event is over, sales volume falls significantly. Over the last twenty years the proportion of total marketing expenditure allocated by consumer goods companies to sales promotions has risen dramatically. Their use is extremely prevalent towards the end of the financial year when marketers are striving to deliver the annual sales budget. Although this objective may be met, the huge sales upswing during the promotion often means scheduling overtime in the factory to meet increased order levels. This is then followed by a period when sales are so slow it may be necessary to lay off production workers. Companies have finally begun to wake up to the fact that this activity is, at best, an extremely inefficient way of running a factory and, at worst, actually results in a major increase in product costs. More recently the supermarket chains, which have traditionally favoured sales promotions because these events allowed them to build inventories at reduced prices, have now realized that the holding and administrative costs greatly exceed any inventory profit from selling the promotional pack at list price. In the US, some manufacturers and supermarkets have now accepted that it would be more beneficial to the consumer if sales promotion activity was cut back severely. The savings all parties make by taking this step can be used to adopt the significantly more customer-oriented concept of offering lower-price products on a year-round basis. This is a very recent trend and, even if it soon gains widespread acceptance, it is horrifying to think of the additional millions consumers have paid out over the years because of the inflated prices charged by manufacturers and retailers seeking to recover the high costs associated with the misuse of the sales promotion tool.

Promotional mismanagement

Mismanagement of promotions can be demonstrated in many organizations by the way marketing determines the advertising budget. As indicated by the infamous quote – 'We know that 50 per cent of our advertising is effective, but the problem is we do not know which 50 per cent' – defining the relationship between advertising spend and product performance is not a simple task. Nevertheless, over the years extensive research has begun to permit marketers to develop a number of scientific tools to enhance their decision making. Under these circumstances, it is worrying to find that as recently as 1988, in a survey of over 1300 UK companies, only a minority were using any of the available sophisticated techniques (e.g. econometric modelling) which can greatly enhance the management of the advertising process. Instead half the respondents indicated that their decision rule was simply to spend what they felt was affordable. This usually means that marketing commits large sums when demand is buoyant and cuts back in a recession. Yet studies of corporate behaviour during the economic downturn at the end of the seventies have shown that this philosophy is guaranteed to weaken the company's market position and it is then poorly prepared to exploit any subsequent market upturn. The other aspect of the 'what seems affordable' budgeting approach is the risk that advertising decisions can be controlled by the demands of the major shareholders. They may insist that a reduction in dividend payments during years of poor financial performance is unacceptable. This can result in the Board deciding that to sustain shareholder dividends promotional spending should be reduced, even though this action will weaken the organization's market position over the longer term and is certainly completely unrelated to any objective of delivering customer satisfaction.

Misconception and real purpose

In addition to misuse and mismanagement, significant monies are also wasted because some marketers seem to believe that any

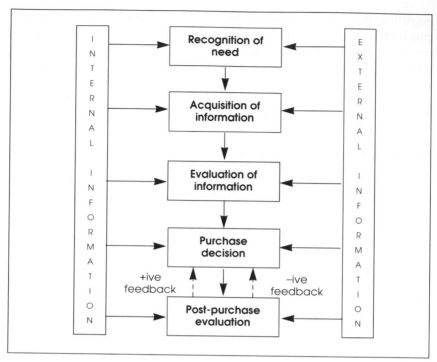

Figure 7.2 A buyer behaviour model

product can be made to succeed by increasing the weight of promotional support. This fundamental misconception explains why companies continue to delude themselves into hoping that, by increasing the advertising budget on (to use the BCG matrix terminology) their Dog products, they will steal sales from the Cash Cow brands in the market.

To understand the real purpose of promotion it is necessary to examine buyer behaviour. A simplified visualization of buyer behaviour (Figure 7.2) shows that customers move through the five stages of recognizing need, gathering information, evaluating information, deciding to buy and then, through post-purchase evaluation, assessing whether the product has lived up to the expectations developed prior to purchase. Throughout this activity the customer is acquiring information from internal and external sources. Examples of the former are personal experience and the opinions of people they trust, such as family, friends, colleagues and professional advisers. It is only when the internal sources cannot provide sufficient information that the customer will listen to the external data contained within the promotional messages of the suppliers.

It can be concluded that the real purpose of promotion is to provide customers with the information that will assist their search to select the product most likely to satisfy their current needs. If, of course, one heavily promotes an inferior product, there may be a brief period when sales increase. Having carried out post-purchase evaluation, however, customers will realize they were misinformed and will (a) cease to buy in the future and (b) vocally act as an internal information source warning others of their unfortunate experience. A graphic example of this effect is provided by the activities of the UK package holiday firms in the mid-eighties who spent millions on advertising campaigns promising dream holidays at rock-bottom prices. Their poor customers were inflicted with the miseries of being packed like sardines in charter aircraft and staying in hotels that bore no resemblance to the luxury surroundings featured in the glossy brochure. In the end the customers reacted by taking their business elsewhere, and part of the cause for the recent decline in the Spanish tourist industry is undoubtedly attributable to the earlier promotional campaigns of some UK tour operators.

CASE STUDY   Using promotions to inform – Mazda (UK)

In the mid-1980s Mazda (UK) faced the interesting situation that their maximum sales were limited to 1 per cent of the UK car market by a gentlemen's agreement between the Japanese Automotive Manufacturers Association (JAMA) and the Society of Motor Manufacturers and Trade (SMMT). The company therefore embarked on a programme to move customers from the small 323 family hatchback to the larger 626 family saloon. Research on UK customer car-buying behaviour revealed that most people, when selecting their next car and drawing up a mental list of possible models, are strongly infuenced by the manufacturers' promotional claims. They then actively gather more background information to arrive at a candidate short list before beginning a round of visits to the various dealer showrooms. However, in the case of existing Mazda owners, research revealed that very few had followed this process. Many (42 per cent) had discovered Mazda through recommendations of friends or relatives. A further 32 per cent apparently came upon the company by chance (e.g. the man who popped out to buy a lettuce and glimpsed the 626 in a showroom).

From this analysis, Mazda concluded that the role of future promotional campaigns should be to reduce the somewhat random information search of potential customers by educating people about the high quality of the product and thereby generate more visits to their dealer showrooms. The specified objective of the promotional campaign was 'to make the models famous' and it was decided that television advertising was the most suitable vehicle to achieve the goal. The campaign for the two models centred

Table 7.1   The difference in pre- and post-campaign research
results for the Mazda 626

Issue	% Change post/pre-test data
Advertising awareness	+650
Proportion of UK car buyers interested in Mazda	+135
Inclusion of model on potential buy lists	+57
Enquiry level at Mazda dealerships	+30

around the theme of 'You'll be amazed by a Mazda' and exploited facts
such as the 626 coming top in a German road test against the Mercedes
190, and being voted top imported car ahead of the Porsche 944 in
America. The success of the campaign is shown in Table 7.1.

A model for managing the promotional process

For the marketer wishing to ensure that promotional activity
successfully fulfils the objective of providing information of benefit
to the customer, one possible approach is to adopt the process model
illustrated in Figure 7.3. As the purpose of promotion is to
communicate information relevant to organizational goals, it is the
corporate marketing strategy that should provide the overall
framework upon which programme planning and implementation
decisions should be based. The marketing strategy will determine
the appropriate positioning for the promotional campaign. Two key
dimensions of positioning are (a) whether price or product
performance will form the main plank of the communication
platform and (b) the degree to which a performance superiority claim
can be justified. As illustrated in Figure 7.4, these parameters offer
the organization four possible positioning alternatives. Where there
is a demonstrable superiority over competition, this performance
parameter can be heavily featured in the information communicated
to customers. An example of a superior value performance claim was
the launch of the Compaq computer, which offered a performance
specification equal to the IBM PC but at a much lower cost. Where
price is the selected competitive weapon, but the magnitude of
difference quite narrow, then the promotional campaign will either
select a non-comparable item (e.g. a supermarket chain which
features own-label price specials in press advertising) or underpin
offered benefits with added assurances such as claims of 'never
knowingly being undersold'.

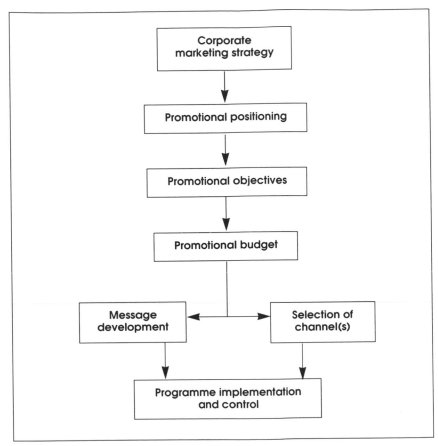

Figure 7.3 A promotional management process model

In those cases where the product delivers tangible superiority over competition it is likely that this will provide a performance-based promotional claim. In the mid-eighties, for example, Ford UK faced the problem of declining overall sales and the fact that their top-of-the-market large car, the Granada, was being seen as desperately in need of a face-lift. Research on the new model identified an extremely positive response to the inclusion of the safety features of anti-lock brakes and security locks as standard equipment, whereas on equivalent competitor models these were either absent or offered only as an added option. These product benefits were heavily featured in the advertising launch which commenced in mid-1985 and, as proven in various research studies, were the vital ingredient which contributed to reversing the decline in the company's overall market share.

	Cost-based	Differentiation	
SUPERIORITY POSITIONING	Leadership value superiority	Leadership performance superiority	TOTAL FOCUSED
	Selective aspect of comparative value	Niche-focused performance claim	

Figure 7.4 Alternative promotional positioning options

In many mature, non-durable consumer goods markets, the actual tangible differences in product performance between brands is often quite small or non-existent. Under these circumstances, any desire for differentiation can only be achieved by creating some form of perceived difference by concentrating on the augmented features of the product. Where there is little to distinguish even the attributes of the augmented product, it then falls to the promotional campaign to be the only mechanism through which to create perceived differences. An example of this situation is provided by the UK market for pot noodles, which are dehydrated snack meals in individual serving size containers, prepared by adding hot water. Introduced in the mid-seventies, by the end of the decade total sector sales had begun to plateau and most brands had moved from promotion to intense price competition to sustain market share. The choices facing the brand leader, Golden Wonder, were to do nothing, move to price-based competition or seek a mechanism to differentiate the brand from competition. Given the minor differences in product performance, the company decided there was a need to reinject a feeling of enjoyment and excitement into product usage situations. This was achieved by the launch of a new television advertising campaign in the mid-eighties based on associating product usage with appealing lifestyle situations. By the use of econometric modelling to assess the impact of the new campaign, it was demonstrated that the new promotional message was the main contributor to delivering a 12 per cent increase in sales over the subsequent 24-month period.

Determining promotional objectives

The primary purpose of promotion is to provide information. To develop an adequate plan and subsequently evaluate the effectiveness of campaign implementation, the marketer will need to establish objectives for the promotion. There is significant variance of opinion on how these objectives should be specified. Some marketers favour sales or market share targets. This can be misleading, however, because product performance in most cases is influenced by the combined interactions of all elements of the marketing mix and the behaviour of competitors. Under these circumstances it is possibly more sensible to restrict promotional objectives to mainly quantifiable communication goals such as desired level of awareness among a target customer group or a single, focused purpose for the information provision activity (e.g. education, brand switching, defence or existing customer reassurance).

Determining promotional budgets

The fundamental factor which should determine a budget is the spending required to deliver fully the specified objectives for the promotion. The theoretical aspects of the relationship between effort and effect are probably best described by the expenditure/impact curve of the type illustrated in Figure 7.5. Such curves exhibit the key features of (a) the existence of a spending threshold below which promotions have no measurable impact and (b) beyond a certain point, information has been delivered to all those to whom it is of interest and further increases in spending have no measurable benefit. Construction of these curves is complex and time-consuming and, once created, changing market conditions may rapidly render them obsolete. Hence the more commonly encountered promotional budgeting techniques are *objective task, share of spend* and *modelling*. The application of each of these can be illustrated by the following examples:

● *Objective task* To generate orders, the ethical drugs sector of the UK pharmaceutical industry is critically dependent upon doctors prescribing their particular brand name product. The primary promotional objective, therefore, is keeping the medical profession updated on the performance parameters and treatment capabilities of their product portfolio. The tasks to deliver this objective will involve a mixture of one-to-one briefings, regular follow-up calls, promotional mailings and, where possible, the

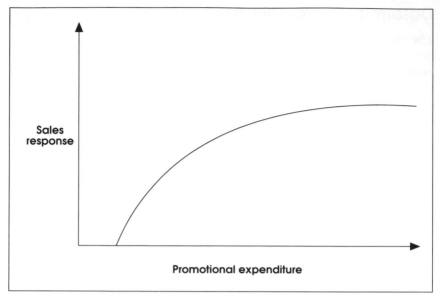

Figure 7.5 A promotional expenditure – sales response curve

attendance of doctors at medical seminars. The number of doctors multiplied by the costs of the promotional tasks per member of the medical professional will define the required promotional budget.

● *Share of spend* In a relatively stable, mature market analysis of promotional spending and brand shares will reveal a linear relationship of the type illustrated in Figure 7.6. Smaller brands tend to overspend relative to market share, whereas the situation is exactly the opposite for brand leaders whose share of spend tends to be lower than their share of market sales. Advertising expenditure in the consumer goods market is extremely well documented because the data are required by advertising agency media planners negotiating with the broadcast and print media suppliers. Hence if a brand objective is to sustain the same level of information provision to customers as in prior years, the share of spend information can be used to estimate the required promotional budget.

● *Modelling* The advent of increasingly sophisticated computer software has greatly enhanced the ability of organizations to build models which accurately describe the interactions of the marketing mix variables and market environment which influence overall sales performance. Hence, once a company has constructed

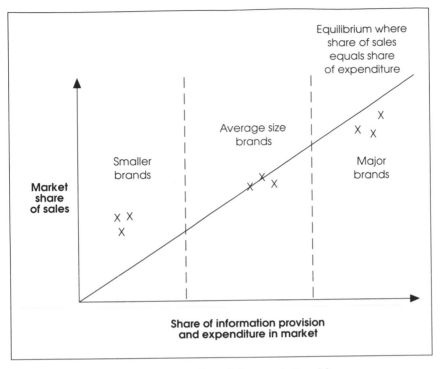

Figure 7.6 Market share/promotional share relationship

an appropriate quantitative forecasting model, this knowledge can be applied to determining an appropriate promotional budget. The Bradford & Bingley Building Society has, for example, developed a formula in which the desired number of new savings accounts opened by customers can be predicted using an equation containing the variables of prevailing interest rates, average earnings, television advertising, press advertising and a seasonality factor.

Message development

No matter which promotional channel is used (e.g. personal selling, advertising, public relations) the attention span of the customer is extremely limited and this severely restricts the time available in which to deliver product information. The message development process, which is executed concurrently with channel selection, is therefore a critical synthesis of encapsulating the promotional positioning strategy into a form which can be effectively communicated in a time-constrained situation. The two key elements of the message will be the communication of benefit and some form of justification to ensure the supplier's product claim is believed. No matter which channel is used, the effectiveness of the message will be greatly enhanced by careful research on the problems, attitudes and general background of the prospective customer. In the world of industrial marketing, the sales force often spends a major proportion of total time meeting with customers to gather this type of data through activities such as visits to client sites, attending exhibitions and arranging industry updating seminars.

Where advertising is the selected promotional vehicle, it is worth spending funds on in-depth market research and not, as regretfully is often the case, merely relying on the 'creative hunches' of the advertising agency's copy-writers. In the eighties, for example, the premium quality UK corn oil brand, Mazola, faced the problem that, although the use of oil for cooking was continuing to increase, most consumers favoured lower-cost blended vegetable oils. Research revealed a growing interest in healthy eating linked to the fact that, for certain cooking preparation situations, the actual taste of the oil used was seen as critical by the housewife.

Development of a new message, therefore, focused on the health implication of 100% Pure Corn Oil plus the importance of using a pure oil in situations such as salads where the oil could influence the taste experience. The message communicated by the new campaign is judged to have been the main factor in the subsequent improvement of the brand's UK market performance.

Promotional channel selection

The channels used to deliver the promotional message have usually evolved over time because they have been found to be the most cost-effective way of delivering information to the customer. Effective communication is most likely where dialogue between customer and supplier can occur. Hence, in selecting a channel, the first choice of the marketer will normally be that of using a sales force that can deliver promotional information through a one-to-one conversation with the customer. Unfortunately, personal selling is an extremely expensive activity. This is why in markets containing many customers, each of whom represents a very small proportion of total sales, organizations are forced to turn to indirect methods such as advertising and publicity to deliver promotional information.

Even within a promotional channel, the marketer will be faced with a reasonable degree of choice across a number of alternative promotional vehicles. In the world of advertising, the choice includes such media as newspapers, magazines, television, radio, billboards or direct mail. Managing vehicle selection given this diversity of choice requires specialist knowledge and it is rarely worthwhile for organizations to build an internal expertise in this area. Hence even very large companies tend to delegate this responsibility to their advertising agency's media planning department.

The channel selection process does offer an important opportunity to recognize that changing conditions may provide the basis for developing new ways of satisfying customers' desire for information. In assessing changing promotional circumstances, the marketer needs to balance the two variables of information content of promotions and the cost of delivery. As illustrated by Figure 7.6, increasing the quantity of information will also increase the cost of promotions. Yet there are several forces acting on the information content and cost of delivery equation. These will, therefore, require careful monitoring because effective management of the channel selection process can create new ways of staying ahead of competition by delivering a higher degree of customer satisfaction. An example of the benefits of exploiting this opportunity are provided by the success of the US corporation, American Hospital & Supply. As their name suggests, the company is a distributor in the medical industry. In the past they relied on the traditional method of communicating to their customers through a large sales force, supplemented with mail shots. They realized that the purchase decision within a major hospital involves the review of a vast quantity of information as the basis for selecting appropriate products. Hence, in the place of visits from a sales force, they offered hospitals the facility of a free computer terminal linked into American Hospital & Supply's order entry/warehouse management system. Once this was proven to be a lower-cost and more efficient way of delivering information, they then began to add facilities to the computer system such as permitting hospitals to compare their product usage patterns with other hospitals and, at no cost, to use specially developed purchase decision support software to assist the hospital to procure and utilize medical supplies.

The American Hospital & Supply situation provides an unusual example of where information content was increased while information delivery costs were reduced. This example represents the ultimate achievement of a company being able to revise the promotional process completely by introducing new technology into

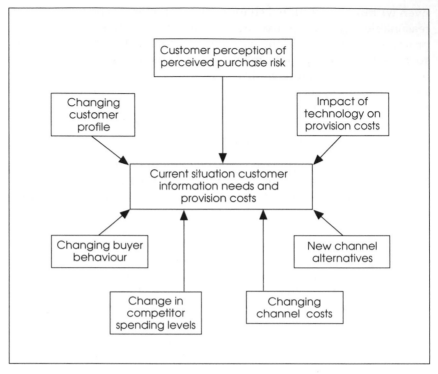

Figure 7.7 Factors influencing promotional costs and information provision needs

the information channel. Achievement of such a radical change in channel systems is not an objective that marketers can expect to achieve on more than a very infrequent basis. Probably a more practical goal, therefore, is to find ways of gradually reducing the cost of information delivery. Characteristically this will occur as the customer begins to need less external information to reach a purchase decision and, at this point in time, an alternative channel might feasibly be introduced. Many office supply distributors have found, for example, that for frequently purchased goods more and more customers are willing to buy from a catalogue and no longer require regular visits from a sales person.

The customer's need for detailed information is also reduced where there has been a decline in their perception of the degree of risk associated with the purchase. This change in perception can be influenced by a customer's growing understanding of a product and/or where there has been a significant reduction in the price of the product over time. This situation is illustrated by the case of personal computers and computer peripherals, where many people are now prepared to buy these through mail order houses that offer standard products at extremely low prices. Those distributors who recognized this trend and moved to using the national press to promote office equipment have enjoyed a significant increase in sales revenue. In many cases their success has been at the expense of smaller local firms who ignored indications of changing customer behaviour and tended to rely on the more traditional approach of regular visits to the customer by their sales force.

The various forces acting on the information content and cost situation are summarized in Figure 7.7. The important principle described in this diagram is that the marketer should not simply base channel selection on the adoption of practices that have been shown to work in the past for a certain market sector. Instead the marketer should continually monitor the external environment and customer information needs with the objective of finding better ways, ahead of competition, of further enhancing the cost-effective delivery of information which can assist the purchase decision process.

Implementation and control

In most organizations implementation of a £1 million project to upgrade a production facility would involve development of planning schedules, specification of performance parameters, detailed reports of senior management, weekly conferences with project staff and careful monitoring of fund outflows. Yet in these same organizations, monitoring of promotional spending of a similar magnitude will probably be restricted to a quarterly report on expenditure versus budget and a cursory review of share of sales versus competition. Even in many of the world's largest multinationals, where promotional budgets read like telephone numbers, one will often find the only additional forms of monitoring are occasional recall studies to check whether copy points in the advertising are being communicated and an annual attitude and usage study to compare the brand's performance against competition.

Given the simple methods described earlier to determine the size of promotional budgets, it is not surprising to find that many organizations also use relatively unsophisticated techniques to assess the effectiveness of campaign implementation. In such situations, the marketer is often forced to rely on personal judgement in determining whether the organization has received a satisfactory return from the promotional campaign. Even in those cases, however, where promotions have no beneficial impact on corporate performance, the costs incurred will still have to be met, either through higher prices or a reduction in profits. In the former case, the burden of poor promotional management falls upon the unsuspecting customers. A decline in profits, on the other hand, will lead to a reduction in employee earnings and/or a reduction in the level of annual dividends. If an organization or an entire industry claims it is oriented towards delivering higher customer satisfaction, then an obvious priority is to seek ways of managing the promotional process more effectively. For if the same information can be delivered at a lower cost or, alternatively, if the quality of information can be enhanced for the same cost, eventually customers will begin to enjoy the benefits of price reductions made possible through improving promotional productivity.

Exploiting the benefits of control systems

Even in those organizations that have recognized the need for effective promotional control systems, there is often a failure to understand the purpose of these controls. Sales management is the area of organizational activity where some of the most sophisticated systems have been developed. These not only identify performance problems, but also provide some degree of diagnosis about the cause of the problem. This is achieved by creating a database which permits the manager to examine the performance of an individual sales person relative to an organizational norm. Using the 'call reports' of the sales force, it is possible to compare activities such as number of calls and size of orders. But if you ask most sales managers how they use this information, their usual response is that they aim to increase sales by identifying ways to improve the selling skills of the sales staff. There is an indirect benefit to the customer in this response; namely, a professionally trained sales person will be a more effective communicator. Nevertheless, even in this situation, the orientation of the control system is towards finding ways of improving the organization's promotional activities, whereas the real focus of control should be on identifying opportunities to increase customer satisfaction through the mechanism of enhancing the quality of the information made available to the market.

EXAMPLE   The case study presented on page 61 (ABC Systems Ltd) gives an example of controls that did not control. Having adopted the various strategic pathways using the processes described in Chapter 5, ABC's implementation of their new policies was accompanied by the creation of improved control systems. One of these was designed to assess the performance of the sales force concentrating on the marketing of standard specified systems where, although sales were forecast to remain stable, evidence of revenue decline was beginning to appear. A standard diagnostic sales control system provided data on weaknesses in closing the sale and order size, which led to the appointment of a consultant to deliver sales training sessions. Although this was soon reflected in a reduction in performance variation among sales staff, overall revenue performance still remained below forecast.

Finally, the marketing director decided it would be useful to talk to people who used to buy from ABC but had switched their allegiance to other suppliers over recent months. He was a little shocked to hear they felt ABC was no longer interested in them because they were small accounts and the company did not really want their business any more. Further investigation revealed that this effect was created in the minds of such customers by the fact that the sales staff tended to communicate only standard information. If they were confronted with either an unusual request or one which would require extensive further research, the customer would rarely receive a satisfactory response. Over time this reduced their faith in ABC's claims of seeking to provide the best possible sales support to the customer.

Internal discussions within ABC revealed that this problem stemmed from the decision to reduce resources allocated to non-growth market sectors, because it had created the impression among the sales force that orders for standard products from smaller customers were to be discouraged. The marketing director was somewhat shaken by this turn of events and in fact accepted that the drive for success had possibly been at the price of customer relations. To reverse this trend and to avoid the problem occurring in the future, the marketing group implemented a series of initiatives such as customer surveys, senior management field trips and a special section in the company newspaper based on customer contributions. All these data sources were designed to monitor carefully the quality of the promotional information ABC was delivering to the market. An interesting side effect of these activities was that, within a year of their introduction, the marketing director was giving serious consideration to whether he really needed the traditional standard control system which measured issues such as number of calls and order size. He was beginning to find that the feedback from regular customer contacts and surveys provided a much better insight into the quality of service being provided by his sales force.

8

Adding satisfaction through pricing and distribution

CASE STUDY   Baby Alarm

Cot death syndrome is the medical term for the tragic situation of apparently healthy babies dying in their sleep. Despite years of research, the exact causes of the illness are still not fully understood. Extensive studies have, however, revealed certain physiological indicators which can be used to provide an early warning of a child at risk. Some years ago a UK electronics company developed a system for measuring these indicators and automatically alerting medical staff of a developing risk situation.

The product was warmly welcomed by the medical profession, but sales remained frustratingly well below forecast. Eventually an external adviser was recruited. His research revealed that although medical professionals were interested in the product they suspected that, given the quite low price, it was likely the system would not fulfil the performance parameters claimed by the manufacturer. The adviser recommended a significant price increase and once this was implemented sales grew very rapidly.

Who should determine price?

The Baby Alarm company set the original price using a technique that is extremely prevalent in the SME sector: namely, first determining product costs and then adding their required unit profit. This method is often referred to as 'cost plus' pricing. It has become infamous as the method used in the defence industry, a method which over the years has cost governments millions in over-priced military hardware. The concept seems reasonable in the sense that the government is the only customer. They inform the contractor of an acceptable profit margin and are prepared to meet this and the costs associated with supplying the required product. Unfortunately, if the defence contractor is unscrupulous and overstates the costs, then this results in the government paying a very inflated price. To protect themselves, governments employ armies of administrators to monitor and audit contractors' activities. But as situations such as the notorious US Air Force 'thousand dollar wrench' (which could be bought in a hardware store for a few dollars) have proved, the contractor is sometimes successfully able to hide the real costs from the government auditors.

Even more important than governments paying more than they should for defence equipment is the fact that cost plus pricing in the commercial sector, as demonstrated by the Baby Alarm case, can result in a price that is very different from that expected by the customer, and hence sales fail to materialize. The reason for this outcome is that to deliver market satisfaction it should be customers, not suppliers, who determine price. This fundamental philosophy can be demonstrated by market research in which a product specification is described to a sample of customers and they are asked to select, from a range of alternatives, the price they would expect to pay. The outcome is usually of the type illustrated in Figure 8.1, where customer response is in the form of a normal curve with the price expected by the majority of respondents falling within a

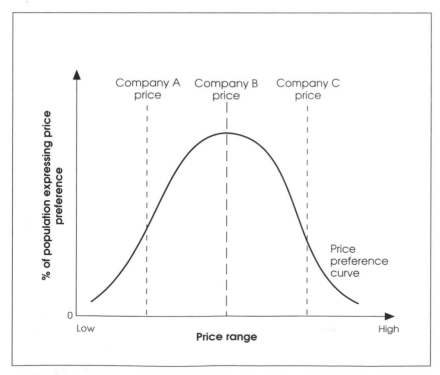

Figure 8.1 A price preference curve

quite narrow range. With three companies – A, B and C – all using cost plus pricing operating in the market described by Figure 8.1, it can be concluded that if all factors were equal the majority of customers would select Product B. Or to put it another way, Company B is more effective in delivering satisfaction over price than its competitors.

Pricing to satisfy customers

Given the important role that price has in influencing customer satisfaction, it is vital that marketers carefully undertake research on customer expectations as the basis for determining the price at which products and services are offered to the market. The process is complicated in many markets because customers have varying product performance requirements and hence differing views of the price they expect to pay. Fundamental to this expectation is the acceptance that high-performance products will cost more than lower-quality products. The interaction between price and performance expectations means that the supplier faces a number of alternative choices in using price as a mechanism through which customer satisfaction in a market can be achieved.

These alternative market scenarios can be illustrated by constructing a price/performance matrix of the type shown in Figure 8.2. The explanation behind the various price/performance offerings in this diagram are as follows:

● *Superiority satisfaction pricing* is delivered to customers who are seeking the best available performance and expect to pay a high price (e.g. luxury sports cars such as Ferrari or Jaguar).

● *Shared benefit satisfaction pricing* is delivered because the supplier is offering high performance and a lower price. This is usually only achievable because the supplier is able to exploit an experience curve effect where, as output increases, costs fall dramatically. By offering the lower price from the outset, the supplier is seeking large orders which accelerate the drive down the experience curve, thereby benefiting themselves and their customers. This approach is very common in the electronics industry and is used by companies such as Texas Instruments when introducing a new generation of microchips to their OEM (original equipment manufacturer) customers.

● *Temporary satisfaction pricing* occurs because, to deliver high performance at such a low price, the supplier is usually offering

		PRICE		
		High	**Average**	**Low**
P **E** **R** **F**	**High**	Superiority satisfaction pricing	Shared benefit satisfaction pricing	Temporary satisfaction pricing
O **R** **M** **A**	**Average**	Status satisfaction pricing	Standard satisfaction pricing	Bargain satisfaction pricing
N **C** **E**	**Low**	Dissatisfaction pricing	Limited satisfaction pricing	Value satisfaction pricing

Figure 8.2 The price/performance matrix

the product at below cost. This situation sometimes occurs in export markets where a producer faces insufficient demand in the home market and 'dumps' product overseas to keep their factories operating at near capacity. Over the longer term, the producer will either have to find a way of bringing demand and supply back into balance (e.g. the domestic demand recovers or capacity is cut back) or face bankruptcy. Whichever the outcome, after a time the extremely low prices offered in overseas markets are then withdrawn.

● *Status satisfaction pricing* occurs in those situations when the customer knowingly accepts a price in excess of the product performance offered. Customer motivation is usually because ownership is perceived to confer some form of status to the purchaser. For example, in the consumer camera market there are individuals who feel they must have the latest technology. Some camera manufacturers therefore launch their latest products at a price somewhere between 10 and 25 per cent higher than they expect to charge over the longer term. Once the 'camera buffs' have been satisfied, the price is then gradually reduced to the level at which the majority of customers are willing to consider buying the product.

● *Standard satisfaction pricing* is achieved through the provision of the performance required by the majority of the customers at a price which is acceptable to the majority of the market.

● *Bargain satisfaction pricing* involves offering the standard product at a lower than usual price. This is typified by the 'special sales' which retailers offer on a regular basis. The risk of bargain pricing is that it may prevail for an excessively long period. This can cause customers to revise their price expectations and consequently react adversely to a return to normal prices at the end of the sale period by switching their loyalties to another supplier.

● *Dissatisfaction pricing* merely means that, having purchased the product, actual performance delivered is the cause of dissatisfaction. Hence the customer will seek to avoid a second purchase. This type of situation can arise because the customer lacks sufficient understanding of purchase alternatives and/or is desperate to buy (e.g. a person on a low income in a period of rapidly rising house prices who is persuaded to accept a mortgage made expensive by being linked to an inappropriate insurance policy).

● *Limited satisfaction pricing* is similar to the dissatisfaction scenario, except that the price may mean there are one or two repeat purchases prior to rejection of the product. This situation is sometimes found in the tourist industry where firms, knowing that most customers only visit a specific holiday location once or twice, believe they can overcharge without doing significant damage to long-term sales.

● *Value satisfaction pricing* offers the basic product to that group of customers who can only afford to purchase a 'no frills' proposition. An example of this situation in the UK is provided by discount supermarket chains such as Normans.

Matching internal and external price satisfaction

There is little benefit in determining the nature of customer performance preference and then providing the required product if production costs do not permit generation of sufficient profit. The customers might be very happy with this situation but individuals such as managers paid on a profit share basis would be extremely

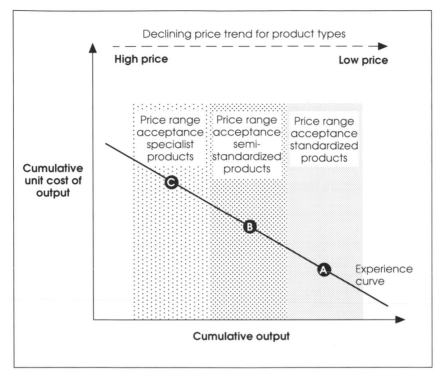

Figure 8.3 Relationship between production cost capability and prevailing range of acceptable prices

dissatisfied. Hence marketers, having determined market preferences, then need to assess the optimum market sector which they should service in relation to the internal capability of the organization.

The usual situation is that companies that supply standard or 'no frills' products have developed a capability to produce large quantities at a low cost per unit. Superior performance products will often involve higher production costs to meet customized specifications and manufacturing processes will be biased towards some form of batch production system. The relationship between production cost capability and product performance is illustrated in Figure 8.3. It can be seen that Company A is more suited to producing standardized products. Company C should focus on supplying specialist specification output. Company B lies between these two companies and may produce some form of mixed output. The type of situation shown in Figure 8.3 is frequently found in the electronics industry among subcontractors assembling circuit boards. A Type A company would focus on supplying high-volume standard boards, probably using automated assembly systems. A Type B company would be best suited to supplying customers seeking circuits which are modified versions of standard circuits. These would probably be manufactured using a semi-automated production system. A Type C company would serve that part of the market where the customer is seeking small quantities of very specialist circuits and the company would probably use a batch system, possibly even involving hand-built 'one offs'.

Pricing policies for further enhanced satisfaction

If organizations existed in stable markets where demand was in balance with supply, competitive pressures were minimal and customer expectations remained the same, then achieving an unchanging equilibrium between price and product performance would be simple. In reality, or course, it is almost impossible to find a market that exhibits these characteristics. Consequently, marketers need to recognize that, as shown in Figure 8.4, there is a number of forces which can dramatically alter the relationship between customer expectations over price and product performance. If these forces are effectively managed, they offer an important mechanism through which to strengthen the organization's market position by delivering enhanced customer satisfaction. The reverse proposition is also valid: by ignoring these forces the organization can place itself in an increasingly vulnerable situation.

Economic forces have the effect of altering customers' propensity to purchase. During an economic downturn, there is a tendency in consumer goods markets to reduce both absolute spending and the proportion of actual spending allocated to what are perceived as luxury goods. If the marketer has access to an economic forecasting model, then it may be possible to restructure the product line in preparation for a near-future change in buying behaviour. In the late eighties, for example, a number of UK High Street retailers such as the Next Group and Queensway apparently misread the impending onset of the recession and continued to operate as if the mid-eighties consumer boom was still in progress. Their behaviour can be contrasted with Woolworths who implemented a product line restructuring programme which was, no doubt, a major contributory factor in the ability of this retailer to sustain a significantly better profit performance than competition towards the end of the decade.

Another effect of changing economic conditions is that customers may begin to seek a substitute product which they perceive as more

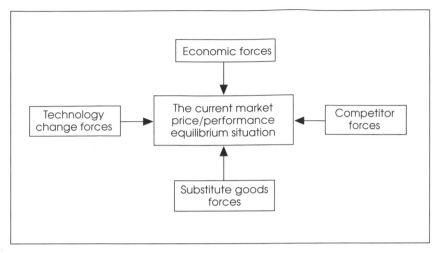

Figure 8.4 The forces acting on market price

affordable. An example of this effect occurred during the period of rapidly escalating house prices in the UK between 1986 and 1989. Many young couples who found they could no longer afford a house switched to buying apartments. The property developers who recognized this trend redirected resources to acquiring large houses and converting them into flats. Evidence suggests that these firms enjoyed a higher profit from their activities than their competitors who continued only to buy land and build starter homes.

The cost of many products is controlled by the availability of suitable technologies. Once a company has invested heavily in a technology, in their desire to sustain a high level of profit, there is a tendency to ignore new developments and continue to market the same product. If this myopic attitude is permitted to go on for too long, there is the possibility that the company may be overtaken by a superior product available at the same price. This situation is currently being demonstrated in the computer printer market where, for some years, the low-cost sector was dominated by dot matrix printers. Although the quality of the print from these machines is lower than a standard typewriter, the cost of alternative technologies upon which bubble jet and laser printers are based meant that these latter products could not compete in the lower end of the IT market. In the last 24 months, however, the cost of these latter technologies has begun to fall dramatically and these printers now represent a major threat to producers of dot matrix machines.

Dominant suppliers in premium quality sectors tend to be less affected by the forces of economic change or product substitution. If the sector offers few opportunities for the introduction of revolutionary new technologies, however, there is the risk that the dominant companies may become too complacent. This may permit new competitors to enter the market and disturb the price/performance equilibrium. Over the last twenty years German car manufacturers such as Mercedes and BMW have enjoyed a period of market growth by exploiting their capabilities to supply superbly engineered luxury automobiles. What they appear to have ignored was the growing technical capabilities of the Japanese who have gradually moved from supplying mass market vehicles to developing also a range of luxury saloon and sports cars. In the last few years Honda, Toyota and Mazda have all launched new product ranges which offered the same performance specification as their German competitors but at significantly lower prices. In doing so, they have totally altered the price/performance equilibrium in this market sector and, in America, already toppled the Germans from their brand leadership position.

Distribution channel selection

Conventional wisdom on the selection of the most appropriate channel through which to distribute products or services tends to focus on the issue of minimum cost. This proposition is usually presented in a simple model involving a number of suppliers and customers. As illustrated in Figure 8.5a, by directly supplying the customer seeking a variety of products (e.g. the consumer buying groceries), the complexity of transactions would be very high. Involving an intermediary such as a supermarket to act as a middleman, will reduce the number of transactions (see Figure 8.5b). This reduction, when accompanied by the intermediary managing shipping, warehousing and breaking down large supplier shipments into the smaller unit of purchase size sought by the customer, will lead to the provision of product to the end user at the lowest possible cost.

The emphasis of this view of channel selection will undoubtedly result in the customer paying the lowest possible distribution cost, thereby receiving satisfaction on the issue of economical pricing. This view of channel selection, however, ignores the other vital aspect in the transaction process: namely, managing the provision of information, which in some cases is even more crucial than lowest possible price.

Total transaction management involves definition of customer

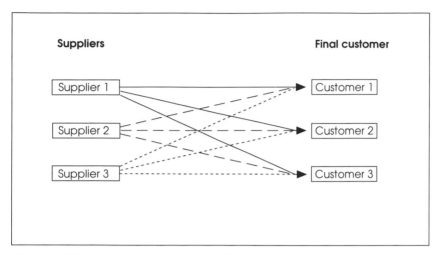

Figure 8.5(a) Transaction flows in a direct market channel

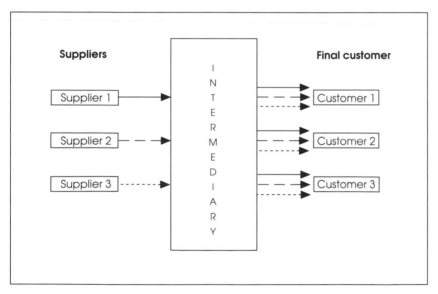

Figure 8.5(b) Transaction flows in an indirect market channel

profile, validating a fit between profile and suitability of the specific product offering, provision of information to assist the customer to reach the best decision, closing the sale and delivering post-purchase service. Effectiveness of this process is most likely to be guaranteed by linking the customer in a one-to-one relationship with the supplier, because direct dialogue between these two parties can ensure that no errors arise in managing the delivery of the product under terms totally satisfactory to the purchaser. To ensure satisfaction, however, one also has to weigh the costs involved in managing this direct delivery relationship. As illustrated in Figure 8.6, interaction between the two variables of control and unit value can be represented as an equilibrium relationship balancing the degree of control the supplier retains over product delivery against the value of the transaction. For a high-value goods such as a large mainframe computer, it is probable that a direct channel between supplier and customer will be mutually satisfying to both parties. At the other extreme, however, the supplier would usually delegate transaction management for a low unit value product to a distributor/ retailer channel and have minimal involvement with the final customer.

Delivering channel satisfaction

Most service organizations (e.g. banks, medical practices, accountants) face the problem that provision of intangible goods often involves detailed discussions between supplier and customer as part of the transaction process. Hence the service sector tends to rely heavily on dealing direct with the customer without the involvement of intermediaries. With the exception of very high value purchases (e.g. capital goods in industrial markets; a very major purchase such as a house in consumer markets), the majority of tangible goods suppliers will utilize indirect channels such as wholesalers and distributors. Passing over authority to others is always accompanied by a loss of control by the delegator. In the case of distribution management, this means that the use of non-direct channels inevitably increases the risk that inappropriate behaviour by the intermediary can result in damage to the customer perceptions over product performance relative to expectation. Consequently, much more important than channel selection based on minimizing distribution costs is the selection and management of channels to ensure that participating intermediaries share a mutual goal with the supplier of desiring to maximize customer satisfaction.

Manufacturers of premium price cars have always recognized the importance of only appointing distributors who have the expertise to manage both the selling and post-purchase servicing of their vehicles. Rolls-Royce, for example, always insisted that the service staff at their dealers were trained at the Rolls-Royce mechanics school. In recent years other manufacturers have increasingly accepted that the behaviour of their distributors can either enhance or reduce customer satisfaction. This has caused companies such as Volvo UK to develop standards of customer care which they insist their distributors either fulfil or risk losing the dealership.

A vital ingredient in the success of IBM has been their emphasis on building and sustaining effective relations with their customers. Traditionally they achieved this by having a huge sales force and servicing their customers mainly through a direct distribution system. They retained this philosophy even after the advent of the personal computer reduced the unit cost of the product and competitors such as Apple began to prove it was feasible for hardware to be marketed through a network of independent distributors. Eventually (and some would say belatedly) IBM accepted that the declining unit value of IT hardware necessitated a much greater reliance upon indirect distribution channels. Nevertheless, in the business machines sector they recognized the importance of not permitting this change in philosophy to reduce their image for customer service. Hence they were extremely selective in their appointment of IBM authorized dealers, laying down strict guidelines over matters such as sales force training and stocking of a sufficiently broad range of products. Other computer companies that put sales volume ahead of customer service in managing indirect channels have frequently found that the poor managerial skills of some dealers have subsequently damaged their product reputation in the business machine market.

In some markets a few intermediaries may dominate the distribution channel and no supplier has sufficient power to dictate desired behaviour to optimize customer satisfaction. This situation has, for example, prevailed in the UK food market for many years where four supermarket chains control over 60 per cent of total market sales. In the 1970s, some chains emphasized low price as their operating strategy. Consequently, the ability to be competitive over delivered costs, not product quality, was the key attribute which they required of their suppliers. Under these circumstances, food manufacturers had minimal influence over quality or product line variety. They were totally in the hands of the intermediaries in terms of the degree to which their products were likely to satisfy the needs of UK consumers. Fortunately for UK food manufacturers seeking to build a stronger reputation for delivering performance-based customer satisfaction, retailers such as Marks & Spencer and Sainsburys demonstrated that UK consumers were willing to meet the higher costs associated with being offered a much wider range of high-quality foods. These two retailers recognized the importance of building a strong relationship with their suppliers based on a mutual goal of seeking to deliver consumer satisfaction. Hence, over the last few years, other UK national chain retailers have increasingly shifted towards recognizing that all members of a distribution channel share the responsibility for acting in ways most likely to meet the needs of the customer. Both suppliers and intermediaries who ignore this trend are likely to find in the nineties that their sales performance will suffer accordingly as their customers seek alternative product sources. The German meat industry, for example, is known to be researching opportunities in the UK for exploiting their capabilities to offer a much broader range of quality butchered meat products. Although there may be some resistance to the slightly higher prices associated with the German approach to meat retailing, if they do decide to enter the UK market, their British counterparts could be in for a very difficult time until they learn how to respond to this new threat.

Distribution policies for further enhanced satisfaction

Similar to the situation described for price, there are few markets where the supplier can afford to be complacent; there are forces acting on the distribution process which can be exploited ahead of competition to bring about enhanced customer satisfaction. Forces which can influence the enhancement of the transaction process, give greater control over the transaction process at the same cost or offer a significant reduction in the cost of distributing the product, are featured in Figure 8.6.

One example of economic forces opportunity is provided by the US West Coast salmon processors. Traditionally their sales of fresh product were limited by the distance the product could be shipped by truck. As per capita income rose in the early eighties, New Yorkers were willing to pay a slightly higher price for fresh instead of frozen seafoods. The salmon companies formed a link with American Airlines who developed specially designed freight 'pods' which permitted the airfreighting of fresh salmon direct into East Coast markets. The producers took control of the transaction process by creating a telesales force to sell direct to up-market restaurants and thereby created an entirely new market opportunity for their product.

A similar example of seeking to exploit improving economic conditions is the Next Group in the UK, which launched a mail order catalogue mainly for up-market customers who, for location or lifestyle reasons, were unlikely to visit Next retail outlets.

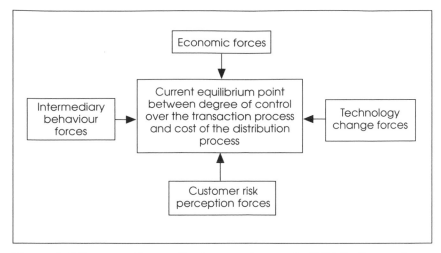

Figure 8.6 Forces acting on the transaction control/distribution cost situation

Unfortunately, soon after launch, the economy began to show signs of a downturn and this was probably a key reason why their extremely innovative approach to channel management has not been an outstanding success.

Economic downturns are usually accompanied by customers being prepared to suffer additional inconvenience in order to purchase their preferred product. Retailers who use catalogue merchandizing can expect to be less affected by a reduction in consumer spending in a recession. The reason for this situation is that many customers become more interested in lowest possible price and are willing to forgo in-store personal service by using the catalogue as a substitute for product information being delivered by sales staff. Hence marketers who recognize this trend, accept less control over the transaction process, and cultivate this type of intermediary are able to satisfy the needs of customers still willing to purchase product if available at a reduced cost through a catalogue.

The catalogue retailing scenario is an example where the customers are the initiators of change by altering their buying behaviour. In other cases, it may be the behaviour of intermediaries themselves that alters the balance of power in a market system. If manufacturers ignore such a change, they may lose control of the transaction process by not being stocked by channel members who are expanding their share of total category sales. During the last few years, for example, many garages in their struggle to remain profitable in the face of poor returns from merely selling petrol have increasingly turned to retailing other products such as groceries, confectionery, newspapers, prepared foods and DIY car-repair products. Manufacturers who recognized this trend at an early stage have subsequently reaped the benefits of directing resources to growing their sales in this sector of the UK consumer goods market. An interesting example of this situation was provided by the late Graham Morgan, chairman of Wrigley UK, who, in response to a question about significant achievements in his career, described his decision to be one of the first UK confectionery manufacturers to develop a much stronger presence on British garage forecourts.

Effective control of transaction management requires a detailed understanding of the perceived risk which the customer attaches to the purchase. When buying a complex, expensive product for the first time, perceived risk is high and customers will expect significant assistance as they move towards their purchase decision. At the introduction/growth stage in PLC, the supplier may manage the market by selling direct and/or use full service, technically skilled distributors. As the product becomes more widely understood, customers will need less support and price will become increasingly important. If marketers ignore this trend and continue to emphasize high-cost, high-transaction control channels, they may miss the opportunity to satisfy the needs of those customers who perceive the purchase risk has declined. An example of this situation is provided in the UK mobile telephone market where, in the early years, most suppliers used their own sales force or appointed full service distributors to market the product. In the late eighties, a number of electronic goods retailers realized that price was becoming an increasingly important factor as potential customers became more familiar with the technology and their perception of purchase risk rapidly declined. These retailers acquired mobile telephones from low-cost overseas producers and mounted advertising campaigns based purely on price comparisons against the better known UK brands. Evidence suggests that certain large UK mobile telephone manufacturers lost sales volume by not recognizing and responding immediately to this change in customer buying behaviour.

The success of the alternative approach to marketing mobile telephones is due in large part to the advances in technology which permitted a rapid reduction in the retail price of the product. Marketers must also be aware that technology can provide opportunities to alter the balance between transaction control and actual distribution costs within a market sector. Advances in IT, for example, have significantly reduced the costs associated with building accurate databases and producing high-quality, personalized printed materials. This in turn has dramatically opened new opportunities in the world of marketing products and services through the medium of direct mail. Insurance companies have traditionally relied on one-to-one contact with their clients using their own sales force or employing brokers. Certain insurance companies recognized that advances in direct mail technology, although representing a reduction in transaction control when compared with personal selling, nevertheless permitted the provision of a reasonable quantity of information, but at a much lower cost. They rapidly proved that it was possible to generate a huge increase in the sale of products such as term insurance and annuities by switching from direct selling to direct mail marketing.

More recently marketers have also realized that IT systems can actually offer increased control over the transaction process. In the past the cost of operating a direct sales force has impelled many food companies to delegate customer management responsibility to sales agents and distributors. The rapidly falling costs of computer-based order entry/stock control systems has meant that manufacturers were able to establish centralized telesales systems which could liaise directly with customers, thereby vitiating the need for agents and/or regional distributors. This was only the first step in regaining control of the transaction process – some manufacturers and their customers have begun to explore 'hard wiring' their computer systems together to automate completely the order entry/distribution management process. The point has now been reached in some organizations where supplier and customer computers work together analysing sales rates and stock levels, and may even revise supplier production schedules with minimal intervention by humans. As experience of these approaches is incorporated into 'thinking systems' based on AI (artificial intelligence) technology, even suppliers who traditionally were forced to delegate channel management because of the low value of individual transactions, will be able to re-establish direct links with the final customer.

Certain German companies have already begun to experiment with this approach to 'intelligent mail order' marketing with, in some cases, catalogue information being delivered via the consumer's own television set. If this new direction in channel management is ignored by UK retailers and manufacturers who decide to rely on the traditional indirect channels, both groups may eventually find they have lost control of the market to those companies who are delivering greater customer satisfaction by exploiting IT to establish closer links between themselves and the ultimate user of their products.

9

Presenting the organization's total commitment to satisfaction

CASE STUDY   Trying times in the water industry

To achieve their goal of improving organizational performance throughout the UK water industry, the British Government decided in the late 1980s to expose the regional authorities to market forces by privatizing them. The subsequent share prospectuses were full of glowing claims of how each company would effectively deliver a much higher level of customer service, once the shackles of public sector control were removed.

Following privatization, managers at all levels were enthused by the exciting opportunities now made possible through access to the funds that they had pleaded for over years to modernize their storage, distribution and treatment facilities. As they embarked on some of the largest civil engineering projects ever seen in Britain, the new entities concurrently invested in computerizing customer service facilities, modernizing their image and training their staff in the skills needed in the commercial world to deliver an appropriate level of customer care.

In the first two years following privatization the industry faced whole series of criticisms over issues such as drought conditions requiring water constraint orders to remain in effect for the foreseeable future, sewage plants causing pollution, beaches failing to meet EC standards due to the local discharge of raw, untreated sewage and senior management being granted large salary increases. Meanwhile, consumers were receiving water bills that were rising at twice the rate of inflation and the industry's statutory watch-dog, Ofwat, received numerous complaints that the new companies were exploiting their monopoly position to sustain exorbitant profits at the expense of their customers.

Employees in the British water industry are genuinely dedicated to utilizing their technical skills to deliver the best possible service to their customers. They are both surprised and confused to discover that, although to them privatization represents a real opportunity to improve service delivery, their image with the general public was probably better when they were still part of a nationalized industry.

In hindsight, if the marketers within the industry had been a little more perceptive about the magnitude of the problems to be overcome in the early years following privatization, then perhaps they would have adopted a much lower profile approach to promoting claims about an ability to deliver an improved level of customer service immediately. If one examines the industry's promotional activities, it does appear that, in seeking to be perceived as totally competent, there has been a failure to appreciate that the multi-faceted interfaces which exist between the water companies and their numerous publics all have to be carefully managed. Each contact point represents a potential banana skin upon which to slip. If the occasional slip is not effectively managed, this situation can rapidly accelerate into a fatal erosion of the market image which companies are striving to establish.

Over the next few years the water companies will be required to make massive revisions to virtually every internal system, structure, procedure and policy across all areas of their operations. During this period of change, it will be impossible to be certain that every customer interface is being adequately managed to er.sure that defined standards of service are being delivered. By adopting a realistic appreciation of the problems associated with managing corporate image during the period when internal processes are undergoing change, then possibly the water companies may be able to reduce the intensity of criticism currently being directed at their industry.

Understanding the organizational points of influence

It would be naive of the marketer to assume that delivery of customer satisfaction merely rests upon providing the market with a product superior to those offered by the competition. In most industrial sectors, the organization is part of a complex web and actions along just one strand can cause vibrations throughout the entire market system. It is frequently the case that problems leading to adverse customer reaction will arise from the least expected source and, unless appropriate actions are immediately implemented, damage limitation can prove to be extremely difficult.

Imagine, for example, that you arrive at work one morning to find that a fundamentalist religious sect has decided your corporate logo represents visual evidence of satanic influences and is recommending that consumers pour your products down the toilet. Your initial reaction is to issue a placatory press release and hope the problem goes away. Of course, if this does not work, you may face a massive bill to repair the damage that has been inflicted on your

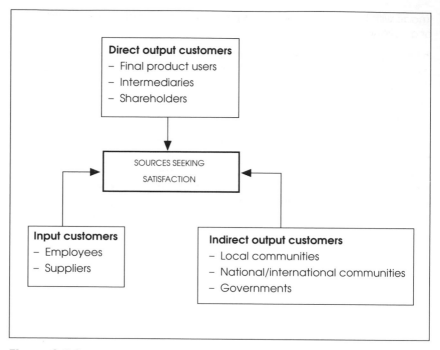

Figure 9.1 Sources seeking customer satisfaction from the activities of the organization

market image. Silly, fanciful example, you may say. Perhaps you might wish to think again, because this was exactly the problem faced by Procter & Gamble in the mid-eighties and resolution ultimately proved to be extremely expensive. If Procter had not, over the years, already made significant investments in creating a capability to manage the various publics who are influenced by the company's activities, it is very likely that the problem over the logo could have had a much more disastrous impact on corporate performance.

A first requirement for any marketer seeking to ensure that the total organization is perceived as delivering satisfaction is to acquire a detailed understanding of the relationships that exist with all external customer groups. One such model is illustrated in Figure 9.1 where the proposed groupings have been classified under the three headings of direct output, indirect output and input customers. Furthermore, within each grouping there are distinct sub-groups, each of which will exhibit specific and, in many cases, conflicting requirements when seeking evidence to confirm any claim that the organization is genuinely oriented to satisfying their various needs.

Seeking convergence of opinion

To move towards the point where the company and its customers share the same opinions about the values exhibited by the organization is a three-stage process. It is comprised of:

1 Determining an appropriate philosophy.

2 Identifying mechanisms whereby internal systems and policies truly reflect this philosophy.

3 Managing interface relationships to ensure internal values are mirrored by the image which all customer groups have of the organization.

To establish an appropriate philosophy will require the marketer to determine carefully what values are considered important in sustaining the core objective of delivering customer satisfaction. Some of these issues will relate to the nature of the products which are to be made available to the market. Further underpinning is provided by desired characteristics for the total organization. Marketers will need to debate these matters carefully with senior management and where necessary undertake research to validate existing perspectives on values appropriate to the organization and the industrial sector of which the organization is a part.

One approach to this task is to create a values diagram of the type shown in Figure 9.2. In the illustrated example, both the product and the overall organizational dimension are each considered best represented by four values. This type of model can be made more informative by entering rating scores for actual performance for each of the selected factors. Having created a decision model, the marketer can use this to prepare a statement of organizational values to be used in guiding all aspects of internal behaviour.

Translating a statement of philosophy into something which can be understood and utilized by all employees is a process over which management experts exhibit a diversity of opinions. Some would argue it needs to be evolved into a simple slogan. John Egan, for example, in seeking to gain internal recognition of the problems faced by Jaguar in the early eighties focused employees' attention by use of the phrase 'in pursuit of perfection'. The Mars Company values are articulated in five sentences which specify objectives for quality, responsibility, mutuality, efficiency and freedom. The diversified multinational company, Johnson & Johnson, has a one-page document to define everyday business and social responsibilities.

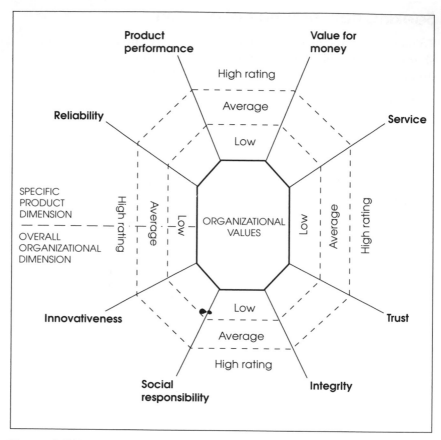

Figure 9.2 Factor definition of desired organizational values

In recent years, the concept that every company should have a
mission statement has gained in popularity. Again the length,
structure and content of this document has been much debated.
Nevertheless, whatever is finally decided about how to articulate the
organizational mission, it is imperative that the final statement
contains a clear definition of the values by which all aspects of both
internal behaviour and market relations can be judged.

Values have no purpose if they are not incorporated into every aspect
of organizational life, from the relationship between a sales person
and a customer through to involving the local community in
discussions on how a tree-planting programme could be used to help
a production facility blend into the local countryside. Hence, once a
statement of values has been created, significant amounts of time and
money will have to be invested in ensuring all systems, policies,

structures and processes are a genuine reflection of the values by which the organization wishes to be measured.

A critical issue in this phase of the process is a genuine commitment by management to sustaining these changes over the long term. Initial changes are often implemented under the guidance of a charismatic chief executive who is seeking to share a vision with the employees (e.g. the complete repositioning of the airline SAS initiated under the direction of their dynamic chief executive, Jan Carlzon). However, most people are not stupid. They realize that no leader is immortal and the next person in the job may have a very different perception of how the company should be run (e.g. Ford Motor Company's criticisms of John Egan's approach to manufacturing and product development immediately following their recent acquisition of Jaguar Cars). To ensure employees do not sit on the sidelines waiting for the next change at head office, efforts must be made to build a senior management team containing people with integrity sufficient to ensure that (a) the new corporate values are adopted across the entire organization and (b) even more critically, these standards will continue to be supported by future generations of management.

Avoiding misunderstandings

In any form of communication, the task of the sender is to encode the message into a form which can be accurately translated and understood by the receiver. Corporate identity is the combined effect of the values which the organization wishes to have contained within all dealings with the various customer groups. How these groups perceive and interpret the information and experience to which they are exposed will lead them to form an image of the organization. Any failure in the communication process has the potential to create an image which is different from that which is desired of the specified corporate identity.

The dilemma facing the marketer is that every activity by every employee has the potential to communicate a message which conflicts with desired corporate identity and thereby alters customer perceptions. The implications of this situation are, of course, that within the execution of employee roles there are potentially millions of opportunities to damage organizational image. Seeking to achieve an objective of zero defects in this area of organizational activity is probably an impossible target. This does not mean, however, that no attempts should be made to improve the image management process.

The traditional approach to image management is to assume that, between them, the marketing and public relations departments could be relied upon to take care of this task. More recently, however, organizations have begun to understand that seeking convergence between identity and image will require an integrated and consistent response across the entire organization. To achieve this task some firms have created a new post at a senior level: that of 'head of corporate communications'. Where this has occurred the marketing staff are sometimes aggrieved to find that the post is filled by an individual from either public relations or the consumer complaints department. If one can persuade these organizations to discuss why a marketer was not appointed to the new role, senior management's explanation is usually that they did not perceive their marketing group as having a sufficiently global view of the organization and therefore would be unsuited to managing this new area of responsibility.

Where the organization's marketers are sufficiently respected by senior management to be assigned the responsibility for guiding the development of a customer-oriented internal culture, the recommended approach is to create the new position of internal marketing manager. UK organizations that have recently begun to move down this path include the Royal Mail, Midland Bank, Trust House Forte and the Rank Organization.

The first step for the individual or department assigned the role of managing total organizational image is to implement studies of internal performance indicators and employee attitudes. This research will determine the degree to which the official corporate values are accepted and understood at every level within the organization. By providing a 'helicopter' view of day-to-day affairs, the data can also provide early warning signs of emerging situations which may eventually develop into problems that could ultimately have a devastating effect on market image. One wonders, for example, whether such approaches, if in place, could have resulted in avoidance of such tragedies as Three Mile Island and the Zeebrugge ferry disaster.

The other key task in organizational image management is to create a system whereby the numerous sources of information related to external events (e.g. market research studies, customer complaints, supplier performance, product returns, press comments, local community relations at plant level) that flow into the organization can be cross-referenced and interpreted. Even detailed information from all these sources is unlikely to provide a complete picture, especially where the market image at either the company and/or industrial sector level is undergoing fundamental change. It will also be advisable, therefore, to fund long-term tracking studies as a way of providing an early warning of any attitude shifts beginning to emerge within the market system.

Over recent years, industry has been aided in these activities by research companies such as MORI who, recognizing a growing new revenue opportunity, have invested in the creation of detailed databases across a broad range of customer groups measuring attitudes to issues such as ethics, profitability and business practices, both in general and in relation to specific industrial sectors. Had more companies in the 1980s recognized the advantages of utilizing the diverse information that flows into an organization and linked this to longitudinal tracking studies, then possibly they could have avoided the adverse reaction from certain sectors of society (e.g. the fashion industry's failure to recognize the sales revenue implications of a growing rejection of the concept of killing animals to make fur coats; criticism of the use of environmentally unfriendly packaging in the fast-food industry). The other advantage of such research is that it may also provide an early indication of a changing attitude that could lead to a new opportunity. All too often, unfortunately, larger organizations' slow reading of a changing situation merely leaves the door open to new sources of competition from smaller, more informed entrepreneurs (e.g. Anita Roddick's perceptive observation of the growing concern about using animals to test health and beauty products, which led to the establishment of her outstandingly successful retail chain – The Body Shop).

Managing the media

Over the last decade the world has experienced an explosion in the application of new technologies that have permitted the media industry to provide people with instant information about events as they are actually happening. Possibly the most powerful recent example of this capability was the attempted overthrow of Mr Gorbachev. The final outcome was significantly influenced by the failure of the coup organizers, during the first critical 72 hours, to block reporting of Mr Yeltsin's activities to create a core of opposition to their efforts to return the country to a more centrally controlled autocracy.

The problem facing the marketer is that not only can the media influence opinions, they also appear to be much more interested in communicating bad as opposed to good news. Make a mistake and the organization can be certain that everyone will be told. Be successful and you will have to work very hard to get your message across. For example, some years ago GEC's sales of electric turbines to the Chinese Government was one of the largest single contracts for capital equipment ever won by a UK company. It was totally ignored by most of the media, rating only a three-line mention on an inside page of *The Daily Telegraph*. It may be frustrating to accept the realities of life, but good news is no news. Hence it will rarely stimulate television viewing ratings or newspaper circulation figures. The media are in the business of generating revenue, not providing channels of free communication for other organizations.

This conclusion does not mean, however, that the marketer should ignore the media. Far from it, in fact, because the media have a power to reach more people more rapidly than can ever be achieved using all the resources available to even the largest of organizations. The first step in developing an effective partnership with the media is to recognize that if a company is at the point where integrity, responsiveness and a willingness to admit mistakes are fundamental philosophies for dealing with customers, then these same values can be used to gain the support of most journalists. For those organizations that have yet to reach this stage in their relationship with customers, then the advice to the marketer must be (a) accelerate your progress to achieve this objective and (b) in the meantime, be very careful how you handle any of your contacts with the media. It may also be a relief to know that journalists' interest in exposing examples of incompetence seem to decline in direct proportion to the degree of success being achieved by the organization. Some years ago, for example, the latest misadventure at British Steel was guaranteed to make front page news. As this company has successfully moved to become one of the most productive steel producers in the world, the attention of the media has virtually disappeared. Now, when the occasional opportunity occurs that might provide some interesting ammunition (e.g. the decision to phase out production at the Scottish Ravenscraig site), even this appears to be of little interest to the popular press.

Corporate advertising

The problems associated with trying to get the media to communicate positive statements about organizations have led in the last few years to a massive increase in corporate advertising. The logic behind this move is quite simple – if the organization is paying for materials, space or airtime it can have absolute control over what is to be communicated.

The objectives of such campaigns can be very diverse, ranging from seeking to influence analysts in brokerage houses to make positive comments about future earnings potential through to educating the general public about an organization's record in building a 'greener world'. Furthermore, it is often possible to complement these campaigns with sponsorship of worthwhile causes such as erecting litter bins in the high street, supporting a national charity or establishing a major research centre at a university.

The risk with all these activities is that, if the organization has yet to establish a reputation for consistent quality and a genuine desire to deliver customer satisfaction, then large-scale corporate advertising or community initiatives may be greeted with suspicion. In fact, there is an ever-present risk that large-scale expenditure on corporate image-building exercises may cause the ever-vigilant journalist to begin to wonder what bad news you may be seeking to hide. Ultimately it must be recognized that a strong organizational image is founded on positive deeds that cause customer groups to develop a trust in the consistent capabilities of the provider. Where research indicates a low awareness for significant genuine achievements in customer satisfaction, then implementation of a corporate advertising campaign is possibly justified (e.g. BP's very successful television campaign to heighten understanding in Britain of the company's very diversified industrial activities outside the UK). In most other circumstances, however, it is probably much safer to deliver superior service, ignore the apparent lure of funding a large corporate advertising campaign and instead leave the grateful customer to promote your achievements through word-of-mouth recommendations to others.

Customers who bite

At trade association meetings and national conferences on the social responsibilities of industry, speaker after speaker will dwell upon their disappointment that they and their companies are just not trusted by the general public. Suffice to say, events over the years (e.g. the thalidomide and Opren drug tragedies; the BCCI banking collapse; evidence of market manipulation by Salomom Brothers on Wall Street; the collapse of the Maxwell empire; mismanagement of child abuse cases by Social Services departments) are more than adequate justification that, for most people, active mistrust of organizations in both the private and public sector is probably the safest option.

In reality, legal and moral misbehaviour by individuals and organizations is nothing new. Unfortunately, the human animal has always been easily corrupted by the incentive of being able to acquire greater wealth and/or power. What does appear to have changed over recent years, however, are the attitudes of the general public. Previous generations grew up believing that senior individuals in large private or public organizations, especially if they held technical or professional qualifications, could be trusted to behave correctly. As the general rise in the level of education has given more people the confidence to question the truth behind what they are told, increasingly members of the general public are willing to challenge the credibility of reassuring statements or the validity of an expert opinion.

This attitude shift is often now collectively labelled 'consumerism'. The modern roots of the movement are founded in the 1960s writings of influential authors such as John Kenneth Galbraith and Vance Packard and the 1962 John F. Kennedy presidential announcement that people have the right to safety, to be informed, to choose and to be heard. Unfortunately, those in industry and government who assumed that the movement would wither and die were in for a rude awakening over the next decade. In no small part the spread of consumerism can be attributed to the efforts of Ralph Nader, who targeted what was then the godfather of the American Dream, the US car industry. By throwing the spotlight on various incidents (e.g. the safety defects of General Motors Corvair; the fire risk resulting from the positioning of the gas tank on the Ford Pinto), it emerged that company executives were well aware of product problems but apparently chose to ignore them on the grounds of damaging corporate financial performance. The lesson to be learned from such situations is, of course, that in today's highly competitive environment consumerism means no company can expect to survive for very long if it fails to put the rights of the customer well ahead of any short-term financial goals. Again, of course, the more enlightened company, which has already achieved a strong market position based on a genuine desire to deliver customer satisfaction, can exploit this attitude shift as another weapon with which to beat the competition. Policies such as instantly refunding money to the customer, offering lifetime guarantees and responding immediately to concerns over the safety of a product by withdrawing it from the market appear to the financially oriented executive as extremely expensive propositions. Compared, however, to alternative options of using massive advertising campaigns to generate sales and/or the financial implications of your company becoming the target of a successful class action suit, then 'putting the consumer first' is not only the most effective way to build customer loyalty; over the long term it is also the most cost-effective managerial philosophy.

'Green' no longer refers to the colour of money

Born out of consumerism were the writings of Rachel Carson who, in her book *The Silent Spring*, documented the case against the hazards of using pesticides. This was followed in 1970 by Paul and Anne Ehrlich's prediction of an eco-catastrophe facing the world unless businesses could be persuaded to develop a sense of responsibility over the impact of their activities on the environment. These prophecies were the basis for spawning a new consumer attitude: namely, that a concerned group of citizens could orchestrate a movement that could eventually lead to a change of behaviour by companies and even by government departments.

Environmentalists is the collective name applied to people who are concerned about the need for human beings actively to protect and enhance the environment as part of a heritage to be passed on to future generations. Although first evident in the late sixties, it has been only in the last few years that the movement has become a force to be reckoned with in terms of its power to change the behaviour of industrialists and politicians. Why the 'Greens' (to give them their more popular name) have suddenly moved in the last few years from being a small minority of often strangely dressed eccentrics to a major force drawing support from all sectors of society is difficult to determine. Part of the reason is probably that the widespread reporting of issues such as global warming, acid rain and holes in the ozone layer has ultimately caused people to realize that planet Earth is a more fragile environment than most of us had previously supposed. This awareness and understanding has been accelerated by the fact that the undesirable outcome of our efforts to exploit new technologies is often a catastrophic side effect (e.g. Chernobyl; the greenhouse effect associated with the burning of hydrocarbon fuels; long-term contamination of water sources from leakage of industrial wastes from land fill sites).

Despite the fact that, for organizations in both the private and public sector, becoming more environmentally responsible is going to cost huge amounts of money to revise products and processes, a failure to respond to such demands could be even more expensive in terms of an eventual loss of customers. An August 1991 *Daily Telegraph* survey revealed that 41 per cent of the British population would be willing to give up the fruits of scientific discovery if they could live in a natural world free from radiation and pollution. There is little to be gained from responses such as those expressed by Sir Walter Bodmer, chairman of the Committee on the Public Understanding of Science. He was quoted as saying, 'Put those who hanker for some new arcadia back into the jungle. Let them roam Epping Forest with a stone axe. By golly, they would be back like a shot.'

A mature and reasoned response for all organizations is to accept that the environment is now a priority item for consideration on their agenda of social responsibilities. Having determined the need for change, the approach must be both sincere and embedded in the foundations of future organizational culture. There is little point in the marketing department issuing a press release proudly announcing that Head Office is switching to using recycled paper, while elsewhere in the company people are working in an outdated and unsafe processing facility known to pose a major environmental hazard. Eventually, somebody in the media is going to notice the image conflict and if, in fact, the plant is the cause of a massive pollution incident, the consequent adverse publicity will rapidly erode customer trust in the quality of the company's products.

As we enter the twenty-first century, responding to green issues is probably going to represent the greatest source of incremental cost that organizations will have to learn to manage if they wish to retain an image of seeking to meet the needs of their customers fully. By ignoring the problem, organizations can probably enjoy a brief period of higher profits. Ultimately, however, as market performance of competitors is seen to benefit from their greater sense of social responsibility, shareholders and employees will vocally demand a change in attitude. At this late juncture, the cost of catching up, let alone overtaking the competition, is liable to bankrupt the organization. The advice must be for organizations immediately to incorporate 'green' into the current statement of organizational values, to make a careful audit of current capability to fulfil the act as a guardian of the environment and evolve a plan that will steadily improve internal standards for this vital area of corporate performance.

For those who reject the above suggestions, there are two additional factors worth considering. First, remember that, if politicians decide to intervene on an issue, the cost of fulfilling mandatory legislated guidelines is often greater than if the event had been handled earlier by voluntary action within an industrial sector. Second, the one area of potential vulnerability of many Pacific Basin producers is their failure to pay much attention to protecting the environment from their industrial activities. As customers become more aware of this situation, and if Western companies have successfully learnt to incorporate safer technologies into their core processes, then ultimately this may prove a vital advantage in the battle to regain market leadership in world markets.

10

Working with others inside the organization to enhance customer satisfaction

Imagine visiting a car dealership, sitting with the sales person ordering your model specification on a computer screen, confirming the production date with the manufacturer's order-entry computer, and then agreeing with the dealer that you will accept delivery in seven days' time. Furthermore, once you own the car, the dealer can monitor mechanical performance of the vehicle using a telephone link modem and, if a developing fault is identified, the dealer's computer will automatically schedule an appointment with their service department and arrange delivery of a loan car to your door. Based on your experience of car ownership you may feel this description of a completely integrated market system sounds like a futuristic 'customer satisfaction heaven', which you will never see in your lifetime. Well, you might be surprised to know that car manufacturers in Japan are already a long way down the road towards turning this fantasy into fact.

CASE STUDY   Ashmore Instruments

Most of us will probably feel more familiar with the scenario facing Ashmore Instruments, a disguised case of a company that manufactures test equipment for the telecommunications industry. Dissatisfied by recent performance the Board accepted the advice of a consulting firm that possibly it was time to persuade both the managing and marketing directors to take early retirement. Their replacements were recruited from another telecommunications company. On their first day, the new directors took a walk through the plant. They noticed a warehouse full of finished goods, racks alongside the production line filled with partly assembled machines and numerous boxes of components stacked in the goods inbound area. A review of the latest financial statements (Table 10.1) confirmed their suspicions that the company had an excessive amount of monies tied up in materials and finished goods.

Table 10.1   Profit and loss statement (£ millions)

Sales		5.0
Cost of goods		3.5
Gross profit		1.5
Other expenses		1.0
Net profit		0.5

Balance sheet

Fixed assets		2.2	Current liabilities	1.0
Current assets				
Cash	0.1		Long-term liabilities	
Debtors	0.9		Long-term loans	2.0
Finished goods, work				
in progress	1.8		Equity	1.3
		2.8	Retained earnings	0.7
Total assets		5.0	*Total liabilities*	5.0

The marketing department response to questions about this situation was that the high debtor level was necessary because applying pressure to customers was not wise, given the level of faulty products returned for repair and also a poor record for meeting delivery dates. The production department explained high stocks on the grounds that they did not trust the sales forecasts and hence plant schedules were based on prior year shipments. Customer product complaints were mainly about teething problems with new products, which tracked back to some fundamental design faults. The work in progress situation reflected problems over component availability and high failure rates in pre-test prior to assembly. The procurement manager felt the late delivery and poor performance of components was only to be expected, given the company's rigid policy of purchasing only from supply sources offering the lowest quotes.

The status of the manufacturing role

Production staff in manufacturing companies rely on sales forecast information to match current output to customer orders. They also need data on future market needs to provide the specifications upon which new product development projects can be based. One would expect, therefore, to find a close working relationship between the marketing and manufacturing departments which, in turn, provides the basis for links with staff in procurement, design, R & D and accounting.

Unfortunately, the scenario at Ashmore Instruments is all too familiar in Western industry: namely, departments not prepared to cooperate which in turn leads to a complete failure to fulfil customer needs. This breakdown in departmental relationships can often be tracked back to the late 1970s. For it was at this time, during moves to sustain financial performance through the manipulation of balance sheets, that production staff demands for funds to upgrade manufacturing performance caused them to be reclassified as the 'second class' citizens of Western corporate life. This unfair treatment eventually led many production managers to withdraw back into their departments and from then on to minimize their interactions with employees elsewhere in the organization.

Over the last few years there has been a growing revival of the view that production executives can make a contribution to delivering customer satisfaction at least equal to, and in many instances greater than, other functional groups within the organization. This change in perspective has been brought about by the political realization that the economic survival of a country depends on the capability of its manufacturing industries to stay ahead of competition in world markets. The Pacific Basin countries who never discarded the importance of sustaining manufacturing capability (e.g. Taiwanese electronics companies; Korean shipbuilders; Japanese camera companies) have, on almost a daily basis, been handed new market opportunities by Western companies that failed to stay in the race to deliver the highest possible level of product quality. The reason for this situation is that the latter have downgraded the importance that should be attached to the vital contribution their production group can make to overall corporate performance.

The path back to manufacturing sanity

Over the last few years companies such as Ashmore, seeking to improve overall performance, have usually turned to concepts such as Total Quality Management (TQM), the computer-based control system, MRPII, or a Customer Care scheme. All these approaches are extremely useful, but prior to implementation it is vital that a way is found to instil a common sense of purpose across all departments in the organization. Michael Porter proposed that one way of describing the unifying purpose of departments is that they all have a role in contributing towards adding value to the organization's products or services. A guru of the movement to rebuild manufacturing competences in American industry, Richard Schonberger, has further evolved this view through the development of the 'chain of customers' concept. This he presents by suggesting to each individual, no matter what their position in the organization, that the person to whom they provide a service is their customer. By seeking to treat this relationship in the same way that the entire organization should respond to external customers, employees will automatically contribute to enhancing internal productivity. Thus, for example, if the marketing department considers manufacturing as an internal customer, they would recognize the need to supply accurate sales forecasts on a regular basis. Fulfilling this need would result in the production schedules being more in line with market demand, which would very probably reduce the monies tied up in finished goods inventories.

The only limitation to Schonberger's 'chain of customers' concept is that it can be interpreted as a one-way process in which the department acts to satisfy the needs of another group within the organization. In reality, of course, the process is a circle not a chain because both parties should be seeking mutual satisfaction from working more closely with each other. The example of marketing providing a sales forecast represents a benefit to manufacturing because it assists their production planning and reduces finished goods inventories. It is also likely that the company will have the right products in stock, which will benefit the marketing group because there will be a concurrent improvement in customer satisfaction over the level of on-time deliveries. Once the customer is no longer angry about late deliveries, it may then become easier for the sales force to raise the issue of slow payment. The consequent decline in the average age of outstanding receivables will satisfy the accounting department's need to ensure efficient management of working capital within the organization.

Dismantling the barricades at Ashmore

The two new directors arranged an off-site residential weekend conference for all levels of management from shop-floor supervisors through to department heads. The keynote speakers were senior managers from other electronics companies who presented case studies of how performance had been improved through the adoption of the 'circle of customers' concept. This was followed by the managing director reviewing the current state of the balance sheet. He closed his speech by summarizing the explanations he had heard from the various departments and expressed the view that, to him, these all indicated a fundamental lack of common purpose within the organization. Participants were then formed into small inter-departmental groups to generate ideas on how the barriers which appeared to exist within Ashmore might be dismantled over time. Possibly the most important outcome of these discussions was the widespread recognition that increased cooperation between departments could lead to performance improvement. Other important decisions adopted by the participants were the creation of an inter-departmental sales forecasting/production scheduling group and the abolition of the company policy of selecting suppliers purely on the grounds of lowest possible price.

The supportive euphoria which existed during the weekend meeting was not easy to sustain back in the workplace. Initially the two directors found that they were frequently being drawn into arbitrating disputes between senior managers concerned about departmental boundaries and retaining lines of authority. Nevertheless, 12 months later, both individuals were very gratified by (a) year-end results in which current assets as a percentage of sales had fallen from 56 to 28 per cent of sales and (b) the results of a survey of customers indicating a much higher level of confidence in the quality of service they now received from the Ashmore organization.

Validity of internal information

Although greater inter-departmental trust is fundamental in the management of internal customer relations, this must also be accompanied by the availability of valid information if the organization is to reach agreement over important operational decisions. The disguised case of Whitworth Ltd can be used to illustrate how errors in information can easily mislead an organization.

CASE STUDY   Whitworth Ltd

The company specializes in the manufacture of programmable control units which are supplied to a diverse range of OEMs. The product line consists of standard, semi-customized and specialist customized control units. Production is highly automated and the largest areas of expense are the indirect overheads associated with R & D, creating software systems for unit programming, test equipment and production automation support staff. Product costs are calculated using a standard cost system in which indirect plant overheads and general administrative costs are allocated on the basis of direct labour hours. Current relationships between costs and revenue are described in Table 10.2. The issue under debate within the organization is that the marketing department is reporting pressure from customers seeking a reduction in the quoted price for standard units. It has been suggested by the marketing director that it would be possible to accommodate a decrease because the market would probably be willing to pay a higher price for the semi-customized and specialist controllers. His view is supported by the manufacturing group which feels that, given the company's highly automated technology, the real cost of production for standard units is probably lower than that reflected by the company costing system. Although the director of finance is sceptical about these claims he approved the formation of a small working party from manufacturing and his own department to re-examine the costing system.

At the first meeting of the group, manufacturing explained that as, over the years, the company had automated the production systems, the relevance of using labour hours as the basis for overhead cost allocation seemed increasingly questionable. As one of the engineers pointed out, one outcome of this situation was the tendency to place great emphasis on reducing the labour content of any product when, in fact, there was

Table 10.2 The current costing and revenue situation at Whitworth ('000)

	Standard units	Semi- customized	Customized units
Quantity sold	100	30	10
	£	£	£
Direct labour	50	21	10
Direct materials	250	159	110
Total direct costs	300	180	120
Indirect overheads	496	208	96
Total cost of goods	796	388	216
General administration	228	112	60
Total costs	1024	500	276
Revenue	1100	570	330
(Average price/unit)	(11)	(19)	(33)
Net profit	76	70	54
Profit as % of sales	6.9	12.2	16.4

Table 10.3 Revised production costs at Whitworth utilizing an allocation of overheads based on total direct product costs ('000)

	Standard units	Semi- customized	Customized units
Quantity	100	30	10
	£	£	£
Total direct costs	300	180	120
Indirect overheads	384	248	168
General administration	196	124	80
Total product costs	880	552	368
Unit cost £	8.8	18.4	36
(Current cost system £)	(10.24)	(16.70)	(27.60)

probably more benefit in considering how to reduce either the cost of components or the time taken to develop the new software systems used to programme the control units.

The accountants were quite interested in the view that plant labour was no longer the real 'cost driver' at Whitworth. Their suggestion was that they should re-examine the formula for allocating indirect and administrative overheads. Initially they examined whether the current accounting system might permit specific overheads to be allocated to the product types. They soon recognized, however, that this would be an almost impossible task without completely redesigning the management accounting system. Instead they decided to try allocating overheads in relation to total direct product costs and the results of this approach are shown in Table 10.3. On the basis of this alternative approach it can be seen that actual unit cost for standard products has fallen from £10.24 to £8.80, whereas semi-customized and customized products have risen from £16.67 to £18.40 and £27.60 to £36.80 respectively. The consensus view of the group was that the revised costs were a more accurate representation of real costs. The finance director accepted their conclusions and requested the marketing department to investigate to what degree customers would accept a price increase in semi-customized and customized controllers if this was accompanied by a price reduction for standard units.

The Whitworth case is not an exception. Many companies over recent years have begun to realize that their information systems, which are intended to provide data on costs, are using assumptions that are no longer valid.

The dangers of using invalid information were popularized by Professors Johnson and Kaplan in their book entitled *Relevance Lost: The Rise and Fall of Management Accounting*. In the place of traditional management accounting practices, they have recommended the abandonment of techniques that merely allocate costs and replacing them with systems which explain the real causes of costs. Once causes or 'drivers' can be identified, employees can then allocate resources to finding ways of more effectively managing costs and thereby improve overall productivity. Gains in productivity provide the basis for delivering greater market satisfaction because the organization can either offer the same product at a lower price or use the higher profit margin/unit to fund product performance improvement programmes.

From 'in stock' to 'Just in Time'

In the fifties and sixties, the orientation of manufacturing was towards building huge-capacity facilities to capture all the advantages associated with exploiting economies of scale. The creation of giant single-site factories meant that the lowest possible unit cost could only be achieved by scheduling long production runs for a product. Unfortunately, the more output the factory produced, the longer this would remain in inventory. Optimizing production and storage costs was achieved through the concept of *economic order quantity*, which permitted the production department to calculate the point at which the combined costs of production and carrying stock could be minimized. As process technologies became more complex, managers increasingly turned to sophisticated computer-based decision tools to manage their scheduling problems. Such systems depend on accurate forecasts of demand and suppliers who deliver raw materials on time. Where forecasts were wrong or inbound deliveries were late, managers would be forced to build 'buffer stocks' into the planning model to avoid disruption of the plant operations. Under these circumstances companies could be confident that product would be in stock, but only by having huge sums invested in finished goods, work in progress and raw materials.

The Japanese solution to this problem was to examine how costs could be reduced by improving the management of their manufacturing systems. One of the largest costs associated with many process technologies is the set-up expense associated with changing a production line from one product to another. These costs were traditionally recovered by spreading such costs over long production runs. The Japanese approach was to place emphasis on ways to reduce set-up costs, which would then permit a factory to produce smaller quantities at the same unit cost. They also recognized that poor quality control results in costs rising because of the need for either rework or scrapping of defective products. Hence, concurrent with incorporation of faster set-up times into their manufacturing processes, they also sought to achieve zero defects through the introduction of techniques under the generic title of Total Quality Management. The various facets of this Japanese manufacturing management philosophy have now been enshrined in the term 'Just in Time' or JIT.

Although JIT was initially perceived as a mechanism by which to reduce current assets, those companies that have adopted the concept have rapidly recognized that it provides numerous opportunities to offer greater customer satisfaction. One benefit of JIT is that the company has greater manufacturing flexibility and hence the marketer is in a position to offer a much wider range of product choice. Delivery times are also shortened and, as the company carries very limited stocks of any item, it is able to introduce a product improvement immediately, without delaying the launch, while the sales force is engaged in disposing of huge quantities of the obsolete product. Finally, as response times are reduced, product produced 'right first time' and internal productivity increased, the consequent cost savings permit the company to pull well ahead of less responsive competition.

Extending the customer circle outside of the organization

Once an organization has developed the level of internal trust, information sharing and employee skills to be confident in their abilities to exploit the benefits of JIT, the next step is for the marketing department to extend the operational philosophy into relationships with both customers and suppliers.

The traditional view of suppliers is that they should be kept at arm's length, provided with the minimum of information and continually pressured to reduce their prices. Not surprisingly, this attitude leads to the development of relationships based on mutual distrust. Yet the most critical aspect of JIT is ensuring that the raw materials required in all value added processes are available when needed. Hence, the more perceptive companies have now realized that successful JIT operations must be based on a relationship with suppliers founded on mutual trust.

The development of closer relationships with suppliers requires the adoption of a reverse flow marketing philosophy. The company will have to spend time determining what is desired of them by their suppliers, while concurrently educating the suppliers on how their contribution to the company's operations can be optimized. Most suppliers prefer stable order patterns, prompt payment and easily administered delivery systems. In the more enlightened companies, this has led to complete delegation of the procurement process to the suppliers. They are authorized to come onto the shop floor, replenish stocks, and prepare a monthly invoice without having quantities checked by the customer, and they are paid within days of invoice submission. These suppliers are also trained in TQM by the company and given delegated responsibility to manage product quality before delivery, thereby vitiating the need for inbound inspection of raw materials prior to use in the production process.

Companies that have moved towards forging close relationships with their suppliers soon find that, not only do they receive better service, but as supplier productivity is improved by stabilized order patterns and simplified administrative procedures, this often leads to a decline in the cost of raw materials. The next step in the relationship is to recognize that in many cases the specialist knowledge of the suppliers can be exploited to enhance further the company's products and/or process technologies. Once this point is reached, the marketing department should seek approval for the adoption of a policy of involving supplier employees in new product development projects and promoting regular interchange of marketing staff between the two organizations.

Moving to forge closer relationships with customers also requires a change in attitudes by both parties in the relationship. The marketing group must adopt the philosophy that the purpose of all activities is to seek to enhance the performance of the company and to place the customer first in any situation. An effective start point in building mutual trust is to invite the customer into the organization and to arrange an interchange between the visitors and employees from all levels within the organization. A frequently quoted example of this approach is the US Milliken Corporation, which has managed to survive and thrive in the textile industry despite intensive price-oriented competition from Third World producers. The company places great emphasis on building close relationships with customers. Visitors to their plants are proudly shown exhibits on the 'wall of fame' providing evidence of how they have repeatedly worked with retail chains such as Sears Roebuck and Wal-Mart in fulfilling the company mission of being 'Milliken: The Home of Quick Response'.

Closing the relationship circle outside the organization

Given the increasing influence of supplier expertise in the development of improved product and process technologies, it is obvious that their potential contribution can be even further enhanced if they can acquire a detailed understanding of the problems facing the company's customers. The traditional management philosophy has been to keep suppliers and customers apart because the risk of bringing these two parties together might eventually lead to the company being cut out of the relationship.

The more progressive organizations have now discarded this philosophy because of the potential synergies which can accrue from bringing together all the parties associated with the successful management of the market system. In America for example, the McKesson Corporation, a distributor of drugs to independent retailers, has moved to link their suppliers and their customers using a computer-based inventory management system. The resultant sharing of previously confidential information achieved a massive reduction in inventories at all levels in the distribution chain from manufacturer through to end-user outlet. Similar approaches are also being adopted in the automotive industry where machine tool companies, component suppliers and the car makers are now working together jointly to eradicate problems in the final product caused by bad design and poor quality.

Time to market satisfaction

The intensely competitive conditions that now prevail in most markets make it mandatory that, in the product development process, the time between idea generation and product launch is kept to a minimum. Furthermore, to be successful a new product must satisfy the two criteria of meeting market need and providing optimal utilization of the organization's internal resources.

	PERCEIVED VALUE TO THE MARKETING GROUP OF THE PRODUCT DEVELOPMENT PROJECT		
	Low	**Average**	**High**
Poor	1. Terminate	2. Low priority	3. Assign to skunk works
Reason-able	4. Low priority	5. Standard project schedule	6. Lead project priority to solve resource problems
Excellent	7. Withdraw project resources	8. Lead project priority to identify complementary opportunities	9. Fast track project

(Left axis: INTERNAL RESOURCE UTILIZATION)

Figure 10.1 A project prioritization decision matrix for optimizing the 'time to market' schedule for product development programmes

Delays in the product development process are often caused because insufficient attention has been given to ensuring there is common agreement over what priority has been given to the various projects currently in progress within the organization. One technique for avoiding this problem is to treat project prioritization as an internal customer satisfaction issue. The marketing department is able to use factors such as market demand, customer needs, competitive pressure, growth opportunities, breadth of product line, product quality and price to classify the priority which they would like to allocate to the product development process. By recognizing and responding to these priorities other departments would then be satisfying the needs of the marketing department.

Other departments can use factors such as capacity, technology, R & D expertise, employee skills, availability of funds and access to raw materials to assess which product development projects represent an optimal use of internal resources. Acceptance of this classification by marketing would then satisfy the internal needs of other departments to make best use of their available resources.

The marketing department can apply a simple scoring system to specify the value of each product development project and position it within the simple classification categories of low, average and high. Concurrently, other departments can apply the same principles to specifying how each project represents a poor, reasonable or excellent utilization of internal resources. The two scores can then be used to locate each product development project within a project priority decision matrix of the type illustrated in Figure 10.1. The project decision strategies proposed by this matrix are as follows:

Cell 1   The low value of the product to marketing and the poor utilization of resources means the project should immediately be terminated because it is of little benefit to the organization or the market.

Cell 2   The poor utilization of internal resources reduces the potential value of the project and hence work should only be progressed on a 'time permits' basis.

Cell 3   Despite the high importance of this project to the marketing department, the organization lacks one or more key internal resources to progress successfully the product development process. In successful companies it is an accepted practice for employees to spend part of their time on projects which they consider offer a personal intellectual challenge. The phrase 'skunk works' is often used to describe these type of personal initiatives. The outcomes are often the resolution of what initially appeared to be totally insoluble problems. Hence the recommended action for projects that fall into Cell 3 is that they be turned over to the company skunk works to see if an innovative solution can be found which will resolve the current resource availability problem facing the product development programme.

Cell 4   Although the company has adequate resources, the low importance that marketing places on the project means it should only be progressed on a 'time permits' basis.

Cell 5   Projects in this cell will be progressed but using standard time-scales and no special priorities can be expected over the allocation of internal resources.

Cell 6   These are important projects which may be constrained by internal development resources. Hence priority will be given to seeking ways of resolving resource utilization problems with the specific intent that current length of the 'time to market' schedule will be reduced.

Cell 7   Although this type of project represents an excellent use of resources, the project is of only minimal interest to the marketing group. Under these circumstances, resources should be redirected into other areas of development activity.

Cell 8   These are important projects but priority should be given to finding new market opportunities which would complement the existing product development idea and thereby gain even greater returns on the internal resources allocated to the programme.

Cell 9   Projects in this cell are important to everybody and offer the greatest rewards if 'time to market' can be minimized. Hence they are classified as fast track programmes and should be given priority by all departments when scheduling every phase of the product development process.

Future satisfaction circles

The usual initial motivation for organizations to form relationship circles linking themselves more closely with suppliers and customers is to improve the productivity of current operations. The complexity of products and processing technologies in most industrial sectors is now at the stage, however, that the likelihood of new products being successfully developed and introduced is also critically dependent upon close cooperation between organizations at all levels within the market system.

Hence, prior to embarking upon any major new product development programme, the producer company marketers should endeavour to involve both customers and suppliers in the planning and implementation phases of the project. Key customers should be invited to provide a detailed scenario of their vision of future market conditions (e.g. size, growth rate, new opportunities, changing customer behaviour) and also the factors most likely to influence their internal productivity. The company's own employees and key supplier organizations should concurrently develop similar scenarios and share this information with the customers. As illustrated in Figure 10.2, the objectives of this process are to identify (a) projects of overlapping mutual interest and (b) opportunities for subsequent problem resolution activities which can eventually further enhance the performance of other partners in the market system alliance.

For the marketer seeking to promote an alliance to improve management of future circumstances, it must be recognized that both the organization's own employees and employees within potential partner organizations may initially greet the idea with great suspicion. Revealing future intentions requires a much greater

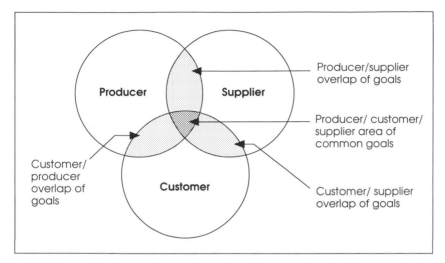

Figure 10.2 Identifying future scenarios of mutual overlap in a customer/producer/supplier satisfaction circle

degree of mutual trust than just working together to solve current problems. Hence it is often a good idea to start with a project about the future in which, if sharing of confidences proves unworkable, no permanent damage would be caused should it be impossible to achieve full and open cooperation between the various partners.

This approach of developing inter-organizational partnership to deal with future management is becoming increasingly common in high technology industries such as computing, precision engineering, communications and health care. Furthermore, in many cases, as the participants come to comprehend fully the complexity of the project tasks, they are now moving to form collaborative partnerships within the market systems between organizations that have traditionally viewed each other as dangerous rivals. The formation of such strategic alliances is, for example, seen as the most likely way that the European IT and electronics industries will ever create a critical mass sufficient to combat effectively the competitive threat posed by Pacific Basin competitors.

CASE STUDY   Seeking to manage the future at Brymor

Brymor Ltd is a disguised case of a company that manufactures components used in the UK new and replacement windows industry. The company supplies 'bar lengths' of four product types (aluminium, thermal break aluminium, composite and uPVC) for customers who fabricate windows and complete window frame kits for customers who do installation work. Approximately half of Brymor sales are to companies that operate in the domestic housing market. The balance of sales is to customers requiring products such as new shop fronts and windows for office buildings or factories.

Established in the late 1970s the company is considered a market leader in the supply of premium quality, advanced design bar length and kit form products. During the housing boom of the mid-eighties, the company moved ahead of competitors through installation of a JIT philosophy across all areas of operation from design through to procurement, manufacturing and product distribution. It also led the industry in developing close links between suppliers and final customers to resolve design, installation and product performance problems rapidly. These close working relationships permitted the company to pick up the early warning signs of the impending downturn in the UK construction industry. Hence, although the company entered the nineties with sales significantly down on prior years, through early restructuring of the manufacturing operation and careful management of assets, it is confident that it will survive the recession while many other competitors are being forced into liquidation.

Following a series of long-term planning meetings, the marketing group decided that, although they had a clear vision of how to optimize near-term market performance, they lacked sufficient understanding of (a) medium-term trends in the UK construction industry and (b) the potential impact of factors such as cost trends for raw materials, the performance capabilities of new forms of composite materials under development in the plastics industry and the benefits of further automation of bar length manufacturing processes.

Selected key customers and suppliers who had made major contributions to the design and implementation of Brymor's JIT systems were invited to attend a conference entitled 'Where Next For All Of Us?'. Delegates were provided with pre-meeting information packs which clearly communicated that the purpose of the event was to examine opportunities for mutually exploiting the benefits of cooperating in the development of new products suited to the market conditions that may prevail during the nineties. To stimulate the broadest possible range of debate, speakers were invited from the worlds of architecture, civil engineering, property development, finance and energy conservation to provide their perspectives on factors that would represent 'performance drivers' as the UK construction industry moved into a recovery phase by the middle of the decade.

The marketing group took care to ensure that delegates perceived the conference as the start point for further discussions and not an event from which major new initiatives could be expected to emerge. Nevertheless, delegates were able to identify a number of areas which offered some very exciting new opportunities. These included:

● new composites which opened up prospects for radically different design shapes for shop fronts and conservatories

● improved bonding agents which could reduce on-site installation times

● a CADCAM network system which, by providing interactive linkage between a fabricator, Brymor and suppliers, might permit development of a much more rapid response to contract situations which in the past appeared too complex to resolve in the time demanded by the architects or surveyors seeking bids on major construction contracts.

These opportunities convinced the delegates that, although surviving the recession was still a priority issue, the scale of potential future success could be greatly enhanced by a more cooperative attitude to new product development. It was therefore resolved that immediate steps should be taken to investigate the creation of a product development centre, resourced by contributions from all levels of the market system, but located within the confines of the Brymor manufacturing site.

11

Service satisfaction – more than just 'Have a nice day'

A common feature of Western nation economies since the Second World War is the massive expansion of the service sector both in terms of contribution to Gross National Product and as a source of employment. Various factors have fuelled this explosion – rising consumer incomes have made the delegation of house repairs to external providers an affordable option, and the purchase of increasingly technologically complex products means that the customer is unable to carry out any needed repairs. Furthermore, as countries acquire economic wealth, they become able to fund large-scale provision of public sector services such as education and health care.

A source of dissatisfaction

A fascinating aspect of the service sector is that it represents the greatest source of customer dissatisfaction. To prove this point merely ask a group of friends to describe recent purchases which have been accompanied by problems. They will usually respond with a long list of complaints about their bank, insurance company, garage repairs, plumber, electrician or telephone company. More rarely will they mention being disappointed with a chocolate bar, breakfast cereal or pair of shoes.

One of the fundamental reasons for this high level of dissatisfaction is that some marketers have yet to acquire an adequate understanding of how to fulfil customer needs through effective management of all aspects of the service provision process. For example, the inexperienced marketer will typically attempt to utilize management concepts that have proved effective in the marketing of branded fast-moving consumer goods. In this latter sector, there is frequently minimal technical differences between competitive offerings (e.g. coffee, beer, toilet soaps) and perceived differentiation is created through heavy promotional spending. Hence uninformed efforts to build market share in the service sector are frequently based upon spending more on advertising than the competition. The approach was popular during the seventies when the US banks were striving to gain a greater share of the consumer financial services market. Although the US banks eventually realized that the technique had only a minor impact on buyer behaviour, the UK banks went ahead and duplicated the error in their fight for market share during the eighties.

In early attempts to understand the differences between the f.m.c.g. and service products, some marketers decided that a key characteristic of the latter sector is the heterogeneous nature of customer need. There is no doubt that this factor is definitely present in many service markets. One example is provided by merely observing the varied nature of the passengers encountered on a Boeing 747 flying from America to Europe. Having determined heterogeneous need was important, these marketers then attempted to exploit this knowledge by expanding the product portfolio to provide a much greater degree of purchase choice. The insurance industry is a very typical example of this type of thinking, which is probably why, in recent years, we have all been inundated with mail shots for a huge variety of new forms of insurance coverage. As was the case of relying on promotional spending, however, most service organization marketing groups that assumed product diversity was the key to success soon found that this approach also had little impact on market share over the longer term.

The characteristics of service markets

Further studies by academics such as Lovelock have demonstrated that in addition to the heterogeneous nature of customer needs, most service markets exhibit the following unique characteristics:

1 The product exhibits a varying degree of intangibility (or, as proposed by Lovelock, 'a good is an object, a device, a thing: a service is a deed, a performance, an effort').

2 The product is perishable and hence if unsold is lost for ever because it cannot be stored for later consumption (e.g. an empty theatre seat).

3 Production and consumption are often inseparable.

4 The provider usually retains ownership and the customer has only temporary access (e.g. renting a car from Hertz).

Research by Professor David Garvin in America has shown that the unique characteristics of service industries cause customers to use a very different range of factors from those that influence purchase satisfaction for tangible goods. The parameters identified by Garvin, ranked in declining order of priority, are:

1 The tangible evidence of service (e.g. physical appearance of facilities and staff).

2 Reliability with which service is provided.

3 A genuine willingness of staff to respond to customer needs.

4 The knowledge exhibited by staff about all aspects of the organization's policies and service provision procedures.

5 The credibility of information communicated.

6 A genuine sense of caring for the customer.

7 The general level of courtesy in dealing with all types of customers and their problems.

8 The communication skills of staff, especially in listening and responding to customers.

Beyond Customer Care

In recent years some management gurus have focused upon the importance people attach to the way they are treated by the employees of the organization, and proposed that the only necessary requirement for delivering satisfaction in the service sector is to be nice to the customer. This has led to a massive increase in the monies both private and public sector organizations have invested in Customer Care training programmes which focus solely on improving the interpersonal skills of employees working at the customer interface. To demonstrate the fallacy of this simplistic philosophy merely ask commuters what they think of British Rail's decision to improve the abilities of their staff to make 'pleasanter apologies' when trains are late arriving at London mainline terminals. These passengers will undoubtedly tell you they would much rather BR put resources into improving the train service instead of sending employees to the company's 'charm school for station staff'.

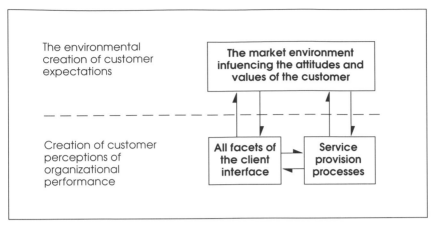

Figure 11.1 The interaction of customer and organization in the service provision process

The reality of delivering customer satisfaction in the service sector is that it cannot be achieved merely by focusing on a single variable such as range of product choice or employee interpersonal skills. Satisfaction occurs when customer expectations are equal to the perceptions formed during all the processes associated with selection, purchase and consumption of the desired service.

As illustrated in Figure 11.1, the parameters that influence customer perceptions are the client interface and the service provision process. The interface components comprise all the facets of the organization with which the customer comes into contact, ranging from personal one-to-one dialogue with an employee through to presence or absence of litter in the car park. The service provision process may be an event which the customer can directly observe (e.g. being served in a shop) or may occur at a location removed from the customer (e.g. administration of an insurance claim). In this latter situation, the customer will use factors such as time and accuracy of response to form a perception about the efficiency of the provision process. The customer can also be adversely influenced by poor linkage within the organization between interface and provision personnel. For example, a sales assistant may fail to record on the order form whether the customer required an overnight or normal delivery. The shipping clerk notes the omission, cannot be bothered to check back with the assistant and assumes 'normal', when in fact 'overnight' was specified. Naturally the customer is very annoyed when the item fails to materialize the next day as promised.

To ensure all aspects of organizational behaviour that can influence

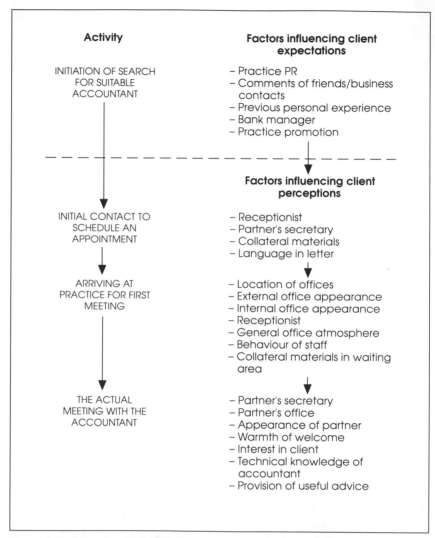

Figure 11.2 Factors influencing the SME owner/manager in the selection of an accountant

customer perceptions are effectively managed, it is necessary for the marketer to develop a complete map of all the activities associated with the service selection, provision and consumption process. It is imperative that this knowledge is formulated through extensive market research and not based on employee guesses about customer needs. The research will involve a number of techniques such as examining the nature of complaints, studying the competition, inviting customers to participate in group discussions, and large-scale mail surveys. These data then provide the basis for specifying policies and procedures for ensuring the organization delivers customer satisfaction.

A typical outcome of such studies is illustrated in Figure 11.2, which describes the influencers of service satisfaction during the search and selection of an accountant by the owner/manager of a small business. This model was created through research by the Plymouth Business School. It is interesting to note that most accountants believe it is only the ability to communicate their technical expertise during the first interview with the client which controls the practice selection decision. As shown by Figure 11.2, however, there is a large number of other variables which influence client perceptions. Furthermore, most of these are related to non-technical issues such as the physical appearance of the practice and the friendliness of the general office staff.

Responding to changing satisfaction criteria

Service organizations are becoming increasingly concerned about the cost of losing a customer to competition. The US supermarket industry estimates that one such customer represents an annual revenue loss of at least $5000. To heighten employee awareness over the need to retain customer loyalty, companies are now installing 'zero defection' programmes which carefully research the causes of customers switching to competitors and then apply this knowledge to revise customer service procedures.

Zero defection studies frequently reveal that the organization, having determined what factors influence satisfaction during the initial selection/purchase cycle, then assumes that these remain unchanged over time. In reality, however, as customers gain experience of the provider, this alters their perceptions and expectations over what they consider is adequate quality of service. To explain this phenomenon, it is necessary to examine the attitudes and values of the customer during the formation of a long-term relationship with the provider. The intangibility of service products causes the customer to mistrust the provider initially and as a result there is an uninformed exchange of information between the two parties. Satisfactory first purchase and post-purchase experience leads to the recognition of common goals. This permits an informed exchange of information and ultimately the establishment of mutual trust and shared goals. As customers move through these various phases their expectations and perceptions undergo change and different aspects of provider behaviour begin to influence delivery of customer satisfaction. If the marketer has not acquired an understanding of this situation there is the risk that customer management programmes will concentrate on those factors important during initial purchase but fail to perform adequately against the different parameters used by loyal customers to assess quality of service.

EXAMPLE   UK banks provide an example of applying the concept of responding to changing needs in the customer relationship. The strategic position adopted by the major UK clearing banks during the 1980s in relation to the SME customers was that of attempting to service the entire market and relying heavily on promotional activity to differentiate themselves from competition. Only the National Giro Bank appeared to compete on a cost leadership basis by overtly offering lower-priced banking services. In a world where most market sectors are in the maturity phase and the level of competition is intensifying, business survival is often critically tied to the abilities of an organization to attract and then retain customers by delivering the highest possible level of service satisfaction. Plymouth Business School research comparing SME owner/manager attitudes during the mid-eighties 'boom' with the early nineties recession revealed that client satisfaction over banking services had declined. In part this was caused by the UK banks recognizing that small business lending is a high-risk proposition in a recession and hence they have changed from an aggressive promotional policy over customer attraction and retention to one involving a somewhat passive willingness to service this client group.

The mutual long-term goal of the owner/manager and the banker is the creation of a successful small business which needs to purchase a broad range of financial services. The mass marketing approach of the banks in the eighties was based on the assumption that, by maximizing the number of clients attracted to the bank, from this source would eventually emerge a crop of growing businesses with whom the bank could have a profitable long-term relationship. The high costs of writing off loans made to businesses which subsequently failed during the current recession must have caused the UK banks to realize that the mass marketing approach in the SME sector is an extremely high-risk strategy.

Press releases by the UK banks indicate a revision in their customer service philosophy by moving towards an approach that reflects the variable nature of the client base and overtly accepts that the bank can expect to make a reasonable profit from only a very small proportion of its SME sector customers. Having decided to be more selective, to sustain customer satisfaction the banks will need to revise their service management philosophies to respond more adequately to the changing needs of their customers over time.

In the case of the client/banker relationship, the two important variables are

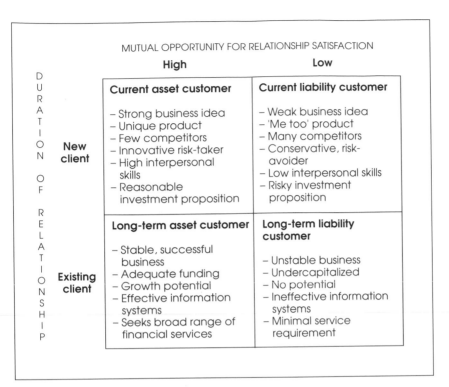

Figure 11.3 A customer service relationship matrix

the length of the relationship and the opportunities for mutual gain. During the early years of the typical small business, owner/manager banking needs are usually restricted to access to an overdraft facility and current account financial transactions. Only after the business has become successful will the client begin to seek additional services (e.g. medium-term loans, pension/ insurance products, computerized transaction services) of a sufficient scale that the bank will begin to obtain an adequate return on the time and effort invested in assisting the client. Some businesses, no matter how many years they trade, will always remain 'one-man' operations, trading near the edge of insolvency and requiring little from their bank other than an overdraft that typically runs close to the bank's authorized maximum lending ceiling.

The two parameters of relationship duration and mutual opportunity can be combined to form a *customer portfolio matrix* of the type illustrated in Figure 11.3. The characteristics exhibited by the long-term asset customers are that they and their bank enjoy a mutually satisfactory relationship. Eventually some of this group of small business customers will go into decline. The bank, therefore, needs to add continually to their pool of current asset customers because it is they who, as their businesses become successful, will form the next generation of long-term asset customers.

The long-term liability customer has been with the bank for some years and the best outcome for both parties is that they terminate their trading activities. The current liability customer has been trading for only a short time, but all the performance indicators (e.g. sales, profits, debtor/creditor ratio) are those of a business which will probably never succeed. Of all potential outcomes, the most likely is that these customers represent the next generation of long-term liabilities.

It is proposed that a bank's marketers can use this type of portfolio approach to classify customer groups and then create the most appropriate form of Customer Care programme to deliver a quality of service compatible with client needs. Fundamental to this process is acceptance of a view that the mass marketing philosophy of delivering equality of service to all customers is inappropriate. In its place, other than ensuring that employees are fulfilling their responsibilities to support effectively the organization's interface with the external environment, the marketer should design the service response to fulfil specifically the varying needs of the different customer types.

It is vital that when owner/managers first contact the bank they do not have too high an expectation that their lending needs will automatically be fulfilled. Hence the marketer may need to assess carefully whether current promotional campaigns are communicating a message of 'We wish to assist where possible' instead of the eighties-type implicit advertising over-promise of 'We are able to help everybody be successful in small business'. Then, as soon as possible, the bank will need to determine whether the new client is a current asset or current liability. Bankers have often told me that being able to gauge correctly the viability of a small business start-up lending proposition can come only through years of experience in the banking profession. Unfortunately, the UK banks tend to use their younger, less experienced loan officers to staff their small business advisory interface. This situation would suggest that most of these loan staff have still to acquire the skills necessary to make an accurate judgement of the potential capability of the new SME owner/manager. In reality, however, the bank's internal records on existing small business customers provide a wealth of both national and regional information which could be used as performance indicators against which to assess the commercial viability of plans presented by people seeking to start their own business. To date, however, there are few indications that the clearing banks have effectively harnessed the potential now offered by linking customized accounting analysis software to an Artificial Intelligence shell. This system would be able to 'learn from information processed' thereby permitting the banks to create a computer-based assessment of new small business loan applications that could be utilized by the most inexperienced of loan officers.

Start-up clients, once identified as current assets, should be (a) told of the bank's faith in the strength of the business proposition, (b) targeted with specific ongoing advisory support and (c) considered for preferential treatment in terms of interest rates on loans, service charges and lending ceiling. The current liability client, on the other hand, should be carefully assessed to determine whether it is the business proposition or the individual that causes the banker to believe that the venture is unlikely to succeed. If it is the latter, and managerial skills enhancement cannot be achieved through persuading the individual to participate in appropriate training, then the bank should constructively communicate its perspective and decline to provide financial services. In the case of an apparent fundamental flaw in the business proposition, if referral to a local advisory service does not lead to a significant improvement in the commercial viability of the business plan, then again the bank may wish politely to decline the opportunity to act as a service provider.

It is very probable that the Pareto Rule exists in the provision of financial services to UK small businesses: namely, that 80 per cent of profit comes from 20 per cent of the client base and 80 per cent of problems are caused by 20 per cent of the clients. The source of the majority of the bank's profits will be the long-term asset customer. It is in the bank's best interests to seek to sustain survival and growth of businesses of this category. Hence the bank should carefully determine whether pro-active advisory support (e.g. inviting the client to special seminars; advising on transaction computerization) may be an appropriate action. Currently, the UK clearing banks appear to wait until the client's annual turnover is in excess of £100 000 before many of these additional facilities are made available. The reasoning is quite understandable – the business needs to be of this size before the bank can expect to receive an adequate immediate return on the provision of such services. However, as client satisfaction should be given priority over immediate gain, this cost/benefit philosophy is possibly inappropriate. Therefore, the bank should move earlier in the life of the small business to make available those support services that can enhance financial performance.

The likely source of 80 per cent of the bank's problems is the long-term liability customer. Under the terms of the Companies Act, a bank that actively promoted termination of trading by a customer business may run the risk of being held liable by disadvantaged creditors. However, from my experience, many small businesses can often benefit from quite simple advice (e.g. revised pricing policy, reduction in production range, more selective acceptance of new debtors) that makes life easier for the owner/manager, upgrades the balance sheet and regains the confidence of their creditors. For the bank to become more actively engaged in this type of role will mean that they first have to gain the trust of the client. This will improve the perceptions that customers hold about the bank, thereby providing the foundations upon which to build an effective working relationship with the less successful businesses within their SME client loan fortfolio.

Enhancing future service provision

Once the marketer has developed an understanding of how to satisfy customers at all stages in the client/provider relationship, new quality of service strategies can be planned which further widen the superiority gap over competition. To commence this process, first it is necessary to accept that few organizations will ever have the internal capability to respond effectively to the highly heterogeneous nature of market need present in most service industries. Furthermore, even in those circumstances where the marketer believes it possible to satisfy all market segments, the question needs to be asked whether scarce internal resources expended on customers who will rarely ever be satisfied might not be better utilized in sectors where quality of service is really appreciated.

One approach to determining future service strategies by market sector is to create a *provision decision portfolio* (or PDP) by analysing the interactions between the two parameters of opportunity to deliver perceived superior service and capability to meet customer expectations. The degree to which perceived superior service can be delivered will be influenced by such factors as number of customers, per capita expenditure, sector growth rate, service requirements, ability of customers to differentiate between suppliers on the basis of service quality, capability of competitors and intensity of competition. Actual performance for each factor is allocated an arbitrary score relative to what would be seen as an optimum condition. The summated factor score will then permit a sector to be rated as a poor, average or high opportunity to deliver perceived service superiority.

The degree to which an organization has the capability to deliver service expectation will be influenced by such factors as physical appearance of tangible facilities, interpersonal skills of interface personnel, capability to undertake the service provision process, process capacity relative to demand, skills to exploit new technologies having potential to enhance provision productivity, financial resources to invest in service upgrade and/or development of new services to sustain service portfolio expansion. Performance for each factor can be scored on an arbitrary scale against the perfect situation. The cumulated factor score can then be used to classify a market sector in relation to the organization's low, average or high capability to fulfil customer expectations. The scores for both opportunity and capability of a market sector can be entered into a PDP matrix of the type illustrated in Figure 11.4. The position of a market sector in the matrix will determine the most appropriate future strategy for the organization as a service provider.

The implications of the nine alternative service strategies described in the PDP matrix in Figure 11.4 are as follows:

Cell 1 represents a situation of low opportunity and low capability.

		OPPORTUNITY TO DELIVER PERCEIVED SUPERIORITY OF SERVICE		
		Low	**Average**	**High**
C A P A B I L I T Y T O M E E T (EXPECTATIONS)	**Low**	1 Immediate termination of provision	2 Phased withdrawal from service provision	3 Last attempt at provision upgrade
	Average	4 Phased withdrawal from service provision	5 Sustain current customer satisfaction	6 Invest in service provision upgrade
	High	7 Reduction in scale of satisfaction provision	8 Invest in customer/ product service provision diversification	9 Invest in retaining service leadership

Figure 11.4 The provision decision portfolio matrix

The organization can never win and hence should immediately terminate activities in this sector. In order not to create adverse reaction among existing customers, the organization should actively assist in the identification of an alternative provider.

Cell 2, although offering average opportunity, is an area where, although the organization can obtain a reasonable revenue, capability to fulfil expectations is low. Over time, therefore, the company should plan to withdraw from this sector through (a) terminating all activities to attract new business and (b) gradually reducing the existing client base by directing them to alternative providers.

Cell 3 is a high-opportunity situation but an area of poor capability. Before finally leaving the sector the organization should be prepared to make one last attempt to invest in a capability upgrade. Should this attempt fail, however, then sector departure must occur immediately because continued failure to fulfil customer expectations will create an adverse image that can detract from the organization's overall service quality reputation.

Cell 4 is a sector where organizational ability is average but opportunity is poor. Over time, similar to the Cell 2 situation, the organization should plan to withdraw from service provision to this client group.

Cell 5 is an area of average opportunity and average capability. Sufficient resources should be allocated to sustain the satisfaction rating among existing customers but no attempt should be made to attract new customers.

Cell 6 is a high-opportunity situation where the organization has yet to acquire adequate capability. Hence the strategy should be investment in a rapid upgrading of factors critical to fulfilling customer expectations.

Cell 7 is a poor-opportunity situation where the capabilities of the organization are probably not appreciated by the customer. Resources can therefore be redirected elsewhere in the organization without damaging customer perceptions over service quality in this sector.

Cell 8 is an area of average opportunity where the organization has recognized superiority to meet customer expectations. Investment should be made to locate new customer segments and/or new service products which provide additional opportunities to exploit the organization's proven areas of expertise.

Cell 9 is the optimal situation where the sector offers high opportunity for superior service and the organization has the capability to fulfil market expectations. Having reached this position, the organization must invest to sustain service quality leadership over competition.

CASE STUDY   Application of the PDP matrix

During research on the provision of accounting services, Plymouth Business School encountered the opportunity to apply the PDP matrix to help a south-west regional practice examine how to plan their future service strategy. Prior to the study the view of the practice was that, although they recognized that variance existed between client groups, they did not feel there was any practical way to use this knowledge to plan future service provision. Hence their marketing philosophy was to treat all clients equally. Their hope was that the overall effect would be to create a positive reputation in the marketplace for delivering satisfactory service.

Using the PDP technique, clients from different market sectors were classified and entered into a matrix of the type illustrated in Figure 11.5. The outcome by cell can be examined commencing with the business start-up client group. Owner/managers from this sector typically seek only year-end

OPPORTUNITY TO DELIVER PERCEIVED SUPERIORITY OF SERVICE

		Low	Average	High
	Low	Start-up businesses	Small farms	Multinational satellite plants
Average		Small retail shops	Medium-sized independent businesses	Receiverships
High		Small guest houses	SMEs seeking to enter export markets	SMEs seeking venture capital and/or a USM listing

(Left axis: CAPABILITY TO MEET EXPECTATIONS)

Figure 11.5 Application of the PDP to a regional accountancy practice

accounts and management of their tax affairs. Relative to the fee which can be charged, the practice rarely receives an adequate return on the resources allocated. Furthermore, many of these clients resent having to use an accountant and hence achieving client satisfaction is very difficult. In fact, in most cases the client would be better off with a smaller practice. Farming, on the other hand, requires specialist accounting knowledge but the long-term prospects for agriculture in the south-west in the face of changes in the EC Common Agricultural Policy (CAP) are not good. Hence the practice should gradually withdraw from this sector. The head office of multinationals will always require the audit/financial consolidation activities to be undertaken by a large international accounting firm. The branch plants, however, often have autonomous authority for projects such as improving the financial management and productivity of the manufacturing operation. Before the practice can be successful in this sector, however, there is a need to upgrade significantly its skills in the selection and installation of computer-based financial control software packages.

Small independent retailers face a bleak future and tend to require only minimal services such as bookkeeping, resolving VAT problems and preparing year-end accounts. Clients typically object to the cost of these services and are difficult to please. Hence the practice should withdraw from this sector over time. The main client base of the practice comprises the medium-size, independently owned businesses that value the services of the accountant. The owners are rarely interested in further growth and the practice, while ensuring that the existing client base remains satisfied, should not be seeking more 'zero expansion' oriented clients. Receiverships are an extremely rewarding source of revenue. However, before any serious attempt is made to persuade the UK clearing banks that they should consider the practice as a major provider of such services, there is a need to appoint more senior staff with the specialist knowledge required to meet customer expectations totally.

The small guesthouse sector provides a steady source of revenue because it involves both accounting services and management of acquisition/ disposition activities. The practice is, however, over-resourcing this area of practice activity and, by delegating some tasks to accounting technicians, senior staff could be released to work with more important clients. In recent years the practice has been successful in assisting a number of regional food processors to enter overseas markets. There are opportunities to exploit this capability further by seeking new non-food SME clients interested in expanding their export activities. Finally, the sector where the practice has already established an outstanding reputation is assisting SME companies expand through the injection of private venture capital or by issuing shares in the Unlisted Securities Market (USM). To sustain this leadership position, the practice needs to continue to invest in further enhancing internal capabilities, to enable them even more effectively to assist SME clients who have plans for aggressive growth requiring the injection of external capital.

12

Public sector services – focus on internal customer satisfaction

The origins of Western-world public sector organizations are rooted in the urbanization which accompanied the industrial revolution. As population density increased in the towns that sprang up around the new factories, the resultant insanitary conditions soon led to major public health problems. As few industrialists felt they had any responsibility for the living conditions of their workers, governments and municipalities were forced to work together in the provision of infrastructures such as roads, clean water, sewage treatment and hospitals.

The evolving dilemma of public sector provision

Nevertheless, it was not until after the Second World War that the majority of the electorate were willing to accept large-scale taxation to support the ideological concept that all the population had the right to equality of treatment in such areas as housing, education and medicine. These rights were encapsulated in the creation of the welfare state and led to a huge expansion of public sector bodies providing socially necessary services. This situation also offered the added Keynesian benefit of creating new jobs through government expenditure and thereby greatly reducing the level of unemployment.

By the early 1970s, this utopian dream had begun to develop into a political nightmare. The post-war expansion of public services was made affordable by a period of unprecedented economic growth. As Western economies downturned during the OPEC oil crisis and inflation rates rose, governments found that the cost of public sector services was greater than their ability to fund these operations through taxation. Furthermore, the strength of the unions in the public sector resulted in confrontations with the workforce as politicians attempted to bring the situation back under control (e.g. the air traffic controllers' strike in America which briefly shut down the airline industry; the hospital porters' industrial action in the UK which reduced the National Health Service merely to a provider of emergency medical services).

Combating inflation through constraining the growth of the public sector became the priority issue on the political agenda of many Western governments in the eighties. A currently popular concept is that industry can provide effective models through which to improve the management of public sector organizations. In the UK, the government placed its faith in the philosophy of 'market forces', which was based on the view that value for money could be achieved by opening up the public sector to competition. Examples of this process included legislation on the provision of cleaning services in hospitals on the basis of competitive tendering and forcing local authorities to place their operatives into Direct Service Organizations, which then had to compete against commercial firms for contracts such as street cleaning or garbage collection.

Despite all these initiatives, over the last decade the gap between demand for public services and the level of services that can actually be provided from the public purse has continued to widen. There is a multitude of interacting variables that have led to this situation (e.g. the rising technological costs of new medical treatments; the continuing slowdown in economic growth reducing the absolute level of tax inflows to central governments; the general demographic trend of an increasing proportion of old people in the population). These variables, when linked with the usual inertia associated with attempts to persuade any large organization to alter dramatically its method of operation, mean that many Western governments have enjoyed only limited success in radically changing the behaviour of the public sector in their respective countries.

Unfortunately, when politicians are frustrated in their endeavours, they have a tendency to search for a new, and preferably simplistic, Holy Grail. In both America and Britain the current fashion is to preach the need for public sector employees to adopt the private sector philosophy of 'putting the customer first'. The case studies presented in the next section illustrate how the UK Government has attempted to utilize this view to enhance quality of provision in local authorities and the National Health Service (NHS).

Being seen to care

EXAMPLE 1　In recognition of National Audit Office recommendations on the need to be more customer-oriented, the chief executive of a local authority hired a national consulting company to advise on how this objective might be met. The consultants' report focused on the need to improve the interface between the council and the general public. They recommended that all staff receive training in Customer Care and that a Customer Enquiry Centre be established in the Civic Centre to direct people to the correct department within the building. Six months later, a survey of people using the Civic Centre indicated no improvement in the council's image (in fact, there were indications from the data of a possible image decline). Furthermore, a survey of employees also revealed that they were not convinced that their more caring attitude was appreciated by the general public.

EXAMPLE 2　In the same geographic area as the council case, the District Health Authority decided there was a need to prove to the local population that the Health Service was genuinely committed to caring for the patients. One of their first projects was to upgrade the way patients were treated upon arriving at the local hospital. The reception area was refurbished, new uniforms issued and staff were put through a Customer Care training programme. Some months later the authority was rather surprised to find little improvement in local attitudes about perceived quality of service when going to the hospital for treatment.

What do the general public want?

It is undoubtedly very discouraging for public sector employees, enthused after participating in a Customer Care exercise, to see little reward for their actions in terms of receiving a positive response from the general public. What in fact has happened in many of these schemes is that they have broken the basic rule of service management: namely, the objective of matching expectations against perceptions. In the past, the general public had developed an expectation that public sector service response would be slow and in many cases they would be told they did not qualify for assistance. Imagine, therefore, what happens when people are suddenly greeted by a smiling, smartly dressed employee who directs them to the relevant department at the offices of their local authority. Service expectations have been raised and they feel more confident that their needs will be met. Once they arrive at the relevant department, however, the same forms need to be filled in, the same wait endured and probably the same answer, 'I'm sorry, but you do not qualify', will eventually be given. Because the initial contact is more welcoming, the gap between expectations and perceptions has been dramatically widened. Consequently, when service delivery shows no sign of improvement, the level of dissatisfaction is greatly magnified.

In fact, it has recently been reported in the UK media that the Civil Service is considering scrapping Customer Care training because there is now research evidence to suggest that the general public is much happier when their case is handled by a miserable, unsmiling public servant!

One of the major obstacles in the public sector is the fact that the system does not take kindly to employees who openly disagree with accepted policies. This is especially true in those situations when such policies are based on the political manifesto of whichever party is currently in power, because open criticism can be rewarded by a budget cut and/or monies being transferred to others who are willing to give enthusiastic support to the views expressed by their political masters. Hence, it is usually only behind closed doors that the competent public sector employee is willing to express doubts about the ability of 'customer first' schemes to achieve anything except increased disenchantment among both the general public and the employees working in the public sector. It must, therefore, be recognized that an alternative marketing philosophy is needed which, by more closely matching expectation to perception, offers the dual benefits of public sector employees (a) re-establishing pride in the fulfilment of their service role and (b) being regarded by the general public with the respect which they enjoyed in the fifties and sixties.

An alternative public sector strategy

Formulating any marketing strategy for the public sector must involve recognition of the fact that there will always be a gap between potential total demand for a service and the actual level of provision which can be afforded. Concepts based on a strategy of 'putting the customer first' are extremely difficult to implement, because in many cases the public sector provider is placed in the unenviable situation of having to say 'No' or 'I'm sorry, you will have to wait'. For example, in the UK, if hip replacement surgery was a private sector product and all patients could afford to pay, there would be an immediate expansion in provision of this treatment and the current two-year waiting list would disappear. For the NHS to achieve the same effect, however, funds would have to be found from within the existing Health Service total budget, with a consequent reduction in the resources available to support other forms of medical treatment.

Public sector organizations will be forced to operate as resource-constrained entities for the foreseeable future. Hence, a marketing strategy which has the outcome that the general public perceive that available resources are being used to maximize service provision productivity would seem to be the only viable long-term solution. Consequently, it is suggested that customer-first concepts be replaced with the generic marketing strategy of 'seeking to optimize utilization of constrained resources by maximizing the added value content of all activities associated with the service provision process'.

Implementation of this alternative strategy can be achieved by public sector employees evaluating their role in service provision and executing only those tasks that add value to the service. For example, the 1988 Educational Reform Act charges local education authorities (LEAs) with the task of enhancing learning quality and public accountability. The traditional response to such legislation is reflected in the views of Ransom and Thomas, two British academics (Clarke and Stewart 1990). They suggest that the role of the LEA should be:

disseminating good practice in curriculum and teaching methods; encouraging clear and consistent thinking throughout the service about educational values and purpose; making staff development suit the needs of institutions ... establishing strategic planning teams to develop shared values, agree programmes and targets, as well as methods for evaluating performance.

Acting on their suggestions could possibly mean an expansion of the number of educational advisers at County Hall running around the area, inundating teachers with requests for data and review papers and requiring attendance at numerous 'coordinating seminars'. Whereas the alternative strategy, which focuses on maximizing added value of any action, would hopefully cause the LEA to decide that (a) most of the new legislation should be autonomously managed by headmasters and (b) the only responsibility of any central planning group is to act as a data coordination unit to assess whether school budgets are being optimally utilized to sustain a specified minimum standard of education across the entire county.

Processes for strategy implementation

A marketing strategy is merely a statement of intent designed to provide management with a yardstick against which to evaluate actual performance. It therefore must be accompanied by appropriate processes to ensure that implementation is a feasible proposition. In the case of the public sector, it is suggested that three major areas will need to be addressed in the implementation process: managerial attitudes, individual staff competences, and overall organizational competences.

Public sector services are typically organized along functional lines and staffed by 'professionals'. The term 'professionals' is ambiguous but in the main refers to individuals such as doctors, lawyers, accountants, engineers and scientists, who are members of a professional body which sets minimum educational standards to be achieved by an individual in order to qualify for membership. The professional tends to exhibit the following characteristics:

1 They participate in protracted specialized training to acquire and prove their expertise.

2 Their membership of a professional body confers a right to decide on the means and ends in their work to a degree which even an employer would have difficulty in challenging (e.g. the rights of senior consultants in the NHS to ignore demands for the government to alter their work practices).

3 They are devoted to the technical aspects of their work to the point of placing this ahead of any organizational objective such as revising work practices to increase productivity.

4 They identify with other members of their profession ahead of any loyalty to their work colleagues or employer.

5 Challenges to their conduct can often only be made indirectly through a formal complaints procedure involving their professional body.

6 Work standards and further knowledge acquisition activities are considered the responsibility of their professional body.

The resultant attitude of many professionals is an unwillingness to place the performance objectives of either superiors who are not of the same profession, or of their employer organization, before the standards and task roles defined by their own professional body. Under these circumstances, it is very understandable why attempts to introduce a more integrated, cross-functional, participative, market-oriented approach to service provision in the public sector are often frustrated. This situation has been dramatically demonstrated in recent years by British doctors who have fiercely resisted changes (e.g. reducing the length of stay in hospital for certain types of surgery) that could improve resource utilization in the NHS. The grounds for their resistance is that only they and/or a professional body such as the British Medical Association have the skills to decide what is clinically appropriate in determining the nature of patient care.

Overcoming attitude barriers between professionals and non-professionals must be the first step in implementing a strategy based on maximizing value added processes within the organization. It is unlikely that the current fashion of bringing in new senior managers from the commercial sector, who attempt to mandate revised working practices, will prove successful in every situation. Instead it may be necessary to instigate internal marketing programmes which promote a change process based upon employees gaining a deeper understanding of each other's needs, perceptions and opinions in relation to their task role of supporting the service provision process. This type of interchange can hopefully provide a solid foundation upon which to begin to identify a set of shared values that will be reflected in a new culture of intra-organizational cooperation.

Accompanying this change, it is also necessary to examine the accepted style of management within the organization. There is a tendency for professionals to consider that authority and decision making should be the preserve of only very senior staff (e.g. the senior consultant in the NHS; the director of finance in a local authority). This somewhat authoritarian approach may have been appropriate in the fifties and sixties. The rapidly changing, uncertain and turbulent environment now facing public sector organizations, however, demands a more flexible and innovative operating philosophy if effective solutions are to be found to the problem of sustaining service delivery in a period of declining resources. Hence the organization should develop internal marketing campaigns which can lead to a change in management style – a style that permits junior staff being granted greater self-decision powers and the discretion to allocate resources without first seeking the approval of a superior.

Staff competence

The insistence of professionals that only they have the necessary skills to make all but the most trivial of decisions means that staff costs in organizations dominated by such individuals can be extremely high. One way of reducing costs, and thereby enhancing value added service provision processes, is to delegate service provision tasks and decisions to individuals who, because they are not members of the appropriate professional body, can be paid a lower salary (e.g. architectural technicians preparing building plans; accounting technicians undertaking audits; nurses prescribing drug treatments). Another, and at the moment apparently more palatable approach, is to broaden the managerial responsibilities of the senior professional (e.g. granting autonomy of financial managerial control to a chartered surveyor who is the director of Property Services; authorizing a headmaster to be responsible for hiring staff and procurement of supplies).

Either approach is doomed to failure unless the individual to whom the new responsibilities are allocated has the necessary technical and interpersonal competences to undertake the expanded task role effectively. Hence, prior to implementation of any employment role-broadening scheme, it is first necessary to put into place a continuing personal development programme which equips nominated individuals with the required skills to perform effectively. This programme will need to contain an appropriate performance appraisal mechanism, career-planning scheme and access to a structured skills and knowledge development system.

Organizational competence

Service provision management

The process of enhancing value added processes in the private sector is greatly assisted by the fact that organizations usually have accounting systems which provide data on the various input costs associated with the production of goods or services. This information can be used to prioritize which activities offer significant opportunities for cost reduction. Unfortunately, the traditional accounting philosophy within the public sector has been an orientation towards determining that total expenditure is within budget and employees are not misappropriating funds. Hence, as Western governments have attempted to introduce the concept of 'value for money', they are finding that very few public sector bodies are able to identify the costs attributable to specific activities (e.g. cost of a medical treatment or per capita expenditure/subject/student in a school). At the moment the universal cry of public sector managers seems to be 'We must have more information before we can begin to control costs'. Having gained the government's agreement on this issue, managers then embark on a massive data-collection exercise using specially developed complex computer systems. Even assuming that these systems can be made to operate effectively, interpretation of the results is usually then delayed while

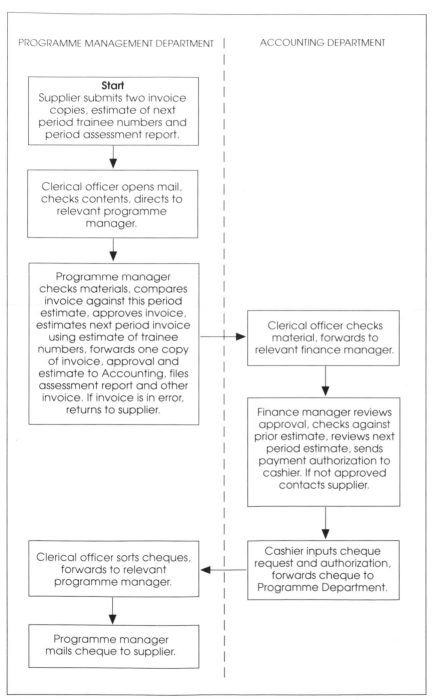

Figure 12.1 Flow chart of the current claim management process

debate rages on which would be the most appropriate performance indicators to be applied in analysing the data. In the meantime, costs are still rising and the gap between service demand and capability to provide continues to widen – an outcome hardly likely to endear the provider to the increasingly frustrated seekers of service from among the general public.

Assuming that the organization genuinely wishes to enhance the productivity of service provision, one alternative to demanding more information before any decisions are taken is to introduce employees to a pre-computer age technique known as *process mapping*. This concept could not be simpler, merely requiring the accumulated experience of the employees and a large sheet of paper. The start point is to develop a chart describing how a process is currently undertaken in terms of the role of people in the organization and the flow of materials and/or information between them. The flow chart then provides a visual description which can be used by the analyst to determine the purpose, location, sequence, people and methods by which a process is carried out within the organization. This knowledge can be used to determine whether costs can be reduced by actions such as eliminating, combining, rearranging or simplifying any of the activities within the process.

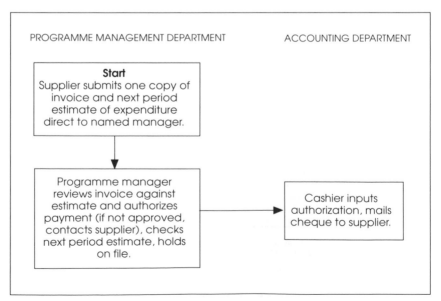

Figure 12.2 Revised claim process flow chart

CASE STUDY   Processing provider invoices

The benefits of flow charting can be demonstrated by examining a case example of the means by which a public sector body processes claims for payment to commercial providers who deliver government training schemes. As is apparent from Figure 12.1, the system is extremely involved and could probably benefit from being simplified.

First, only one invoice is needed from the supplier, who is also in a much better position to estimate the next period expenditure based on expected trainee numbers. The period assessment report is not usually read and hence the procedure can be abolished. Finally, by naming the programme manager on the materials submitted by the supplier, the claim can immediately be directed to the relevant manager without involvement of the clerical officer. Then, by permitting the programme manager complete authority over payment authorization and dispute resolution, the task of the Accounting Department can be radically simplified. A final refinement is to have the cashier mail cheques directly to the supplier. The impact of these changes is summarized in the revised flow chart shown in Figure 12.2.

Reducing errors

In recent years there has been growing recognition of the fact that one of the most expensive activities within most organizations is rectifying mistakes. Phillip Crosby, as Director of Quality for ITT, popularized the idea of replacing the conventional quality control approach of inspection, checking and testing with the philosophy of persuading people to 'get things right the first time'. By setting the ultimate objective of zero errors, he confidently predicts that any organization can rapidly reduce operating costs by at least 20 per cent.

Without waiting for a detailed computer-based costing system, once a public sector organization has developed an understanding of process flows it is then in a position to reduce costs further by immediately launching an internal marketing campaign to promote the benefits of zero defects. Again it is possible to apply techniques that were around long before the arrival of the computer. The approach is collectively known as *statistical process control* (SPC) and, despite its frighteningly complex name, is actually a set of simple techniques designed to measure and quantify the nature of errors occurring within the organization.

CASE STUDY   Expense claim processing errors

Following complaints about the time taken by the Finance Office to reimburse employee expense claims in a local authority, a clerical officer was allocated the task of identifying the cause of the problem. The individual took a batch of claims, identified those where further information was required prior to completing the payment process and then analysed the nature of the information errors. The percentage breakdown on the types of information error was as follows:

	% of total expense claims
Numerical addition error	4.3
Incorrect expense rate used	3.7
Error on prior approval form	2.4
Incorrect payroll number on claim	1.8
Claimant not signed claim	1.2
No departmental approval signature	0.8
Prior approval claim not provided	0.6

Although the percentage occurrence for each error is quite small, when combined they represent a total error level of 14.8 per cent of cases where the Finance Department will have to return the form either to the claimant or the department head in order to rectify the problem. As an isolated issue, the cost of these errors is negligible. Imagine, however, if every process activity within the entire local authority is running at an average error level of 15 per cent. Should this be the case, the cost implications of this type of inefficiency are mind-boggling, as are the resources which would be released following a successful campaign to persuade employees to move towards fulfilling the objective of zero errors. Furthermore, because no doubt many of these errors have a direct impact on service provision, imagine the image benefits associated with customers no longer being on the receiving end of frequent intra-organizational decision errors.

Information system competence

Despite the above criticism of managers' demand for better information systems before they can act to add value through cost-reduction initiatives, ultimately no public sector organization can be expected to optimize service provision processes without access to timely and accurate information. The power of the modern computer to store and process data causes this technology to appear extremely attractive as the most effective way to create decision support sytems. A frequently articulated complaint of managers in the public sector is that their data-processing staff lack the abilities to provide these systems. Although this criticism may be valid in some situations, the more usual cause of the problem is that information users lack even a basic understanding of information technology and are therefore unable to describe their real needs adequately to the systems designer. This problem is not unique to the public sector – the same weakness is to be found in many commercial organizations. Consequently, if public sector organizations wish to upgrade the power of their information systems, in many cases the most appropriate initial action is to implement training programmes to enhance the computer literacy skills of their line managers.

Structure competence

In situations where the organizations can control events through creation of a monopoly, external conditions are stable, resources are unconstrained and the nature of product demand remains unchanged over the years, then despite the bad connotations associated with the term, Max Weber's recommended structure of a bureaucracy still remains a most effective way to manage. In a bureaucratic structure, processes are effectively discharged through the mechanisms of a clear specification of tasks, formalized procedures, hierarchies that carefully define the degree of decision-making authority at each level, and career progress based on formal qualifications linked to specified years of service.

Unfortunately, if the organization is suddenly required to be more responsive, to cope with resource availability problems and rapidly changing market conditions, then the bureaucracy will probably fail to fulfil its responsibilities to act as an effective provider of services. This, of course, is the situation facing most public sector bodies and, as the most obvious characteristic of these organizations, it is usually assigned a high priority in projects to improve the productivity of public sector employees.

Although it is easy to criticize the rigidity of the hierarchical systems that are still so very prevalent in the public sector, coming up with proven formulae to restructure these organizations is possibly one of the most difficult tasks facing senior management or their external advisers. Examination of the various attempts that have been made over the years by both academics and management consultants to find the perfect organizational structure can only lead one to conclude there is 'no such animal'. At best all one can suggest is that management should seek to develop the most appropriate structure through which to fulfil the assigned service provision responsibilities. In adopting this approach there is, however, adequate evidence to suggest that fulfilling certain objectives will prove beneficial. These include:

● Creating flatter organizations by seeking to reduce the number of levels within the structure.

● Delegating decision making as far down the organization as possible and concurrently permitting the most junior of staff the opportunity to gain a high degree of personal control over their assigned work tasks.

● Ensuring there are effective communication channels to permit the rapid, accurate flow of information down, up and across the organization.

● Where solutions require inter-departmental inputs, moving from a rigid functional system to one based upon multi-disciplinary teams of either a temporary or permanent nature, depending on the nature of the task being undertaken.

In defence of heresy

No doubt there will be some readers who are deeply convinced of the merits of public sector organizational strategies based on the philosophy of putting the external customer first. They will therefore feel obliged to reject the proposed alternative of giving priority to improving internal productivity. Certainly, one must expect vocal non-acceptance by politicians, consulting firms specializing in customer care and senior managers recently hired to implement customer-first initiatives. I would ask all these people, however, to consider the declining employee morale in the public sector, to examine the statistics for stress-related illness or attend a customer care training session and observe the body language of the participants. Perhaps this may persuade them to reassess the validity of their current views on this issue.

On more than one occasion my views have been met with the response that Japanese firms such as Toyota and Honda have convincingly demonstrated that the customer first/emphasis on quality of service approach is a certain path to success. I would be the first to agree with such an opinion. However, it is imperative to comprehend that the Japanese were only able to implement such strategic concepts subsequent to the creation of a highly motivated and committed workforce. Hence, all I am suggesting is that what should be put first is not the external customer but, instead, internal marketing programmes designed to improve internal organizational attitudes and competences.

The next agenda item – the customer

It is mandatory that management of change programmes should be accompanied by regular surveys of employee attitudes and opinions. Hopefully, the results of such tracking studies will begin to indicate that (a) employees are regaining a sense of personal satisfaction about their contributions to value added processes and (b) the organizational culture is moving from confrontation towards inter-departmental cooperation. It is only at this point that public sector marketers should start to emphasize the importance of establishing mechanisms to enhance customer perceptions over the quality of service provision.

Compared to a commercial firm, a public sector organization faces a number of unique operational characteristics which can greatly complicate the management of service quality. These include:

● Huge variation in the expectations and needs of external customer groups. Take, for example, a local authority department responsible for rehousing homeless families. The families are seeking help, the electorate may require that limited assistance is rendered in order to avoid paying more local taxes, counsellors may support or oppose increased taxes depending on their political persuasion, and government departments may be seeking to curb total public expenditure as a mechanism to defeat inflation.

● The provider has only minimal control over the demand for services because these are influenced by external variables such as economic conditions, government legislation, local or national pressure groups, population shifts and changes in the socio-demographic structure of the population.

● Minimal authority to implement actions which can move the organization nearer to the point of supply and demand equilibrium. In the private sector, a firm can respond to supply/demand imbalances by steps such as altering price, redesigning product performance characteristics, modifying the product portfolio, closing obsolete facilities and, through access to external funds, undertaking investment in capacity expansion. If such steps prove ineffective it can also apply the ultimate sanction: complete withdrawal from the market. Such freedoms are unavailable to the public sector because there is rarely sufficient consensus among the general public to grant their elected representatives a mandate to carry out significant restructuring of the service provision processes or structures. As demonstrated by the Conservative Government's attempts to overhaul the UK Health Service, the speed with which even the most well-meaning initiative can be implemented will greatly depend upon whether opponents decide to create obstacles by invoking the cry that service availability will be curtailed.

Given these characteristics and assuming that politicians, members of watch-dog committees and senior management are genuinely committed to enhanced service provision in the public sector, then all these interested parties need to reconsider their approach to the issue of managing quality. The current view on this issue appears to be that quality is a matter of requiring public sector bodies to meet nationally specified standards (e.g. maximum waiting times for medical treatment; responding to a planning application within six weeks; rigid timetables under an Environmental Protection Act concerning the frequency of site visits to catering establishments).

The unfailing popularity of holding up commercial firms as examples of excellence over the management of quality makes it worth examining them to find whether they still use the concept of rigid standards, inspection and control. The answer of course is that they do not. The secret to the much publicized success of the Nordstroms, Millikens and 3Ms of this world is that they have empowered their workforce to manage quality. The role of senior management is not to lay down rigid guidelines, but instead to nurture an internal environment that can sustain the vision of effectively delivering customer satisfaction.

These observations of good practice must surely lead to the conclusion that the way forward in the public sector is to abolish rigid, mandated guidelines and empower the workforce to become the real owners of the service provision process. To achieve this goal, however, senior management must create systems and policies that enable the newly empowered employees to discharge their responsibilities effectively.

As firms such as the bank First Boston of America have found, it is impossible always to provide instant positive service to every customer. Often they will have to wait and sometimes it is necessary to refuse a request. Under these circumstances, however, it is amazing how dissatisfaction can be reduced by keeping the customer informed. This can be achieved, for example, by actions such as a visual display screen in the bank foyer informing customers of current wait times for teller service, or by providing a detailed and honest explanation of why a loan request has been refused.

At the moment most public sector marketers could not adopt this approach because senior management has yet to provide the information systems which permit employees (a) to know the actual resources available for specific services and (b) to forecast possible future changes in the magnitude of service demand and in the scale of the provision gap created because of internal resource constraints.

Unfortunately, for this objective to be met, most senior managers still need to understand that the real purpose of collecting information is not to improve their control over employee performance, but to provide a support system to enhance the capabilities of the employees to make better decisions and to provide the customer with an accurate statement of the status of their request for service.

Accompanying this improved access to information, employees (having agreed to the feasibility of fulfilling an assigned responsibility) must be granted the authority and trust to make autonomous decisions about the best use of available resources. In theory this move is already occurring in some areas of the public sector. For example, under the UK Government's LMS programme, headmasters are granted control over their school budget. In reality, however, the control previously executed by the Local Education Committee is now replaced by the appointment of a Board of Governors with executive authority to over-rule decisions and a national audit control system that will curtail most attempts by teachers to try innovative, flexible, new approaches to education. The reason for the apparent unwillingness of senior public sector management to release their control over resources and major decision making is difficult to understand. Possibly they perceive this scenario as having implications for the future security of their own jobs, or feel that it represents an erosion of their powers to influence events within the organization. If these explanations are correct, then it reflects a lack of understanding among senior managers of the true nature of their executive role.

The effectiveness of any public sector organization depends on its ability to gain the support and cooperation of the various committees and monitoring bodies responsible for overseeing that the organization is operating within the various statutory guidelines that govern its existence. By delegating more activities to lower-level staff, senior managers will then be able to give more attention to working with these external influencers, gaining their understanding of the dilemmas created by resource constraints, seeking guidance on appropriate future policies, reviewing the benefits of revising structures, systems or procedures and developing valid arguments for approaching central government with proposals for incremental funding to overcome critical imbalances in service provision.

None of the above proposals will ever be able to overcome the insurmountable obstacle that the capacity of a society to support the provision of public services is defined by the size of the nation's

Gross National Product. Nevertheless, executing internal marketing strategies to enhance the value added component of internal processes through improved employee attitudes linked to further development of appropriate individual and organizational competences can significantly enhance service provision productivity. This outcome will create a much greater level of customer satisfaction than can ever be expected from expenditure on schemes where the apparent primary objective is for the general public to be regularly instructed to 'Have a nice day'.

13

Satisfaction on an international scale

Since the early mists of time, when people first recognized that not all their needs could be met from the area immediately surrounding their cave, there has been trade between the nations of the world. Regretfully, the activity has frequently been accompanied by war and the oppression of entire civilizations as governments have striven to gain control of markets or scarce resources (e.g. the Spanish invasion of South America to acquire gold and silver; the creation of the British Empire).

Moving beyond domestic boundaries

In the present day, the exploitation of overseas markets has increasingly become a priority issue within even the smallest of companies. At a national level, governments seek to stimulate greater exports because, as graphically illustrated by the Japanese, this can enhance the total wealth of the nation, stabilize the currency and contribute to lowering the rate of domestic inflation. The individual firm usually has much less grandiose reasons for seeking international sales and commonly encountered justifications include:

● Breathing new life into a product which, in the domestic market, has already moved into the decline phase of the PLC (e.g. the much criticized endeavours of certain Western nation food producers in aggressively marketing powdered milk as a baby food in the less developed countries of the world).

● An inability to be highly profitable at home in the face of intense competition from other domestic producers (e.g. the reason given to me by another Japanese company about their perspective on Sony Corporation's initial entry into the US television set market).

● A desire to develop a sales base in an overseas market ahead of other competitors (e.g. the post-war battles between Pepsi and

Coca Cola to be first in gaining sole bottling rights in various communist countries around the world).

● Overseas markets are larger and hence offer greater revenue opportunities than the domestic market (e.g. the Danish manufacturers of food-processing equipment).

● The total revenue required to recover the product development investment cannot be obtained from domestic sales (e.g. British Aerospace's executive passenger jet, which has now also been successfully marketed to the Japanese as a search and rescue aircraft).

● Access to new opportunities following the removal of trade barriers (e.g. the post-1992 Single Market) or politically motivated constraints to the free flow of goods (e.g. the post-communist free market environment now evolving in the European Eastern Bloc countries).

All these reasons are extremely logical and no doubt seem very laudable to both the employees and shareholders who benefit from the incremental profits generated from overseas sales. On the other hand, when seeing such reasons in management texts or hearing them expressed in meetings with companies, it is surprising how rarely there is ever mention of perceived opportunities to deliver satisfaction to the customer in the overseas market. Many companies would argue that this issue is implicitly enshrined in their mission and corporate strategy statements and therefore does not require repetition when defining goals for non-domestic activities. Perhaps this is the case. But on the other hand it is probably not unreasonable to suspect that, for many companies, the real explanation for this omission is they assume that what satisfies their home market will also be good enough for their international customers. Certainly, this is my experience of some US corporations who seem to believe the entire world is desperate to purchase their products as one way of gaining access to the 'American Dream'. Such attitudes, however, can be extremely dangerous because, as even the masters of marketing such as McDonalds and Procter & Gamble have discovered during their early attempts to enter Pacific Basin markets, what works in one country will not always immediately succeed in another.

Added obstacles to satisfaction

A popular perspective among some futurists is the imminent huge potential for the universal brand which will permit large conglomerates to dominate an industrial sector across world markets with a single, uniform product formulation. Finding examples of companies that have already achieved this goal as a means of justifying the validity of this perspective is, however, far from easy. For with the limited exception of certain consumer (e.g. soft drinks) and industrial categories (e.g. jet aircraft), the citizens of planet Earth have annoyingly exhibited huge variance in their opinion of what constitutes the optimal performance characteristics for their preferred choice of product.

Only a cursory examination of this situation will of course reveal that this variance of need is a reflection of the cultural differences that exist between countries around the world. Culture is an extremely complex idea which is far from easy to define. Within the context of business management, it is usually considered to comprise the seven elements of economic structure, language, education, aesthetics, religion, politics, and social values. All these variables can influence the nature of market demand. It is, therefore, worthwhile examining their potential to create obstacles to delivering customer satisfaction.

Over recent years television reports of drought and famine in Africa have graphically brought to our attention the very low standard of living that prevails in so many nations. In relation to much of the output of the industrialized nations, the low per capita income in these poorer countries severely limits opportunity for significant additional sales volume for such products. Furthermore, a low GNP will also typically result in a poorly developed economic infrastructure, which means that, even if people could afford the products, there are not the distribution and storage systems required to protect products adequately during their journey from producer to final user. The importance of infrastructure is evidenced in recent comments on the Russian economy by Western experts who have been quoted as believing that up to 80 per cent of agricultural output is irrevocably damaged before it reaches the shops due to the obsolete state of the country's transportation and freight-handling facilities.

Inextricably linked with the marketing process is the provision and comprehension of information. Language differences have provided a rich vein of anecdotes about how companies have failed to manage this variable and thereby lost sales in overseas markets (e.g. the General Motors Nova car which, when pronounced as two words, 'no va', in Central America, translated into 'not go'; a Parker Pen advertisement in Latin America which gave a false impression that the product helped prevent pregnancies; the Kentucky Fried Chicken claim of 'finger licking good' which, in Iran, came out as 'so good it will eat your fingers'). Language differences also extend into non-verbal areas which, although less likely to affect advertising claims, will require understanding by company representatives in their negotiations with both potential customers and intermediaries (e.g. the British habit of removing a jacket to indicate the start of serious discussion has completely the opposite meaning to German executives).

Many products, especially in the industrial goods sector, require advanced technical skills to understand both their operation and maintenance. Literacy levels will also affect whether product instructions can be understood. In those countries where only a small minority of the population enjoy the advantages of formal education, this will severely restrict sales opportunities for more than the simplest of products.

Aesthetics, those elements concerning colour, sound and form within each society can, similar to language, create barriers to effective communication (e.g. a brand of John Player cigarettes marketed in a black carton failed in Hong Kong because the colour is seen as conveying bad luck). This factor is especially important in relation to product design, and it is interesting to note that the early failure of Japanese cars to penetrate European markets has been attributed to their somewhat oriental appearance.

Religious values can have a dramatic effect on both the attitudes and buying behaviour within a country. Consumption patterns may be specified (e.g. the taboo against beef for Hindus, pork among Muslims and Jews) and very often the role of women as consumers or consumption influencers may be severely restricted. Unfortunately, religious divisions between countries (e.g. the Islamic Fundamentalists' views of America as the devil) and within countries (e.g. India) may also be reflected in an adverse reaction to products, depending on whether the supplier is prescribed as an acceptable source by the country's religious leaders. As with religion, in some countries strong political convictions can influence customer behaviour. Consequently, one will find that varying political ideologies can create almost insurmountable barriers to the creation of trading relationships (e.g. America's ongoing feud with Castro's Cuba; the unwillingness of the Chinese Communist Government to open their borders to many Western nation suppliers).

The anthropologist would probably argue that social values should not be separated from religious or political issues because in many cases personal behaviour in a society is formed by the effect these factors have on the attitudes of the individual. Nevertheless, the company seeking to determine opportunities in a new overseas market will need to acquire a detailed understanding of the social values of the individual because they can have an important impact on buyer behaviour (e.g. the importance of the family unit and the respect afforded to the family patriarch in certain societies could lead to an adverse reaction to the Western habit of directing advertising specifically at teenagers; the commercial suicide which would accompany a promotional campaign featuring the liberated, decision-influencing type of woman in many Middle Eastern countries).

An international success model

The classic economic theory of success in international markets is centred on the concept of comparative advantage (e.g. access to low-cost labour or plentiful raw materials to support a highly competitive price; a well educated workforce capable of developing and manufacturing products which are technically well in advance of competitors from elsewhere in the world). This concept can certainly be made to fit certain examples, but leaves many other situations completely unexplained. For example, given the climate, limited availability of land and high labour costs, how have the Dutch been so successful in the export of fresh cut flowers? Why has Sweden been able to dominate the world market for high voltage transmission equipment?

In an attempt to explain these numerous exceptions, during the late eighties Professor Michael Porter of Harvard embarked on a global research project with the objective of creating a more complete theory to describe the processes of effective international market management. By drawing upon the concepts contained in his latest book, *The Competitive Advantage of Nations*, it is possible to propose that in addition to comparative advantage there are three other key factors (Figure 13.1) that will significantly influence an organization's abilities to deliver customer satisfaction adequately in overseas markets.

These additional factors are the nature of domestic demand, the operating philosophies of the organization and the capabilities of key suppliers. After having examined the fuller discussion of these factors provided in the subsequent section of this chapter, I hope the reader will accept that there is an important unifying principle concerning the performance potential of international operations:

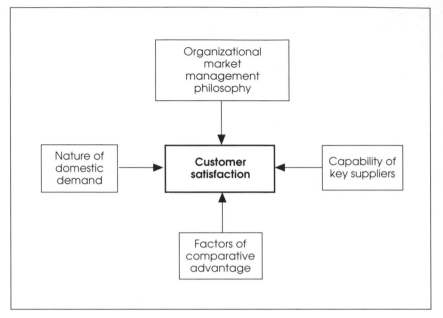

Figure 13.1 Variables influencing the delivery of international customer satisfaction

namely, that no company can expect to succeed overseas unless it has already achieved leadership in delivering customer satisfaction within its domestic market. Or to put it another way, 'Make sure you have made the grass as green as possible on your side of the hill before you start casting envious eyes over somebody else's pastures'.

Satisfaction success factors

On more than one occasion, most managers have mentally cursed the apparently impossible product performance or service requirements which customers can demand of the organization. It is important to realize, however, that a key outcome associated with attempts to respond to such pressures is often a much improved product. The relentless demand of the American citizen for a faster and more consistent response has led US corporations in sectors such as banking and fast foods to evolve standards of service provision which have subsequently served them well in world markets. Pressure for new features and further miniaturization from Japanese consumers means that survival for this country's manufacturers of electronic goods is critically dependent upon an ability to incorporate the latest technological advances into products more rapidly than competition. Sustaining performance in this environment means that, for the leading Japanese manufacturers, the conditions encountered in most overseas markets must come almost as a welcome relief after the intensity of competition they face at home.

Another example of a demanding domestic customer is provided by the Germans who have a reputation for being intensely interested in technical reliability: it is claimed they spend more time reading product usage instruction manuals than any other nation in the world. Under these circumstances, it is not surprising that German engineering firms such as Mercedes Benz and Siemens have few problems in fulfilling the needs of international customers for technically reliable products capable of meeting operating requirements, even in the face of difficult climatic conditions ranging from the equator to the arctic.

In an increasingly competitive world it is only the most myopic of organizations that do not accept the important contribution suppliers can make to achieving and then sustaining a leadership position. The support provided from this source, which initially served the organization so well in delivering satisfaction in domestic markets, is also a vital ingredient as moves are implemented to expand overseas. Some firms, in recognition of the importance of this factor, will actually seek to persuade their suppliers to accompany them into international markets by offering incentives such as guaranteed orders from the new assembly plants being opened in foreign locations and unrestricted access to draw upon the resources contained within the company's international marketing operation.

Examples of the vital support provided by a strong domestic supplier infrastructure include the software houses which have made significant contributions to the success of US computer giants such as IBM and Hewlett-Packard, the benefits to the Japanese machine tool industry of having access to world-class domestic suppliers of numerical control units, and the enhanced competitiveness given to the Swedish ball-bearing industry by their own steel industry's skills in producing the highest possible grades of specialist steels.

It is often only in hindsight that one can identify the unique characteristics of a company or an industrial sector that have led to attainment of a leadership position in their domestic market and then propelled them to success on an international scale. Nevertheless, there are many examples to demonstrate that a specific organizational philosophy has been a vital ingredient in meeting the objective of delivering satisfaction better than the competition. The Japanese attitude towards consensus management, and the important contribution that operatives can make to cost reduction and quality improvement have, for example, played a vital role at home and then abroad in their car industry. In many cases, a key stimulus to create an appropriate philosophy comes from the pressures associated with intense domestic competition between the leading national firms. This ongoing struggle, for example, between Digital Equipment, Data General, Hewlett-Packard and IBM has certainly placed added pressures on each company to outperform the others in the American market. Ultimately the nation benefits because survival of the fittest has effectively prepared these firms to go on to succeed against foreign competitors in other markets around the world.

Last but not least in the equation are those variables that lead to the creation of a comparative advantage, initially in the battle for domestic sales and subsequently in overseas markets. There is a multiplicity of variables which when combined in various ways can lead to organizations being endowed with advantage over competition from elsewhere in the world. Human resources, for example, whether these are reflected by access to low-cost labour or a pool of highly educated technical staff, can have a major influence on industrial productivity. There can also exist abundant physical resources which can act as a catalyst for the successful establishment of a new industry (e.g. the coal deposits of the Ruhr, which strongly influenced creation of the German chemical industry). Other contributors to factor advantage include the general knowledge content of the society (e.g. the 100 per cent literacy rate achieved in Korea), infrastructure to assist the flow of goods or information and access to capital resources to finance industrial development.

In determining potential access to a source of comparative advantage it should be recognized, however, that just because one exists which has the potential to enhance industrial performance, this does not guarantee that the nation concerned will always exploit the consequent opportunity. The British education system, for example, still produces a high knowledge content output, yet for social reasons some of the finest minds are attracted not into industry but instead favour careers in the upper echelons of the civil service. In America students who graduated with degrees in advanced technology in the eighties were frequently lured away from industry by the quick money to be made by applying their skills to playing junk bond monopoly on Wall Street or trading in the pit at the Chicago futures exchange.

In certain circumstances, comparative advantage can evolve out of a situation where initially the company is at a disadvantage versus competition. Italian steel producers, for example, in the face of high costs and no local materials, pioneered the development of high-productivity mini-mills that employ scrap metal as the feedstock. Initially producers for the Italian car industry, firms such as Danieli have subsequently become world leaders in the supply of the technology to other countries. This need to respond to cost pressures, which eventually enhances the capability of certain firms to deliver even greater customer satisfaction, is one that is frequently encountered in the economic history of nations. Other recent examples include the development of float glass technology by Pilkington, the Japanese car industry's move to robotic assembly systems and the switch to prefabricated homes in the Swedish construction industry.

Selecting overseas opportunities

Companies will offer a very diverse set of reasons for explaining how they embark on determining which countries should be targeted in a programme of international expansion. High on this list is market size (which is why some firms are currently trying to succeed in Japan); geographic proximity (a major reason for the strong presence of US corporations in Central and South America); absence of language barriers (the US thereby presenting a strong attraction to British companies); similar cultural values (a factor that appears to have influenced the new Australian entrepreneurs of the eighties to mount take-over bids in Britain); poorly developed capability of existing domestic firms (an opportunity that until recently has repeatedly assisted the global expansion of the US oil exploration industry); and the availability of public sector grants designed to stimulate inward investment (a major factor in the location decision of Pacific Basin countries when determining their entry strategy into Europe over recent years).

Similar to the responses discussed earlier over the issue of why go overseas, one rarely encounters a market selection strategy overtly based on opportunities to deliver a superior level of customer satisfaction. Again, some companies will respond that this factor is not mentioned because it is implicitly contained within the internal managerial processes of identifying any new opportunity at home or abroad. Furthermore, it is virtually impossible to dispute the validity of such statements because there are numerous variables that will ultimately determine the success or failure of a company's

international strategy. Nevertheless, it does not seem unreasonable
to suggest that some companies would have encountered fewer
problems during the initial phases of their launch into certain of
their overseas markets if closer attention had been paid to assessing
their capability to deliver a level of satisfaction higher than that
offered by well entrenched competitors (e.g. Marks & Spencer in
Canada; the UK software company Logica in America; Campbell
Soup Company's range of condensed soups in the UK; Gerber Baby
Foods in Brazil; Kentucky Fried Chicken in Hong Kong).

Managing risk and satisfaction during market entry

In any situation where an organization lacks experience, there is a
greater risk that mistakes will be made. Gaining a complete
understanding of customer needs in overseas markets will take time
and over this period the company is vulnerable to counter-attacks
from competition. The most likely source of this threat will be
domestic competitors who can exploit their vast store of accumulated
understanding of local market conditions. Furthermore, these firms
are often able to invoke the claim that sustained purchase loyalty by
the customers is beneficial to national interests. The strength of this
latter defence will vary in direct relation to the depth of patriotic
fervour within the country (e.g. the well orchestrated activities of
French industry in blocking entry of agricultural produce from
Britain and selected manufactured goods from Japan). Finally, on top
of all these problems, the company must also weigh the additional
risk associated with a change in political climate and/or shift in social
attitudes that could lead to the company losing the entire overseas
investment it has built up over the years (e.g. the sequestration of
Western firms' assets following the Islamic Fundamentalist
revolution in Iran).

One strategy to protect against such risks is to minimize the
company's level of direct involvement in the overseas market by
delegating such activities to other organizations. Unfortunately, this
action creates another type of risk: those responsible for delivering
customer satisfaction in the overseas market may have very different
ideas on how best to manage this process. This can eventually lead to
a worst case scenario in which the quality of customer service is
disrupted while the various parties attempt to resolve their
disagreements. Recently, for example, the Japanese car manufacturer
Nissan decided that the operating strategy of Nissan UK (the

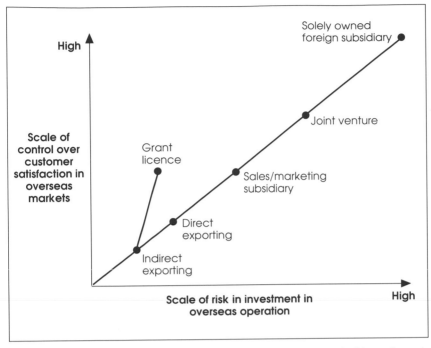

Figure 13.2 Balancing customer satisfaction control against investment risk in overseas markets

company to whom they had granted sole distribution rights in Britain) across areas such as pricing and product mix emphasis, was not compatible with their own long-term aims for the UK market. The resultant legal battle received widespread coverage in the UK media and very probably raised questions in the minds of potential customers about the advisability of buying a Nissan car while this dispute was being resolved.

One approach to determining an appropriate market entry strategy which balances control over customer satisfaction against the risk associated with the scale of the overseas investment is illustrated in Figure 13.2. The lowest possible financial risk is that of indirect exporting where the supplier has minimal involvement in the product after departure from the country of origin. Under these circumstances, the supplier cannot expect to be able to exert any influence over the marketing of the product in the overseas market.

Slightly more control can be gained by appointing a representative in the market to act as the foreign distributor. The supplier and the distributor share the mutual goal of ensuring the product is

successful. In those cases where a synergy of capability emerges from
linking product knowledge of the supplier with the distributor's
understanding of local market conditions, this will often prove to be
a winning combination (e.g. the activities of the UK manufacturer of
earth-moving equipment, JCB, in various markets around the world).
It is also important to recognize that if, at a later date, the supplier
intends to establish a foreign subsidiary, then the distributor may
also have a role in the future as a joint venture partner or acquisition
candidate (e.g. 3M's market development strategy in the
Netherlands; Canon's approach to building their photocopier
business in the UK).

A somewhat tangential strategic alternative is to grant a licence to an
overseas producer. The supplier will provide the necessary
technological support to help the licensee acquire an understanding
of relevant production technologies and in return receives a royalty,
typically calculated on the basis of a defined percentage of
subsequent sales. Under the terms of the licence, the supplier will
probably attempt to retain some degree of advisory influence on how
the product should be marketed. Nevertheless, having granted the
licence, the two risks that exist are:

● low royalty revenue because the licensee does not market the
   product effectively; and/or

● by granting the licence, the supplier is actually providing
   knowledge that ultimately assists in the creation of a new source
   of future competition (e.g. the American decision to grant a
   licence to the Japanese to manufacture the first generation of
   transistors).

Where a company determines there is a need to develop a closer
relationship with international customers, a common solution is to
open sales and marketing operations in overseas locations. For those
firms where it remains cost effective to source markets from domestic
production facilities (e.g. service sector firms; manufacturers of
low-volume, high-value, advanced technology products), no further
investment in overseas assets will be necessary. Many multinational
or global firms find that for cost reasons, tariff barriers and/or
political pressures, however, it eventually becomes advantageous to
establish foreign production operations.

One way of controlling the risks associated with investing in foreign
operations is to share them with others through the creation of joint
ventures. Another advantage of this approach is that it may be
looked upon with favour by many foreign governments: in those

cases where the venture partner is a local company, they feel their nation will gain a greater share of profits and fuller understanding of associated new technologies. India and Mexico, for example, until very recently have been especially restrictive about foreign companies owning more than 50 per cent of any venture in their countries.

The critical issue determining the long-term success of joint ventures is that all parties share similar long-term goals and have the same philosophy over fulfilling customer needs. Successful ventures are very similar to a good marriage: if all parties honestly seek to work together, drawing upon each other's unique skills, then the relationship will prove to be extremely rewarding. IBM in Japan, for example, has achieved almost an 'insider' relationship through the creation of numerous different partnerships (e.g. Nippon Steel in systems integration: Fuji Bank in financial systems; Ricoh for distribution of computers at the lower end of the market).

Other joint venture relationships have proved less rewarding for at least one of the partners. In 1956 Xerox Corporation joined with Rank Organization in the UK to form a 50/50 venture Rank–Xerox which was granted an exclusive licence in perpetuity to manufacture and sell photocopiers outside North America. Subsequently Xerox began to feel the terms of the original licence were too generous. Over the years, there have been periods when relations between the two companies have been strained by negotiations to revise the terms of the venture agreement. In other cases, differences of opinion between the partners have led to dissolution of the venture (e.g. termination of the Rank-Toshiba television manufacturing venture in the UK) with, in many cases, one of the firms selling its equity position to the other (e.g. Goodrich's investment in Yokohoma Rubber and GE Corporation's sale of shares to Toshiba).

The popularity of the joint venture approach seems to show dramatic swings over time. In one decade a company may be openly saying, 'Never again, next time we will operate alone', yet within only a few years the chairman feels 'it is the only way to go' when planning new overseas activities. At the moment, for example, it seems to have widespread appeal among companies seeking to respond to the post-1992 Single European Market scenario (e.g. Philips and the US-based Whirlpool Corporation in the European home appliance market). Another popular stimulus for the formation of a joint venture is the perceived impossibility of a single company affording the massive R & D costs associated with developing new advanced technology products (e.g. the $1 billion venture known as

MegaSubmicron between Philips and Siemens to manufacture semiconductors capable of competing against the Pacific Basin producers in world markets).

Where the company decides to go it alone in the creation of a foreign subsidiary the choice is between acquiring an existing firm or establishing a 'greenfield site' operation (e.g. Murata's recent move to open a factory in south-west England). There are arguments both for and against either alternative. An acquisition offers the attraction of already having an established base of customers and employees with extensive experience of local market conditions. The new owners can, therefore, reasonably expect sales revenue to grow faster than if they decide to establish their own new overseas subsidiary. Unfortunately, however, if the acquisition decision proves to be wrong, company resources have to be directed to remedying the problem. In the most extreme situation, the acquisition can act as a severe drain on corporate resources to the point where attention is diverted away from sustaining customer satisfaction in the domestic market and eventually the only way out is to dispose of the acquisition at a loss.

A tragic example of this situation is Midland Bank's purchase of the Crocker Bank in California. The take-over was originally heralded as the move that propelled Midland into a leadership position in the world of international banking. Unfortunately, the subsequent problems over the Crocker loan portfolio eventually required Midland to sell the operation to Wells Fargo and concurrently transfer liability for Third World loans to their UK balance sheet. Some commentators have argued that Midland's subsequent poor performance in the UK market can be explained by the fact that senior management attention was so deeply committed to the Crocker problem that satisfaction of domestic customers ceased to be a significant corporate objective. The timing of this internal attitude shift could not have been worse because, in the eighties, changes in financial services legislation triggered a massive increase in the intensity of competition between service providers in the UK. Hence, as other banks such as National Westminster and Barclays were investing in systems and human resource initiatives designed to enhance their capability to satisfy customer needs, Midland's domestic banking operations faced severe problems in attempting to mount any response that could adequately defend their threatened market position. Eventually, in order to survive Midland was forced to merge with the Hong Kong and Shanghai Bank. This provides a graphic example of the damage that can be done to an organization's capabilities to sustain domestic customer satisfaction by an ill-conceived decision to seek growth through the high-risk strategy of launching into overseas markets.

Why go international?

For large companies committed to sustaining continued growth over the long term, it is widely accepted that this goal can only be achieved by establishing successful operations in the Triad Markets of the Pacific Basin, the Americas and Europe. This is especially true in those sectors where scale of operation has a major influence on performance (e.g. semiconductors, computers, aviation, industrial chemicals, pharmaceuticals, cars and electronic consumer goods). As the giant multinational and global manufacturers have sought to expand their international activities, they have demanded the same level of assistance from banks and other professional advisers that they had previously come to expect in their home markets. To fulfil this customer need, many of the larger service providers such as banks, accountants, lawyers and management consultants have also found it necessary to expand the scale of their international operations.

For smaller companies (especially those based in a country such as the US where the huge domestic markets offer reasonable opportunity for growth through enhanced delivery of customer satisfaction) it is not unreasonable for them to ask, 'Why bother risking the core business by expanding overseas?'

There are possibly two issues that need to be considered when responding to this question: (a) surviving a growing competitive threat and (b) acquiring understanding of new opportunities to deliver customer satisfaction.

Factors such as the political appeal of reducing barriers to trade by the formation of new economic unions (e.g. between European countries; the relationship evolving between Mexico, Canada and the US), and the impact of advances in both communications and transport which are narrowing differing cultural attitudes around the world, do mean that even small companies can expect to face increasing threats from the entry into the home market of new competitors from overseas. Waiting until the enemy has arrived on your shores rarely proves to be a satisfactory defence. The most effective form of defence is offence. Hence the smaller firm might consider entering the home market of the potential new threat and learning how to defeat them at source. If this concept does not appeal, then consider the fact that alliances are often safer than battles. The firm could explore the formation of links with potential competitors (e.g. acting as distributors for each other's products) and in this way defuse the threat while concurrently mutually learning about new ways to deliver customer satisfaction.

This latter perspective of learning new business methods from international activity is in fact the most important justification to support the argument that all firms should at least examine overseas market opportunities. It is often said that 'travel broadens the mind' and nowhere is this more apposite than in the world of business. Too many firms suffer from the myopic attitude 'not invented here' when relying only on internal capabilities to develop new solutions, and entire industrial sectors are often conceited enough to believe their methods of operation must be superior to any counterparts located outside their own national borders.

A major benefit of entering overseas markets is that the firm is exposed to new ideas, processes and approaches that can eventually be incorporated back into sustaining the customer satisfaction leadership position in the domestic market. Hence, at minimum, all companies should allocate some resources to visiting other markets and evaluating the potential for overseas expansion. Even if no immediate opportunities are identified to outperform existing firms, the knowledge gained will (a) provide an early warning of the scale of potential future threats and (b) assist in defining the actions necessary to be eventually in a position to compete successfully overseas. Finally, there is the third benefit that just seeing new ways of doing things can often be a major incentive to embarking on innovative new customer satisfaction projects back at home.

14

The benefits and challenges of implementation

Although most people over the age of forty can tell where they were when John F. Kennedy was assassinated, probably very few can answer the question, 'Where did you see your first Toyota?' For me, if my memory serves me correctly, it was many years ago in London when a friend proudly showed me his first-ever company car. Certainly, there was nothing about his innocuous little two-door saloon that would lead one to expect that by 1990 the manufacturer would be the third largest car company in the world with sufficient cash reserves ($22.5 billion) to purchase the shares of Ford and Chrysler and still have several billion dollars in change.

EXAMPLE   Given that Toyota emerged from the ashes of a defeated Japan in 1945 to move to such a dominant position in the global car market in less than half a century, it is obviously a company that can provide some valuable insights into the strategies and management processes required of world-class organizations. The corporate philosophy, which is still closely supervised by the 76-year-old president, Schoichiro Toyoda, is that of customer satisfaction. Delivery of this goal is founded upon a dedication always to seek to upgrade all aspects of the company's operations. Toyoda's view is that 'our current success is the best reason to change things . . . we are permanently dissatisfied, even with exemplary performance'. The key phrase at Toyota City is '*kaizen*', which means continuous improvement.

Critical to the achievement of continuous change is R & D, which tripled from $750 million in 1984 to $2.2 billion by 1989. This expenditure has not been restricted just to supporting new product development. It has also been vital in the company's search to find ways of improving the quality, productivity and efficiency of their manufacturing operation. They have led the world in the development and application of JIT to the point where they operate a 7–10-day order to delivery cycle in Japan and can produce more models than the Ford motor company at half the level of man-hour input per model.

Their skills in JIT also extends into new product management. Toyota is now at the stage where, with techniques such as prototype testing in parallel with development of manufacturing machine tools, they have reduced the time from concept to showroom delivery for new models to only four years. This contrasts with five years at Ford and seven at Mercedes. And they still find time to give careful attention to even the smallest detail that could further improve the performance of their new cars. At their Shibetsu 1235-acre test facility, for example, they have created special circuits that exactly mimic various road conditions around the world, such as the Koln to Hanover autobahn, the Ghent to Brussels autoroute and Interstate 91, which runs from Hartford, Connecticut, to the Canadian border.

The company appreciates that their position as a global company requires them to expand overseas, exploiting opportunities for comparative advantage in manufacturing as well as moving both product development and assembly operations nearer to the customer. They already have an engine block plant in Indonesia and expect to have two full-scale production facilities in South East Asia by the year 2000. America is a vital market which is why they formed a joint venture with General Motors in 1983 to build the Corolla in Fremont, California. This was followed in 1988 by the opening of their Camry plant in Georgetown, Kentucky. There is already a design centre at Fremont and, in 1994, this will be complemented by the opening of a test-track facility in Arizona. Their entry into Europe has been at a slightly slower pace, but already they have constructed a manufacturing plant in Derbyshire and sited a design centre in Brussels.

Toyota was one of the earliest of the Japanese car companies to realize that over time they would face increasing competition at the bottom end of the market from developing countries such as Korea. Hence, they have been gradually moving up-market, seeking to use product performance-based differentiation to protect themselves from competitive threats based solely on price. Their ability to interpret and respond to changing market needs is reflected in another Toyoda comment:

'We have learned that universal mass production is not enough; in the 21st century you will need to personalise things much more reflecting individual needs. The winners will be those who target narrow customer niches most successfully with specific models.'

Their latest endeavour, the Lexus luxury sedan, is a reflection of this latest strategy and exploits all their accumulated understanding of manufacturing technology. It has usurped the leadership position of Mercedes for engineering quality but is constructed using only one-sixth of the labour input. Within only a few months after launch it was outselling Mercedes, BMW and Jaguar and moved the company into a leadership position in the luxury segment of the US car market.

Conflicting organizational priorities

Most texts describing a radical new way of doing things will caution that the change can only succeed through securing the commitment and involvement of the senior management. Unfortunately, as demonstrated by Professor Piercy's research at Cardiff Business School on implementing marketing strategies, the power within many organizations is often vested in senior managers who have yet to accept that adopting a customer-oriented approach should be given more than a minimal priority on the corporate agenda. Examples that support Piercy's conclusions which I have encountered include senior partners in legal and accountancy practices and senior managers in sectors such as banking, capital goods manufacturing, electronics, civil engineering, electronics and biotechnology. Recognition of the magnitude of the risks associated with continuing to have many UK companies ignore the importance of adopting a customer-oriented approach, especially when seeking to survive in world markets, has now resulted in the Chartered Institute of Marketing announcing a major new initiative to ensure that marketing is seen as a Board-level issue and no longer treated as a minor, specialist activity which can be delegated to middle management.

Although it seems likely that marketing will eventually be seen as vitally important within all organizations, this promise is of little comfort to the marketer facing a situation where current senior management are not expected in the immediate future suddenly to accept the benefits of becoming a more customer-focused operation. My experience is that these marketers find case materials such as the Toyota story very interesting, but understandably respond by pointing out that a move to introduce similar concepts within their organization is inevitably bound to fail because it is in conflict with the prevailing corporate culture. Some feel the safest approach is to avoid 'rocking the boat' by carrying on and discharging their managerial responsibilities in the same way as they have done in the past.

On the other hand, there are a few brave souls who feel there is some degree of merit in the alternative perspective of deciding that change has got to begin somewhere. So why not start within the marketing department and accept that new approaches may be in conflict with attitudes prevailing elsewhere in the organization? Assuming that this idea appeals, observation and personal experience of a number of such situations suggest it is important that the approach is carefully structured, that the initial attempt is undertaken with no fanfare and that, at least in the early stages, it is primarily intended as a low-risk test of the managerial capabilities of individual marketing staff. This latter objective can usually be achieved by focusing on small-scale personal projects involving changing internal

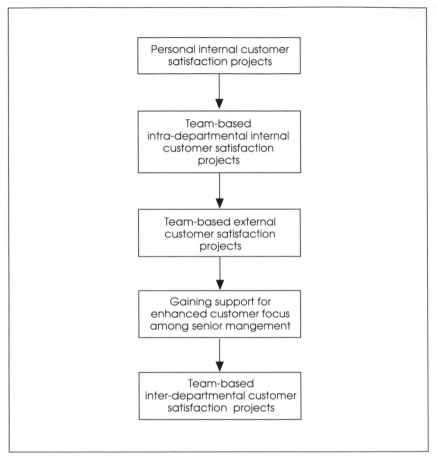

Figure 14.1 Process flow for a marketing group seeking to create a more customer-focused organizational culture

departmental processes where, if things go wrong, it will have minimal impact on corporate performance.

Assuming a review of individual personal project outcomes proves positive, then the change process can be progressed through the subsequent phases described in Figure 14.1 of intra-departmental team-based customer projects and then external customer satisfaction initiatives. Evidence of the benefits from these activities provides the basis for gaining the support of senior management; and once this has been achieved, the marketing group can move into the final phase of involving other departments in developing a more customer-focused attitude across the entire organization.

Marketers as a breed tend to gain greatest satisfaction from the initiation of projects which can be completed within a relatively short time-span. If the reader shares this inclination, then it is necessary to provide a careful warning about the flow model shown in Figure 14.1. Each phase will usually take many months to complete and hence even the most optimistic time schedule for completion of the entire process is that it will take at least three to five years.

The personal project phase

Experience of working with this technique has shown that marketing staff will react positively to this first phase of the initiative if it is clearly presented as (a) the start point of a long-term programme to move the organization towards becoming more customer-focused and (b) providing an important opportunity for further self-development of their managerial skills.

Staff should be required to develop their own specification for an appropriate project but cautioned against selecting a topic that cannot be completed without either significant incremental resources and/or demanding so much time that their ability to discharge current job responsibilities is impaired. A possible process flow model that staff might find useful in managing their customer satisfaction project is shown in Figure 14.2. In presenting this approach to staff, they should be cautioned that rushing into the project with a preconceived solution is the fastest way to fail. It is vital that all the elements of the base-line study, as summarized in Figure 14.3, are carefully examined. Staff should take the time to ensure that they have an adequate understanding of issues such as:

● Who are the actual customers? What is it they are seeking?

● Which subordinates may be involved, and what are their current contributions to service provision? Do they and you have the skills to handle task modifications?

● What are the components of the provision process? Can they be measured? Does sufficient autonomous authority exist over processes and/or resources to revise or eliminate certain procedures?

● How can level of satisfaction be measured? Is it possible to use existing performance indicators or will new measurement techniques need to be developed?

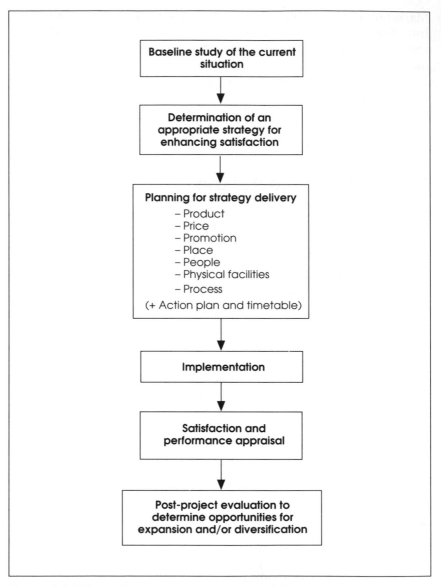

Figure 14.2 Flow of events for a customer satisfaction improvement programme

The base-line study will provide the foundations for defining an appropriate strategy to be used in guiding the planning phase. Factors in the plan requiring attention will be heavily influenced by the nature of the actual project. One possible checklist which can be

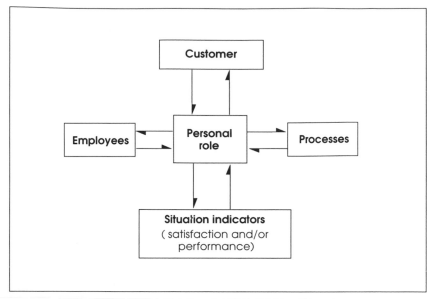

Figure 14.3 Determination of factors of influence within the base-line study

useful in the preparation of the plan is a modified version of the '7Ps' of service marketing, namely:

1 *Product* – will this be modified or is a new product required?

2 *Price* – this is not your cost, but the cost implication for the customer in terms of any need to fund new resources, time required to install or utilize a modified product and the personal psychological cost for the customer of being prepared to accept a change in the way things are done or new procedures to be learnt.

3 *Promotion* – the actions necessary to communicate the change to the customer effectively, to overcome their concerns and respond to any post-acceptance problems that may occur.

4 *Place* – the systems, location and logistics of service delivery.

5 *People* – the possible need for more employees or the acquisition of new skills or attitude shifts by existing staff responsible for service provision.

6 *Processes* – the activities and procedures associated with adding value to the various provision tasks.

7 *Physical facilities* – the physical resources required to undertake and distribute the various services.

Contained within the plan should be a timetable and statement of actions necessary for completing the project. These provide an important framework against which to manage the implementation phase. Once implementation has commenced, it is necessary for actual progress and fulfilment of satisfaction parameters identified in the base-line study to be measured on a regular basis.

EXAMPLE of an individual project   Denise Wilkinson is section head of a small team within the marketing department of Glastonbury Ltd, a disguised case based upon a medium-sized processing company which supplies a range of products to both the retail and catering sectors of the UK food industry. Her team's primary responsibilities are to prepare financial forecasts and operate the intra-departmental management accounting information system required by marketing staff engaged in budgeting, planning and performance assessment activities. On a 'time available' basis her team also offers a service of preparing in-depth reports analysing specific performance situations. The internal customer group that makes greatest use of this latter service are sales staff who depend on the team to produce performance reviews for use in major presentations to national account customers.

In seeking to identify a personal project Denise recalled a recent conversation with the sales director in which he commented on how important the reports were to his national account team and expressed the regret that there were not the resources to provide similar output for sales staff working with smaller, regional customers.

Denise gave some thought to various ways this request might be fulfilled. She was aware that the sales force had recently been equipped with laptop computers and modems which permitted them limited access to the order entry and finished goods system within the company's mainframe facilities. One of her team was forever playing with the company systems and she involved him in the project. Over the next few weeks, in after-hours sessions, they evolved a modification to the laptop software that would permit a sales person, by linking into her department's analysis kit, to extract customer sales data and then convert these into visual materials which could be printed off for presentation to the client.

Having created the first prototype, they obtained approval from the sales director to train one of his field staff in the use of the system. Trials over the next month proved that the system was a very useful new tool in negotiations with customers over issues such as store-level performance, product stocking decisions and assessment of in-store merchandizing plans. These results rapidly convinced the sales director that the system should be made available to his entire sales force.

Intra-departmental team-based satisfaction projects

A characteristic of Western society is a strong belief in protecting the rights of the individual to hold an opinion at variance with the majority. An unfortunate cultural consequence of this situation is that Westerners do not easily adapt to the idea of working in group situations. Furthermore, if their first exposure to group working is when an organization is seeking to make radical alterations to strategies and policies, group productivity may be impaired because individuals will be influenced by one or more of the following factors:

● A fear of anything new that makes the future seem more uncertain.

● Change is often initially accompanied by the need to do more work to meet specified project completion dates.

● A preference to do those things that are familiar and avoid new activities which feel strange or foreign, because this may entail moving away from well established habits.

● Concern over personal abilities to acquire new or different competences.

● Avoidance of situations which can lead to just too many surprises.

Another factor that also has to be recognized when seeking to introduce a team-based problem-solving approach is that marketers and sales people tend to have difficulties in working together effectively. To survive in the field, sales people have learnt to be self-responsible and to reach decisions rapidly with minimal input from others. They are also oriented towards tactical solutions capable of influencing near-term events. Marketers, in contrast, are more concerned with medium-term strategic issues and, because they operate in an office environment, will tend to review major decisions with their superiors in the corporate hierarchy prior to implementation.

Most organizational development experts would recommend that internal performance-enhancement projects should from the outset be team-based initiatives. However, personal experience of the problems described above leads me to caution the reader against using a participative project management approach until after a significant number of staff have successfully completed individual customer satisfaction projects. For, having seen for themselves the benefits of the internal customer concept, marketers and sales people seem much more open to the idea of working with others to improve departmental productivity. As a result, a newly formed team is keener to take on a new challenge and will actively seek ways to avoid personality clashes, which could impair group productivity.

Unlike the individual project phase, the problem to be studied by a group should be selected by the head of the marketing operation, because this individual is in the best position to determine which areas of the operation must be improved. It is vital that the first ever attempt does not fail and therefore the head of marketing is strongly advised to bring together a group of junior staff most likely to approach the assignment with enthusiasm and energy. The team should be carefully briefed on the objectives of the exercise and a leader nominated who will be responsible for coordinating the project. Once the experiment is under way, the head of marketing should then actively work with the leader to provide support in areas such as coaching the team when obstacles emerge, protection of the group from external criticism and fulfilling requests for access to necessary or additional resources.

A very typical outcome of successful programmes is that, even before the pilot project has been completed, other staff begin to develop an interest and seek approval to form work teams to undertake similar initiatives. Under these circumstances, enthusiasm gains a momentum all of its own and the benefits start to become evident, not just within the department – they soon spill over into improved relationships with others both inside and outside the organization.

Managing promotion of the benefits of both the pilot and subsequent larger projects requires careful consideration. As stressed in an earlier chapter, the purpose of promotion is to provide information of benefit to customers and they tend to prefer to obtain this from trusted, internal sources. Hence, within the department, let the project participants lead discussions with colleagues. If a manager from another department inquires about the scheme, respond by persuading him to let his staff come and talk to your people. Many TQM texts stress the importance of clear, simple displays to communicate achievements. These can be invaluable catalysts for raising the curiosity of visitors and stimulating pride of achievement by the work teams. It is vital, however, that these materials are created and managed by the teams. The senior manager who starts putting up such materials himself runs the risk of being seen as attempting to claim ownership for what has been achieved by others.

The nature of team-based projects

The selection of suitable intra-departmental projects will be influenced by factors such as the assigned role of the marketing department, organizational structure, nature of the marketing mix, processes by which relationships with external customers are managed and the characteristics of the industrial sector of which the organization is a part. In virtually all cases, however, in one way or another projects usually share the common objectives of seeking ways of improving communications through greater sharing of information, reducing the time taken to reach decisions and minimizing errors in managerial processes which are currently damaging external customer perceptions of the operational effectiveness of the organization.

EXAMPLE The outcome of the team-based project approach can be illustrated by a further example drawn from the Glastonbury case (see page 204). Responsibility for management of the product range is split across three brand groups. Wherever possible the company attempts to offer the same below-line promotions to all customers. In certain cases, however, because a customer does not carry certain products and/or the promotion is not compatible with an intermediary's merchandizing plan, field sales staff will seek permission from the brand groups to revise the promotional schedule for specific customers. This activity frequently involves the sales force having to discuss proposed changes with all three brand groups. After they have authorized the change, it is the latter's responsibility to inform the order entry team of the revised programme. The process can be extremely time-consuming and at times has led to errors on issued invoices because the order entry group have not been kept up to date on all the changes that have been agreed.

The team allocated the task of examining this problem at Glastonbury was composed of two brand assistants, two field sales staff and the order entry team supervisor who was nominated as group leader. After considering a number of alternatives, the final recommendation of the team was that:

1 To minimize the time to obtain a decision, the sales force should be able to have any brand group authorize changes to a promotional schedule even when the products involved are the management responsibility of another brand group. Certain guidelines would be established, however, (e.g. maximum permissible promotional allowances as a percentage of the selling price; sufficient on-hand finished goods; product was not on promotion in the prior period) which the authorizer would not be permitted to breach without first gaining approval from the relevant brand manager.

2 An electronic mail system should be established summarizing all promotional programmes. Then when a brand group member authorized a programme revision, it would be their responsibility to enter the agreed exception into the EMS file. These data would be accessed by the order

entry staff to ensure that customer invoices contained the correct
promotional allowances.

3 Denise Wilkinson's group be asked to develop software which (a) uses
order entry data to monitor sales promotion expenditure and (b)
generates a regular analysis comparing planned versus actual
expenditure. The purpose of this system would be to ensure that the move
to permit any brand group to authorize promotional changes across the
entire product range did not result in decisions that unwittingly led to
overspending of the total sales promotion budget.

External customer satisfaction projects

A common characteristic of companies with a reputation for
consistently delivering customer satisfaction, such as IBM, GE
Corporation and 3M, is their dedication to carefully tracking market
performance using some form of customer satisfaction index (CSI)
system. Hence the recommended first step for a marketing group
embarking on a programme to improve external customer
satisfaction is, first, to determine which factors are critical to the
customers in terms of influencing their overall satisfaction with the
organization.

Research techniques to acquire this knowledge include focus groups,
customer surveys, analysis of customer self-administered response
forms and a review of internal data describing various aspects of
organizational activity. Internal activity analysis has been greatly
simplified in recent years because moves by companies to
computerize the data management systems means that it is now
feasible to undertake virtually instant comparisons of actual versus
desired service response achievement. One of the pioneers of this
approach, Federal Express, for example, can use their shipment
tracking system to supply employees as they arrive for work with
detailed feedback on the previous day's actual service level
performance across the entire organization.

Organizations rarely have the resources to remedy every area where
the CSI rating indicates improvement is needed. Hence the research
on performance achievement must also permit determination of
which factors are most urgently in need of attention. The other
complication facing a marketing group implementing a programme
to improve CSI ratings is that certain issues will require significant
input from other departments. At this stage in the process of
strengthening the degree of customer focus within the organization,
it is extremely unlikely that such assistance will be forthcoming and,

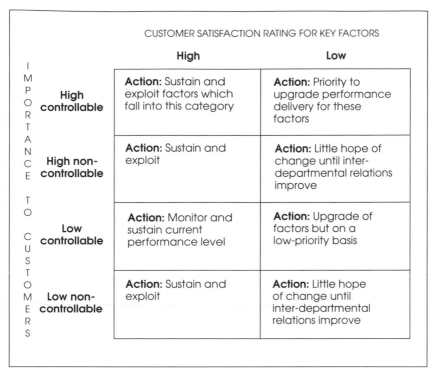

Figure 14.4 A CSI response matrix

therefore, certain actions to enhance customer satisfaction will have to be postponed until sometime in the future.

Once the performance rating/feasible response information has been collated, it is then possible to determine appropriate actions that will form the basis of new external customer satisfaction projects for marketing staff by constructing a CSI response matrix of the type shown in Figure 14.4. The three factors influencing future response in this case are current satisfaction ratings, importance of factors to the customer and whether the marketing group has sufficient autonomous control to implement an appropriate response where dissatisfaction has been identified.

In developing a CSI response matrix, it is very probable that different customer groups will exhibit variance over which factors are important to them in determining their satisfaction with the current performance of the supplier organization. Thus, where an organization operates across a number of market sectors, it is often necessary when attempting to identify customer satisfaction projects

		CUSTOMER SATISFACTION RATING FOR KEY FACTORS	
		High	**Low**
I M P O R T A N C E T O C U S T O M E R S	**High controllable**	Provision of adequate quality range of food service products at competitive prices. **Action:** Sustain and exploit	Provision of advisory and promotional support to assist distributor develop new key accounts. **Action:** Investments in new support schemes
	High non-controllable	Response to enquiries about invoice errors by accounting group. **Action:** Sustain	Poor response time to request for special (non-inventory) order items **Action:** None, due to attitude of manufacturing department
	Low controllable	Provision of sales promotion to support distributor activity. **Action:** Sustain	Provision of merchandizing materials to assist distributor sales force. **Action:** Consider developments of new materials over the medium term
	Low non-controllable	Response to enquiries about status of shipments in transit. **Action:** Sustain	Speed of development of new/improved product formulations of interest to distributor key customers. **Action:** None until manufacturing are willing to commit resources to support expanded product development activity

Figure 14.5 Glastonbury CSI response matrix for the catering sector distributor customers

to construct a whole series of sector-specific response matrices. For example, at Glastonbury Ltd, in addition to the matrix for the catering sector shown in Figure 14.5, it also proved necessary to develop three further matrices to describe the situation for retail distributors, supermarket chains and UK consumers.

Gaining senior management support

The 'how not to' approach

Once ongoing monitoring of CSI ratings indicates that the marketing department projects are beginning to be reflected by an improvement in external customer satisfaction, consideration should be given to persuading senior management to recognize the benefits of adding their support to the initiative. In those organizations where the marketing department feels it has a poor image at Board level, there is often a tendency to call upon the services of an international management guru or consulting firm to sell to senior management the idea of incorporating greater customer orientation into the organizational culture.

The natural inclination of such external advisers is to gain control of the change process, because this will maximize their fee income. Hence their presentation is likely to contain very persuasive arguments to justify senior managers being the first group to receive specialist development assistance at a comfortable venue well away from the company offices. Should this proposition be sold to the organization, the usual outcome on the return of these managers from their cloistered retreat with a world-famous organizational development expert is the presentation of new tablets of stone to the organization. For some reason, presumably to make sure everybody fully grasps the importance of senior management decisions, it is currently very much in vogue that the presentation should include a laser light show. Then, in conditions one would normally associate with a discotheque, the chief executive will enthusiastically announce that 'Together we are going to put the customer first'. Reading between the lines, we also know he means 'and if you fail, I will want to know the reason why and I will make your lives very uncomfortable'. To make sure the message is spread even to the remotest corner of the organization, it is also likely that the company's PR department will distribute thousands of video copies of this speech in which the chief executive is the star in a low-budget rerun of Elvis Presley's last appearance at Las Vegas.

The keynote address is then followed by managers being told to prepare plans on how progress will be achieved in their respective departments. Alternatively, if one is really unlucky, everybody will be given a detailed glossy brochure produced by the company's very expensive external advisers on how the programme should be implemented. Then it's back to the Boardroom and a period of self-congratulation for all concerned.

Unfortunately, this behaviour pattern could not be more
inappropriate. If declining standards of customer service have
reached the point where they have become the priority agenda item
of senior management, then it is extremely likely that internal
processes and systems are in need of a drastic overhaul. This activity
will probably have to be accompanied by a large-scale employee
development programme to upgrade the competences of the entire
workforce. Change of this magnitude will undoubtedly encounter
the problems of obstructive behaviour by demotivated staff,
misallocated or inadequate resources, and policy changes in one
department affecting productivity elsewhere in the organization.
This last effect is the outcome of single departments failing to ensure
that the timing of their process revisions are compatible with actions
planned by colleagues in other departments (e.g. a move to alter
finished goods stocking levels by the distribution manager should
first be discussed with manufacturing and procurement to avoid an
adverse impact on both the production scheduling systems and
contractual obligations with raw material suppliers).

The potential of these factors to act as barriers to progress will
probably not have been included in senior management
deliberations on how to improve customer satisfaction within the
organization. Day-to-day operational details are something they
rarely have to confront while overseeing operations from their
top-floor executive suites at head office. Even if the workforce fails to
notice this omission in management's new plans, its effects will
rapidly become evident as the project implementation phase gets
under way. The typical reaction of senior management when the
project subsequently grinds to a halt is to identify a convenient
scapegoat (e.g. rigid-thinking middle managers or the inflexible
attitude of the unions). Any reason will do, just as long as it
conveniently saves them from having to accept that the whole sorry
state of affairs is actually their fault.

Instead of participating in the development programme offered by
expensive external advisers, what senior management should have
done was to have 'got their hands dirty' by participating in a
base-line study to comprehend the current state of internal and
external customer relations. This knowledge would then have proved
invaluable in developing a feasible plan that would ultimately have
the potential to deliver improved customer satisfaction.

In his book, *Creating Value for Customers*, the Canadian management
consultant William Band provides a graphic insight into what can
happen if senior management do not truly comprehend the

magnitude of the task confronting them. The example company, a major producer of food ingredients, convened a customer satisfaction council which determined that, against the parameters of (a) actions clearly visible to the customer and (b) the capability for implementation in 90 days, there were three areas of immediate opportunity within the organization.

A vice-president was assigned to each project. By the end of the first month all three project leaders had to report that what had seemed like a simple task at the outset was actually composed of numerous complex, interacting variables. The project to improve telephone answering manners revealed a completely untrained order entry team and a telephone system rendered virtually obsolete by years of expenditure cuts and refusals to invest in new technology. The individual charged with improving the visual appearance of company trucks found the entire operation had been subcontracted to an outside firm and no appearance standards had ever been specified in the supplier contract. The only contractual performance requirement was lowest possible freight costs.

The third project was to improve the management of the complaint procedure. This revealed that many complaints were ignored or blamed on another department and nobody was held responsible for monitoring the outcome of each customer enquiry. Even more worrying was the discovery that friction between departments was so intense that it would probably be impossible ever to obtain total agreement on the most effective system for managing complaints in the future. To quote Band's observation of this live scenario:

... senior executives gained first-hand experience in trying to solve customer problems; and they also gained a much more realistic view of the challenges they were asking their employees to tackle.

A safer approach to gaining support

The usual benefit of successful marketing department projects to improve CSI ratings is the development of much closer working relationships between the marketing team and key external customers. This latter group are often then very open to the suggestion that their assistance would be greatly appreciated in selling the benefits of the concept to the marketing group's own senior management. There is a whole range of different mechanisms by which the selling process might be undertaken (e.g. formal meetings between senior managers from the customer and supplier organization; inviting customers to address an internal seminar organized by the marketing group; complimentary letters or phone calls from customers to the chief executive of the supplier organization). But whichever method is selected the objective is always the same: to gain acceptance among senior management that organizational performance can be enhanced by ensuring customer satisfaction becomes a Board-level agenda item. Once this has been achieved, the next step is to review with senior management those areas of the CSI response matrices where satisfaction ratings can only be enhanced through the cooperation and assistance of other departments across the entire organization. Once senior management have been persuaded of the need for action over these issues, then the marketing department can be safely assured that moving into the final phase of inter-departmental projects to increase customer satisfaction will proceed because they are now considered an important aspect of the need to change organizational culture.

EXAMPLE of an inter-departmental project at Glastonbury   Studies by Professor Boothroyd of American companies where the organizational culture is dominated by the views of the manufacturing group have shown that a very common outcome is the emergence of technical specifications for products which do not make best use of existing production capacity and, in some cases, do not really meet the specified needs of the customer. The recommended solution for companies facing this situation is to utilize a concept known as *design for manufacturability* (DFM)

A well documented example of the benefits of applying DFM is provided by Black & Decker. At one time the company produced different models for each of their markets around the world and faced situations such as having over 100 different motors for its range of power tools. The effect on product costs and post-purchasing product servicing of this situation eventually began to affect market performance as the company attempted to respond to newly emerging competitive threats of Pacific Basin producers entering world markets. Black & Decker has responded by adopting DFM with the objective of fewer product variations, fewer parts (e.g. the number of motors to be reduced eventually to only five) and fewer production technologies while concurrently expanding the breadth of the product line.

In a review meeting between marketing and production at Glastonbury to discuss the CSI response matrix for the catering sector (Figure 14.5), it was pointed out that speeding up new product development and reducing response time for special orders was constrained by the fact that the company currently lacked adequate production capacity to meet the demands even for existing food service items. As investment in factory expansion was not deemed acceptable for the foreseeable future, the marketing and manufacturing group agreed to cooperate in a DFM programme to reduce product formulation diversity which could subsequently release production capacity that could be allocated to special orders and new product development. The guidelines agreed by the inter-departmental project team were to examine opportunities that might fulfill the criteria of:

● Minimize the number of product formulations.

● Minimize process manufacturing steps to reduce machine downtime.

● Develop formulations acceptable to customers which could have multiple product applications.

● Minimize processes that can lead to backtracking or duplication of activities within the production process.

● Create greater standardization across special order formulations to reduce product diversity.

● Consider subcontracting where this either released production capacity and/or reduced finished goods costs.

Sustaining satisfaction demands unceasing vigilance

In the opening chapter it was noted that many American corporations, having established the market standard for customer satisfaction in their sector of industry, then permitted themselves to be overtaken by their Pacific Basin competitors. Hence it cannot be over-emphasized that, having expended massive time and effort to create a base of loyal customers, the organization must remain ever vigilant to avoid mistakes that can damage their market reputation.

For example, I am a huge fan of the car manufacturer Volvo. At the moment both of the cars in my family are Volvos. One of them, a Volvo 480 ES Coupe, has the potential to be the most satisfactory car that I ever hope to own. The design is visually appealing and the road-handling characteristics are outstanding. Unfortunately, since I bought the car it has been plagued by niggling faults – two broken clutch cables, certain plastic fitments cracking or breaking off, a leaking window seal, a major brake fluid leak in the master cylinder and burnt-out blower motor plus associated wiring harness. Not what one would expect of a company with a global reputation for quality. Furthermore, when I exchanged experiences with other 480 owners, my stories paled in comparison with some of theirs.

In the next few months, the 480 is due for replacement. My local Volvo dealer was honest in responding to my critical comments, admitting the model did exhibit teething problems that took a surprisingly long time to overcome. He is confident that, on the basis of national warranty claim figures for the model, all the bad times are behind them. Possibly he's right, but I'm sufficiently unsure that I will probably also look at cars from competitors such as Mazda, Nissan or Toyota. And if I like what I see, Volvo may have lost my allegiance for ever.

If only a small minority of pre-1991 480 owners share my opinion, and our negative comments have a limited influence on people considering their first ever Volvo purchase, then even these conservative assumptions must represent a significant potential loss in the company's UK sales revenue over the next few years. One can only theorize on the reasons behind the managerial mistakes which must have occurred sometime during the development and launch programme for the 480.

The issue for the reader, however, is not the story itself. Much more important is the message behind the event: namely, if problems can occur in a company with such an outstanding track record for both superiority of product and innovative approaches to improving employee working conditions, then think how much more likely it is that even more disastrous mistakes might be made in your organization. It cannot be over-stressed that delivering superior satisfaction requires adoption of the Toyota concept of *kaizen*, or continuous improvement accompanied by a relentless vigilance to sustain the standards that have already contributed towards the creation of a loyal base of customers. For neither standing still nor temporarily slipping backwards can ever be entertained as viable options for those organizations in both private and public sectors whose strategy is based upon a genuine commitment to putting the customer first.

Monitoring and responding

Companies which have adopted the response decision model of the type shown in Figure 14.4 soon realize that a key influence on customer opinions is the performance of competition. Many are now, therefore, also monitoring CSI ratings for other organizations that they consider as 'best-in-class' for specific activities. These data can then be used for determining which are the organizations to beat. The majority of organizations will face the situation that they are being outperformed by the market leader. The usual response is to implement actions that permit them to close this satisfaction gap.

Buzzell and Gale's comparative research on the PIMS database has revealed, however, that programmes designed merely to match the 'best-in-class' competition for customer satisfaction will have a limited impact on the organization's overall financial performance. If an organization wishes really to benefit from customer satisfaction enhancement programmes, then it has to fulfil standards much higher than those already established in the market by competition. This objective is usually achieved by sustained investment and effort that eventually permits the company to catch up and then gradually move ahead of the market leader (e.g. IBM's long battle to defeat Apple in the personal computer market). The alternative approach is to specify a new standard well in excess of anything ever considered by the rest of the industry and to 'leap-frog' the competition by being the first organization to meet this goal (e.g. the price/quality combination offered by the Toyota's Lexus in the luxury car market; the processing power of the Cray computer; Toshiba's introduction of flat screen technology in the UK television market).

Although the financial rewards from a successful leap-frog strategy can be outstanding, the marketer must realize that the competition is unlikely to sit passively by and watch itself being overtaken in the market. All you have done is merely to move ahead in a never-ending race. Having accelerated the pace of events, leadership retention will require a scale of ongoing total organizational effort and investment at least equal to that which was committed to achieving the 'best-in-class' rating for delivery of total customer satisfaction.

References and further reading

Argenti, J., *Corporate Collapse: The Causes and Symptoms*, McGraw-Hill, 1976.

Band, W.A., *Creating Value for Customers: Designing and Implementing a Total Corporate Strategy*, J. Wiley, 1991.

Barratt, J. and J. Downs, *Organizing for Local Government*, Longman, 1988.

Belasco, J.A., *Teaching the Elephant to Dance*, Hutchinson, 1990.

Boothroyd, G. and P. Dewhurst, *Product Design for Assembly*, Boothroyd-Dewhurst Inc, 1987.

Broadbent, S. *The Advertising Budget*, NTC Publications, 1989.

Buzzell, R. D. and B. Gale, *The PIMS Principle, Linking Strategy to Performance*, The Free Press, 1987.

Cannon, C. (ed.) *Advertising Works*, Volume 4, Cassell, 1987.

Chaston, I., *Managing for Marketing Excellence*, McGraw-Hill, 1990.

Clarke, M. and J. Stewart, (eds.) *General Management in Local Government*, Longman, 1990.

Crosby, P.B., *Quality is Free*, McGraw-Hill, 1979.

Culyer, A.J., A.K. Maynard and J. W. Posnett, *Competition in Healthcare: Reforming the NHS*, Macmillan, 1990.

Dudley, J.W., *1992 Strategies for the Single Market*, Kogan Page, 1989.

Garvin, D.A., *Managing Quality: The Strategic and Competitive Edge*, The Free Press, 1988.

Handy, C.B., *Understanding Organizations*, 3rd edition, Penguin, 1985.

Hickman, C.R. and M.A. Sivla, *Creating Excellence*, Unwin, 1985.

Hirsch, F., *The Social Limits to Growth*, Routledge and Kegan, 1977.

Johnson, H.T. and R.S. Kaplan, *Relevance Lost: The Rise and Fall of Management Accounting*, Harvard Business School Press, 1987.

Kao, J., *Entrepreneurship, Creativity and Organizations*, Prentice Hall, 1989.

Katz, R. (ed.) *Managing Professionals in Innovative Organizations*, Ballinger Publishing, 1989.

Kotler, P., *Marketing Management: Analysis, Planning Implementation and Control*, 7th edition, Prentice Hall, 1990.

Kotler, P. and A. Andreasen, *Strategic Marketing for Nonprofit Organizations*, 4th edition, Prentice Hall, 1991.

Lovelock, C., *Service Marketing*, Prentice Hall, 1984.

Moss Kanter, R., *The Change Masters*, Unwin, 1983.

Oakland, J.S., *Total Quality Management*, Heinemann, 1989.

Ohmae, K., *The Borderless World: Power and Strategy in the Interlinked Economy*, Collins, 1990.

Peters, T., *Thriving on Chaos: Handbook for a Management Revolution*, Knopf, 1987.

Peters, T.J. and R.H.Waterman, *In Search Of Excellence: Lessons from America's Best-run Companies*, Harper & Row, 1982.

Piercy, N., *Market-led Strategic Change*, Thorsons, 1991.

Porter, M.E., *Competitive Advantage: Creating and Sustaining Superior Performance*, The Free Press, 1985.

Porter M.E., *The Competitive Advantage of Nations*, Macmillan, 1990.

Price, F., *Right First Time*, Gower, 1987.

Slatter, S., *Corporate Recovery: A Guide to Turnaround Management*, Penguin, 1987.

Schonberger, R.J., *Building a Chain of Customers*, Hutchinson, 1990.

Strong, P. and C. Robinson, *The NHS Under New Management*, Open University Press, 1990.

Waterman, R.H., *The Renewal Factor: Building and Maintaining your Competitive Edge*, Bantam Press, 1987.

Index